The Digital Currency Revolution

Mark Mobius · Lourdes Casanova ·
Sharwari Pandit · John Ninia

The Digital Currency Revolution

Central Bank Digital Currencies, Crypto, and the Future of Global Finance

Mark Mobius
Dubai, United Arab Emirates

Sharwari Pandit
Cornell Univerity, SC Johnson School
of Management
Ithaca, NY, USA

Lourdes Casanova
Cornell Univerity, SC Johnson School
of Management
Ithaca, NY, USA

John Ninia
Cornell Univerity, SC Johnson School
of Business
Ithaca, NY, USA

ISBN 978-3-032-02818-1   ISBN 978-3-032-02819-8 (eBook)
https://doi.org/10.1007/978-3-032-02819-8

© The Editor(s) (if applicable) and The Author(s), under exclusive license to Springer Nature Switzerland AG 2025

This work is subject to copyright. All rights are solely and exclusively licensed by the Publisher, whether the whole or part of the material is concerned, specifically the rights of translation, reprinting, reuse of illustrations, recitation, broadcasting, reproduction on microfilms or in any other physical way, and transmission or information storage and retrieval, electronic adaptation, computer software, or by similar or dissimilar methodology now known or hereafter developed.

The use of general descriptive names, registered names, trademarks, service marks, etc. in this publication does not imply, even in the absence of a specific statement, that such names are exempt from the relevant protective laws and regulations and therefore free for general use.

The publisher, the authors and the editors are safe to assume that the advice and information in this book are believed to be true and accurate at the date of publication. Neither the publisher nor the authors or the editors give a warranty, expressed or implied, with respect to the material contained herein or for any errors or omissions that may have been made. The publisher remains neutral with regard to jurisdictional claims in published maps and institutional affiliations.

Cover credit: Image by White Star Media

This Palgrave Macmillan imprint is published by the registered company Springer Nature Switzerland AG
The registered company address is: Gewerbestrasse 11, 6330 Cham, Switzerland

If disposing of this product, please recycle the paper.

To my dear husband, Soumitra, to the extended Casanova family, and to our grandchildren, Kian and Kiara who, we hope, will continue enjoying the pleasure of reading and learning from books. To my students at the Emerging Markets Institute at Cornell University, a source of inspiration and excellence.

Lourdes Casanova

My thanks go out to all the very capable people who contributed to this book and to my friends around the world who give comments and ideas. Also thanks to my family: Pamela, Mark Edward, Matt, Amy, Jamie, Janet, and Hans J for their support. Finally, thanks to the staff at Mobius Investments who followed our trajectory and contributed ideas relevant to investment progress.

Mark Mobius

To my parents, Mrunalini and Rajesh Pandit, and my grandmother, Mitravinda Appalwar; to the extended Pandit and Appalwar families; and to my husband, Dhruva Katrekar—thank you for your quiet care and loud cheerleading. I also wish to thank my professors, teachers, mentors, and collaborators at Cornell University, whose guidance has given meaning to my curiosity—and to that of many others like me.

Sharwari Pandit

Thank you to all who helped bring this book to life, especially those generous enough to offer time and insight during interviews. I also want to acknowledge my family: thank you to my parents Jerry and Evelyn Ninia, my brother James, and my sister Christina for their constant support. I also extend my thanks to all

professors, faculty, and staff members of Cornell University whose guidance and encouragement helped shape the path that led to this book.
John Ninia

Foreword

Although the epicenter of Digital Currency Revolution: Central Banks and the Digital Currency Age is central bank digital currencies (CBDCs), it is much more than just a book about CBDCs. Indeed, the authors fill the canvas by including private digital currencies, such as cryptocurrencies, and their relationship to CBDCs.

When they discuss the origins and purposes of CBDCs, Casanova, Mobius, Nina, and Pandit perform admirably. They use case studies to clearly illustrate their points. The authors present the pros of CBDCs, their cons, and everything in between. Their treatment is comprehensive and clear. To assist readers in navigating this new, and at times, opaque realm, The New Money Order contains two most welcomed appendices: one for acronyms and another for definitions.

With that brief overview and praise, I will now turn to my concerns regarding CBDCs. When it comes to the evaluation of new innovations and their potential adoption by governments, my lodestar is John Stuart Mill (1806–1873) and his exposition of classical liberal ideas contained in On Liberty (1859). In short, Mill (and this author) regarded individual liberty as an intrinsic good.

Given that liberty criterion, how do CBDCs fare? Not well. With CBDCs, the State would have the ability to surveil and control all transactions that individuals make with sovereign legal tender.

This level of control over individuals, enterprises, churches, non-governmental organizations, etc., if exercised, would be total.

It would be control the likes of which even Thomas Hobbes (1588–1679) didn't envision in his classic Leviathan (1651). This type of control can't even be found in The Communist Manifesto (1848), which was penned by none other than Karl Marx (1818–1883) and Friedrich Engels (1820–1895).

But, officialdom argues that we should not worry about the weaponization of CBDCs and their potential to rob people of their liberty. After all, they assert that there would be laws to prohibit such infringements and thefts.

In the real world, however, governments engage in anomie, a word derived from the Greek anomos, which means lawless. Worryingly, the embrace of anomie is becoming more prevalent with each passing day. Just think about how the U.S. dollar and its infrastructure have been weaponized. If we move from the monetary side of the picture to the fiscal side, think about how countries in the Eurozone flout their own Maastricht Treaty—a treaty that sets rules on the ratios of deficit and debt to GDP. As we move closer to the world of democratic despotism, a world anticipated and analyzed so brilliantly by Alexis de Tocqueville (1805-1859) in his classic Democracy in America (1835), CBDCs would likely play a pivotal role. Recall that, in Tocqueville's despotism, the authorities would not wield rifles and bayonets, but would operate as shepherds tending flocks of compliant sheep. What better way for shepherds to keep flocks in check than CBDCs. Indeed, a CBDC would give even the most kindly shepherd the potential to surveil and control every transaction that members of his flock wanted to make.

Prof. Steve H. Hanke
The Johns Hopkins University
Baltimore, USA

Acknowledgements

This book is the product of a collaborative effort, enriched by the insight, dedication, and intellectual contributions of a group of talented students at the Emerging Markets Institute (EMI) at Cornell University. Their expertise and commitment have been invaluable throughout its development.

We are deeply grateful for the intellectual and analytical contributions of **Abhi Das** (Dyson, Cornell '25) and **Gabriel Carvalho** (Cornell Rawlings Presidential Scholar, Cornell '27). Their work was instrumental in shaping the core themes and technical depth of this volume. Special thanks to **Tin Nok (Talia) Mak** and **Maryam Albakry** (Cornell '26), for their copy-editing support. We also extend our appreciation to **Carlos Eduardo Bernos Amoros**, whose expertise played a critical role in completing this book.

We acknowledge the research contributions of **Omeir Zafar Fazal, Grace Heskial, Sasha Phelps, Mini Ge, Shravan Lad**, and **Danna Jumbo Rodríguez**, all of whom interned at EMI in the summer of 2025. Their efforts added meaningful substance to the research process. Additional thanks go to **Srinica Hampi, Akash Kakkar,** and **Ain Razalin** (MBA '25), whose diligence was essential to the project.

We are also indebted to all the chapter contributors who brought their unique expertise to this wide-ranging and global discussion: **Puraav Karnavat, Lucea Wright, Suudharshan Vaidhya, Advik Singh, Ofosuah Frimpong, Jacob Chizunza, Nigel Chimhofu, Chase Young, Tyler Parente, Pratham Rawat, Chris Goranov, and Kaleb Kavuma**. Finally, we extend our heartfelt appreciation to **Nicholas Anthony** from the Cato

Institute's Center for Monetary and Financial Alternatives and **Ankur Singh**, from the Reserve Bank of India, **Anne Miroux**, faculty fellow at EMI for the countless discussions and feedback about the subject; and colleagues at Cornell University for their continued support.

While many individuals contributed to the success of this work, any errors or omissions remain solely the responsibility of the authors.

Executive Summary[1]

Digital Currency Revolution: Central Bank Digital Currencies, Crypto and the Future of Global Finance, explores the transformative potential of Central Bank Digital Currencies (CBDCs). Unlike decentralized cryptocurrencies, CBDCs are government-issued, programmable, and centrally controlled. They promise faster payments, greater transparency, and expanded financial access, but also raise concerns about Privacy, Cybersecurity, and disruption to traditional banking and the financial sector at large. We argue that broad adoption will depend on balancing these trade-offs while aligning incentives across key stakeholders.

Through historical context and global case studies—from China's e-CNY to Nigeria's eNaira—the book shows that technological capability alone isn't enough. Successful CBDC adoption requires public trust, robust infrastructure, targeted activation, and integration with existing financial ecosystems. In many cases, well-established private payment platforms already serve users' needs more effectively, making CBDCs redundant unless paired with thoughtful regulation and user-centric design.

Ultimately, the book suggests that CBDCs will play a role in the future of money, but they are not a guaranteed solution. Countries like the U.S.

---

[1] Central Bank Digital Currencies (CBDCs), stablecoins, and cryptocurrencies are dynamic and rapidly evolving areas of research, policy, and practice. The information contained in this book reflects the status of initiatives at the time of writing. As such, specific projects, regulations, and developments described herein may change, and no guarantee is made as to their future applicability or accuracy.

are choosing alternative paths, focusing on Stablecoins and Blockchain innovation, while others like Dubai lead in asset tokenization infrastructure. The book concludes that the future of finance will be diverse and competitive, driven more by policy choices, and ecosystem readiness than by digital currency alone.

Contents

Part I From Barter to Mobile Payments

1 Introduction to CBDCs   3
   1.1 What Is a CBDC?   5
   1.2 Why Are CBDCs Emerging Now?   5
     1.2.1 The Rise and Rise of Digital Payments   6
     1.2.2 Bringing Financial Services to the Underbanked   7
     1.2.3 The Shifting Tectonics of the Global Economic Order   8
   1.3 Risks and Challenges   9
     1.3.1 Balancing Financial Privacy and Surveillance   9
     1.3.2 Disrupting Traditional Banking Systems   9
     1.3.3 Countering Cybersecurity and Operational Risks   10
     1.3.4 Navigating Legal and Regulatory Hurdles   11
     1.3.5 Building Financial Literacy   11
   1.4 Stakeholder Perspectives   12
   1.5 Digital Sovereignty and the Reinvention of Monetary Systems   14

2 Money: Yesterday, Today, and Tomorrow   15
   2.1 From Barter to Digital Exchange: The Global Evolution of Money   16

	2.1.1	Defining Money: More Than Just Paper and Coins	17
	2.1.2	Barter Economics: The Foundations of Value Exchange	17
	2.1.3	The Coin Era: Metal Currencies and the Standardization of Value	18
	2.1.4	Early Paper Currencies: Flying Money on Textiles	19
	2.1.5	The Gold Standard: Monetary Stability and Global Decline	19
	2.1.6	Contemporary Forms of Money: Fiat Currencies and Their Limitations	21
	2.1.7	Card-Based Transactions: Convenience, Security, and Systemic Challenges	21
2.2	Mobile Payments: Redefining Financial Transactions in the Digital Age		23
2.3	The Future of Money: Cryptocurrencies, CBDCs, and the Next Financial Paradigm		23
2.4	The Rise and Fall of Global Currencies and the Power of Pegging Currencies		24
2.5	Pegging the U.S. Dollar: From Spanish Legacy to American Identity		25
2.6	The Erosion of the Spanish Dollar and the Shift to Gold		25

3 Pain Points in Financial Systems: Financial Inclusion — 29
   3.1 Structural and Infrastructural Social Barriers — 31
   3.2 Conclusion — 36

4 CBDC Systems Engineering — 37
   4.1 Digital Ledger Architecture — 39
   4.2 Blockchain Architecture and Validation Frameworks — 42
   4.3 Data Storage and Security — 47
   4.4 Token-Based Versus Account-Based Models — 49
   4.5 Balancing Privacy, Compliance, and Security — 50
   4.6 Smart Contracts — 52
   4.7 Cross-Border Interoperability — 54
   4.8 Artificial Intelligence and Machine Learning — 56
   4.9 Quantum Computing and the Security of CBDCs — 57
   4.10 CBDC Energy Needs and Environmental Impact: A Comparative Analysis of Digital Currency Systems — 59

	4.10.1	Current Energy Landscape of Financial Systems	59
	4.10.2	CBDC Energy Consumption Characteristics	60
	4.10.3	Comparative Analysis: CBDCs Versus Traditional Banking	61
	4.10.4	Cryptocurrency Energy Consumption Benchmarks	62
	4.10.5	Environmental Impact Assessment	63
	4.10.6	Design Considerations for Energy-Efficient CBDCs	63
	4.10.7	Policy Implications and Strategic Considerations	64
	4.10.8	Implications	65
4.11	Building Digital Currency Systems That Endure	65

Part II The Ins and Outs of CBDC Technology

5 CBDC Launch: e-CNY in China and eNaira in Nigeria — 69
5.1	CBDC Case Study—China	70
	5.1.1 Mobile Payments	73
	5.1.2 China's e-CNY: A Strategic CBDC at the Nexus of Innovation and Global Ambition	78
5.2	CBDC Case Study—Nigeria	82
	5.2.1 Digital Payments	84
	5.2.2 Nigeria's eNaira: A CBDC Caught Between Ambition, Public Resistance, and Policy Reinvention	87
	5.2.3 Looking Ahead: Lessons from CBDC Launches in China and Nigeria	92

6 Mobile Payments: Pix in Brazil and UPI in India — 93
6.1	CBDC Case Study—Brazil	95
	6.1.1 Digital Payments	100
	6.1.2 Mobile Payments in Brazil: Pix	102
	6.1.3 Drex: Brazil's Programmable CBDC for Inclusion and Digital Sovereignty	106
6.2	CBDC Case Study—India	109
	6.2.1 Mobile Payments	110
	6.2.2 CBDCs in India	116
	6.2.3 Divergent Models, Shared Ambitions	122

7	**Experimenting with CBDCs: Ghana, Peru, The Bahamas, Zimbabwe, Kenya, and the Eurozone**	125
	7.1 Ghana's eCedi Project	127
	7.2 Peru: Bridging Rural Gaps Through Gradual Digital Inclusion	132
	7.3 The Bahamas: Pioneering the World's First Retail CBDC	135
	7.4 Zimbabwe: Digital Currency as Crisis Control	139
	7.5 The Digital Euro	142
	7.6 M-Pesa and CBDC Prospects in Kenya	144
	7.7 Lessons and Diverging Trajectories: Global Insights from Early CBDCs	144

Part III Stablecoins, CBDCS, and Competing Visions of Digital Money

8	**Cross-Border CBDCs: mBridge, Agora, and the Others**	149
	8.1 CBDC Effects on Financial Stability and Subsequent Effects on Currency Valuation	151
	8.2 Impacts on Forex	155
	8.3 Project mBridge	156
	8.4 Project Digital Euro	158
	8.5 Project Agora	160
	8.6 Other Projects	162
	8.7 Will the Cross-Border CBDCs Work?	163
9	**Stablecoins: An Alternative to CBDCs**	165
	9.1 What Are Stablecoins?	166
	9.2 Use Cases of Stablecoin and Key Growth Drivers	168
	9.3 Challenges for Stablecoins in a CBDC World	170
	9.4 Stablecoins in a CBDC World	173
	9.5 Tokenization of Assets	175
	9.6 Key Players in the Crypto Space	179

10	**The Debate over CBDCs**		185
	10.1	Advantages of CBDCs	185
	10.2	Fiscal Sustainability and the Elimination of Physical Currency Costs	186
	10.3	Expanding Financial Inclusion	187
	10.4	Technological Sovereignty and the Preservation of Monetary Authority	190
	10.5	Policy Precision and the Fight Against Illicit Activity	191
	10.6	Drawbacks and Concerns Surrounding CBDCs	192
	10.7	Disintermediation of the Banking Sector	194
	10.8	Systemic Cybersecurity Risks	195
	10.9	Barriers to Adoption and Market Readiness	196
11	**2025, a New Opportunity**		199
	11.1	The Digital Euro: An Exercise in Building Consensus in 2025	200
	11.2	China and India: Staying on Course	201
	11.3	United States: Drawing a Line in the Sand	203
	11.4	A GENIUS Move?	208
	11.5	A Red Carpet for Crypto and a Closed Door for CBDCs in 2025	211
	11.6	More Than a Token Gesture—Dubai's Visionary Ecosystem for Tokenization	213
		11.6.1 A Blueprint for the Future	215
	11.7	Case Study: EMAAR	216
	11.8	Looking Ahead: What Does 2025 Promise?	219
12	**Moving Forward**		221
	12.1	The Road to Adoption: Key Drivers	222
	12.2	Challenges to Overcome	223
	12.3	Opportunities for Growth	224
	12.4	Exciting Areas of Growth: What Is Next for CBDCs?	225
	12.5	The End of the Beginning: Charting the Future of Money with CBDCs	226

Appendix   229

References   243

Index   259

About the Authors

Dr. Mark Mobius is synonymous with emerging and frontier markets investing with a reputation as one of the most successful and influential money managers over the past 30 years. He is Chairman of Mobius Emerging Opportunities Fund.

Dr. Mobius is widely known as a pioneer in emerging market investing. In 1987 he was appointed by Sir John Templeton to run one of the world's first emerging market funds. Dr. Mobius went on to spend more than three decades at Franklin Templeton Investments, most recently as Executive Chairman of the Templeton Emerging Markets Group. Under his leadership, the group's assets under management grew from US$100 million to a whopping US$50 billion with the successful launches of numerous investment funds focused on Asia, Latin America, Africa, and Eastern Europe.

Dr. Mobius has also contributed to developing international policies for emerging markets. He served on the World Bank's Global Corporate Governance Forum as a member of the Private

Sector Advisory Group and as co-chairman of its Investor Responsibility Task Force in 1999.

He earned his Ph.D. in Economics and Political Science from the Massachusetts Institute of Technology in 1964. He has also studied at Boston University, University of Wisconsin, Syracuse University, Kyoto University, and the University of New Mexico.

Dr. Mobius has won numerous industry awards and has authored 13 books, including *The Inflation Myth and The Wonderful World of Deflation*, which has gained international acclaim. In October 2022, World Economic Forum selected the book as one of the five must-read books on inflation.

Lourdes Casanova and Rob Cañizares Director Emerging Markets Institute, Senior Lecturer Cornell S.C. Johnson College of Business, Cornell University. Formerly at INSEAD. Awarded in 2025 as a Fellow of the Business Association of Latin American Studies, in 2024 the Euroknowledge Global Thought Leader by Foreign Investment Network. Named one of 50 most influential Iberoamerican intellectuals, one of 30 most influential Iberoamerican women intellectuals by Esglobal. Fulbright Scholar, Masters University of Southern California, Ph.D. University of Barcelona. Her research focuses on the internationalization of emerging market multinationals.

Co-editor with F. Cahen A. Miroux: From copycats to Leaders: Innovation from Emerging Markets. Cambridge University Press with A. Miroux: The Era of Chinese Multinationals. Academic Press. Elsevier 2019. Emerging market multinationals Report 2024, 2023, 2022, 2021, 2020, 2019, 2018, 2017, and 2016. Co-author with P. Cornelius, S. Dutta: Entrepreneurship and the Finance of Innovation in Emerging Markets. Academic Press. Elsevier. With J.

Kassum: The Political Economy of an Emerging Global Power: In search of the Brazilian Dream, Palgrave Macmillan 2014, author Global Latinas: Latin America's emerging multinationals Palgrave Macmillan 2009. Former member Global Agenda Council, Competitiveness in Latin America World Economic Forum, B20 Task Force in G20 summit, Los Cabos (2012). Board member Boyce Tompson Institute. Co-founder Ithaca Hub of Global Shapers. Op-ed writer Latin Trade, Agenda Publica contributor to CNN en español, El País The Economist, Latin America Advisor of The Dialogue and Voice of America.

Sharwari Pandit read law at the National Law School of India University (NLSIU), and graduated with Honors from its B.A., LL.B program in 2017. During this time, she served as Editor of the Socio-Legal Review and Deputy Chief Editor of the National Law School of India Review in 2016-17, which has been cited by the Supreme Court of India on multiple occasions. Sharwari's research at this time focused on issues related to regulation of emerging technologies, and has contributed to academic publications such as the March of the Law (Vol. 10) and the Cyber Crime Laws (Handbook Vol. 1). In 2017, Sharwari was also nominated by the National Law School of India to undertake an academic term at Queen Mary University of London.

Sharwari started her career with Unilever as a Fellow in their legacy Unilever Future Leadership Program, focusing on India and Singapore during her training. From 2018, Sharwari practiced law as an in-house Legal Counsel specializing in technology and Privacy laws at Unilever, where she also supported advocacy and regulatory policy efforts for the Asia Pacific region in the field of e-commerce, data Privacy and anti-counterfeiting regulations. This included engagement with the

Government of India and the Federation of Indian Chambers of Commerce & Industry (FICCI).

In 2023, Sharwari graduated with a Forte Fellowship from the Cornell Johnson Graduate School of Management with a Masters in Business Administration. During this time, she also served as a Fellow at the Emerging Markets Institute. Sharwari's research on Central Bank Digital Currencies, transformative digital payment systems, and financial inclusion in emerging markets has been published by The Diplomat and the Organisation for Economic Co-operation and Development (OECD), among others.

Currently, Sharwari Pandit is a management consultant at McKinsey & Company at Washington, D.C.[1] During her tenure at McKinsey, Sharwari has advised leading global banks, financial institutions, and Fortune 500 technology companies on issues related to risk and regulatory practices, digital strategy, and financial growth.

John Ninia is Co-Founder of Mobius Investments, a global investment firm specializing in emerging and frontier markets, along with Mark Mobius. He plays a central role in shaping the firm's macroeconomic outlook, investment strategy, and thematic research, with a particular focus on technology, energy, and financial systems in developing economies. He integrates deep fundamental analysis with the strategic use of derivatives to optimize portfolio performance, hedge risk, and capture high-conviction opportunities in complex market environments.

John began his academic career as a Hunter R. Rawlings III Research Scholar at Cornell University. While conducting research at Cornell's SC Johnson College of Business and the Emerging

---

[1] All research conducted, resources leveraged, and opinions expressed belong in entirely to the Author and have been made in a strictly personal capacity. They do not represent the opinions or positions of any other organization. All contributions, errors, and liability are the Author's own.

Markets Institute, he focused on the evolution of mobile payment platforms in Asia. His early work on China's digital payment systems catalyzed his long-standing interest in the transformative potential of digital finance, including Central Bank Digital Currencies.

His decision to relocate to Dubai during the COVID-19 pandemic marked a turning point in his professional development, immersing him in one of the world's most dynamic fintech ecosystems. From this global hub, John has led investment research across Asia, Latin America, and the Middle East, examining how digital infrastructure, monetary innovation, and regulatory frameworks influence capital markets. These experiences have informed his nuanced perspective on how CBDCs can reinforce, or disrupt, Financial inclusion, monetary sovereignty, and cross-border settlement systems. Informed by both on-the-ground exposure and institutional investment experience, his work continues to explore how central banks, investors, and innovators navigate the complex trade-offs at the core of digital monetary transformation.

List of Figures

Fig. 4.1	Global CBDC development status as of May 18th, 2025 (*Source* Atlantic Council CBDC Tracker (https://www.atlanticcouncil.org/cbdctracker/); Accessed May 2025)	38
Fig. 4.2	Comparative ledger system attributes in CBDC design (*Source* Designed by Gabriel Carvalho)	41
Fig. 4.3	CBDC network architecture in a permissioned distributed ledger setting (*Source* Designed by Gabriel Carvalho)	43
Fig. 4.4	CBDC consensus mechanism selection tree (*Source* Designed by Gabriel Carvalho)	46
Fig. 4.5	Conceptual triangle illustrating the core trade-offs in CBDC design—privacy, security, and regulatory compliance (*Source* Designed by Gabriel Carvalho)	51
Fig. 4.6	Conceptual model of a CBDC-based welfare disbursement system using smart contracts (*Source* Designed by Gabriel Carvalho)	53
Fig. 4.7	Quantum threat to CBDC systems (*Source* Designed by Gabriel Carvalho)	57
Fig. 4.8	Classical versus post-quantum CBDC security stacks (*Source* Designed by Gabriel Carvalho)	58
Fig. 4.9	Annual energy consumption comparison across financial systems, highlighting CBDC potential for significant energy savings (*Source* Designed by Gabriel Carvalho)	60

List of Figures

Fig. 5.1	Mobile banking penetration in China compared to other countries (%), 2024 (*Source* Statista Consumer Insights [https://www.statista.com/forecasts/1452621/share-of-online-mobile-banking-users-in-selected-countries-worldwide]; Accessed June 2025)	73
Fig. 5.2	E-commerce payment methods in China (in %), 2023 (*Source* EMI research team based on data from Statista)	77
Fig. 5.3	Digital payments transaction values (in billions) (*Source* Statista Market Insights, 2025 [https://www.statista.com/outlook/fmo/payments/digital-payments-worldwide?currency=USD]; Accessed June 2025)	78
Fig. 5.4	GDP per capita in current U.S. dollars of Nigeria, 2001–23 (*Source* World Bank, 2025 [https://data.worldbank.org/indicator/NY.GDP.PCAP.CD?locations=NG]; Accessed June 2025)	83
Fig. 6.1	The number of mobile cellular subscriptions in Brazil from 2015 to 2028 (per 100 capita) (*Source* Statista Market Insights [https://www.statista.com/]; Accessed June 2025)	97
Fig. 6.2	The graph shows the growth in digital payments, net banking, and digital investments, emphasizing the rise of digital finance over the years (*Source* Statista Market Insights [https://www.statista.com/]; Accessed June 2025)	97
Fig. 6.3	Biggest e-commerce payment brands in Brazil as of December 2024 (the use of multiple platforms is common) (*Source* Statista Market Insights [https://www.statista.com/]; Accessed June 2025)	101
Fig. 6.4	Value of real-time payments in Brazil with local scheme Pix from 2020 to 2024 (in million Brazilian real, and estimates in U.S. dollars) (*Source* Statista Market Insights [https://www.statista.com/]; Accessed June 2025)	103
Fig. 6.5	Credit card and digital payment trends in India, 2019–2023 (*Source* Statista Market Insights [https://www.statista.com/]; Accessed June 2025)	110
Fig. 6.6	Market share of payment apps in India's UPI, share of transaction volume processed via these payment apps in April 2024 (*Source* Statista Market Insights [https://www.statista.com/]; Accessed June 2025)	111
Fig. 6.7	Volume of digital transactions in India in FY24, by mode (in billions) (*Source* Statista Market Insights [https://www.statista.com/]; Accessed June 2025)	114
Fig. 6.8	Transaction value across sectors in India in FY23, by payment method (%) (*Source* Statista Market Insights [https://www.statista.com/]; Accessed June 2025)	115

Fig. 6.9	Mobile payments usage by situation in India, 2024 (% of respondents). India, four waves from April 2023 to March 2024, 4032 respondents, 18–54 years (*Source* Statista Market Insights [https://www.statista.com/]; Accessed June 2025)	116
Fig. 7.1	Individuals using the Internet (% of population) vs commercial bank branches (per 100,000 adults) (*Source* World Bank, World Development Indicators [https://data.worldbank.org/indicator]; Accessed November 2024)	133
Fig. 7.2	Transaction value by market in billions ($) (*Source* Statista Market Insights [https://www.statista.com/]; Accessed November 2024)	134
Fig. 8.1	U.S. Dollar (USD) to Nigerian Naira (NGN) exchange rate, 2021–25 (*Source* Google Finance [https://g.co/finance/USD-NGN?window=5Y]; Accessed June 2025)	153
Fig. 8.2	U.S. Dollar (USD) to Indian Rupee (INR) exchange rate, 2021–25 (*Source* Google Finance [https://g.co/finance/USD-INR?window=5Y]; Accessed June 2025)	154

List of Tables

Table 3.1	Top 10 emerging markets by GDP and unbanked population (2021)	30
Table 4.1	Comparison of key consensus mechanisms for CBDC design	45
Table 4.2	Comparison of DeFi and CBDC smart contracts	54
Table 4.3	Energy consumption comparison across different payment systems per transaction, showing CBDC efficiency relative to traditional methods	61
Table 5.1	Timeline of key milestones in the evolution of mobile payments and digital currency in China (2004–2023)	76
Table 5.2	Key categories of digital payment methods and their features	76
Table 5.3	Indirect distribution of e-CNY via the two-tier system	80
Table 5.4	Key design factors underlying China's CBDC technology model	81
Table 5.5	Timeline of key milestones in the evolution of mobile payments and digital currency in Nigeria (2007–2025)	85
Table 6.1	Timeline of key milestones in the evolution of pix in Brazil (2020–2024)	103
Table 6.2	Timeline of key milestones in the evolution of UPI in India (2003–2024)	112
Table 6.3	Key categories and methods of digital payment implementation in India	113
Table 7.1	Timeline of key milestones in the evolution of ZiG in Zimbabwe (2024–2025)	141
Table 9.1	Crypto ecosystem: platforms, exchanges, and newcomers	183

Part I

From Barter to Mobile Payments

1

Introduction to CBDCs

Main Messages

- Central Bank Digital Currencies (CBDCs) are state-issued digital forms of money, representing Legal tender and regulated by central banks. Unlike Bitcoin, CBDCs are centralized and can complement physical cash or a country's Monetary policy.
- CBDCs can improve financial transparency, reduce transaction costs, and expand access to underserved populations. They also enable faster payments and enhance monetary sovereignty in the digital age.
- Key concerns include Privacy, Cybersecurity, and disruption to commercial banks. Success depends on adoption from consumers, financial institutions, fintechs, and governments, each with unique interests and expectations.

The past decade has been one of the most tumultuous in modern history, marked by a pandemic, massive geopolitical shifts, and multiple technological breakthroughs that have created a "tipping point" for many countries, communities, and economies. Every aspect of human life has been disrupted, including the nature of money and its influence on the global economic system.

The contribution of Abhi Das to this chapter is gratefully acknowledged.

One could argue that the 2008 financial crisis acted as a first catalyst for the emergence of alternative financial systems. Although the traditional banking system survived the crisis, it did so at the cost of significant public trust. Coincidentally, Bitcoin was created during that period, filling the trust gap and sparking interest in Blockchain-based technologies. This momentum eventually led to the development of other Blockchains and digital assets.

During this time, government intervention, technological innovation, and commercial enterprises have enabled the rapid scaling of digital payment systems and Cross-border payments worldwide. However, it was with the introduction of Blockchain technology and the emergence of a new class of financial instruments that the very nature of money, as we understand it, was altered. Cryptocurrencies and Stablecoins have expanded the scope and function of money. While governments worldwide adopt a range of stances toward these "alternative assets," it is clear that their adoption is on the rise and unlikely to cease anytime soon.

As these new technology-based financial instruments began to gain significant traction, governments and regulators around the world developed their perspectives and positions on engaging with these innovations. It is far from surprising that key financial and government institutions have also begun experimenting with new tech-based tools at their disposal. The development of Central Bank Digital Currencies, or "CBDCs," was an inevitable next step by governments seeking to leverage these technologies to offer faster, more accessible, and digital native forms of currency. For some, CBDCs can be another step toward Financial inclusion. For others, it may be a way to compete with private digital payment providers. Over the past five years, as more governments and central banks have begun to roll out pilots, a plethora of use cases have emerged. Different models and approaches to developing a CBDC emerged, with a range of design choices for governments based on their primary drivers for creating a CBDC. The introduction of pilots worldwide has been accompanied by a more holistic understanding of the risks, opportunities, and challenges that CBDCs can pose for governments and their citizens.

That is our inspiration for writing this book—to introduce you, our reader, to the new face of money. In this book, we plan to explore the current innovations related to CBDCs, the broad spectrum of CBDCs being launched by countries around the world, and the potential risks, challenges, and opportunities associated with the adoption of CBDCs. We will also explore the implications of CBDCs in a broader context, including their potential to disrupt cross-border payment systems, their implications for the global economic order, and their forward-looking impact on economies worldwide.

But before we delve into these themes, let's start with a quick introduction to the key player in our discussion—the CBDC.

1.1 What Is a CBDC?

At its core, a CBDC is a digital representation of a country's sovereign currency, issued and regulated by its central bank and designed to serve as a form of Legal tender. CBDCs are different from cryptocurrencies, which tend to be decentralized, not backed by any authority, and largely unregulated. CBDCs represent a direct claim on a country's respective central bank, just like physical cash. In most contexts, CBDCs have been designed to complement and not replace cash. The motivation to explore CBDCs has multiple origins. The rapid growth and popularity of private digital payment platforms, such as Alipay and UPI, and cryptocurrencies like Bitcoin, have posed a challenge to the traditional role of central banks in ensuring monetary sovereignty. Although these technologies are now under increased regulatory scrutiny and oversight, they have managed to offer mainstream alternatives to the traditional, legacy banking infrastructure. The growing user base has threatened to displace state-backed monetary systems. Regardless of how they choose to respond, the one thing that key financial institutions cannot do is ignore the disruption wrought by advances in technology and alternative financial instruments. In many countries, CBDCs are the public-sector's response to this. In such countries, the central banks and governments position it as a secure, centralized, and sovereign digital currency that can balance innovation, inclusion, Privacy, and trust.

As of June 2025, 137 countries are exploring CBDCs of which three, Bahamas, Jamaica, and Nigeria have launched it, 49 are in the pilot phase (Atlantic Council 2025). There are two main types of CBDCs: Retail CBDCs, accessible by the general public for everyday transactions (functioning as digital cash), and Wholesale CBDCs, restricted to financial institutions for interbank settlement and improved large-scale financial operations.

1.2 Why Are CBDCs Emerging Now?

The global push toward CBDCs stems from a combination of economic, geopolitical, and technological factors. In our opinion, there are three primary drivers that have set the stage for a broader reset of financial regulation and experimentation with CBDCs: first, a flurry of technology-led innovation created a foundation for the explosive growth of digital payment systems, Blockchain-based digital assets (e.g., cryptocurrencies, Stablecoins, etc.); second, the rapid expansion of access and Financial inclusion to large swathes of unbanked and underbanked populations in developing and less developed economies; and finally, broader geopolitical shifts and a gradual reordering of the global economic order. Together, these three drivers have triggered a fundamental reimagining of the very nature of money and its use, control, and exchange in the past decade.

1.2.1 The Rise and Rise of Digital Payments

The introduction of digital payment capabilities has been one of the most disruptive financial innovations in the past twenty years. At the time of writing, estimates of the number of people who use digital payment services indicate that anywhere between half to two-thirds of the global population uses some form of digital payment. Regardless of the exact number, we can safely assume that billions of users have been able to access financial services, conduct real-time transactions from remote locations, and reduce (if not nearly completely remove) their dependence on physical cash to make payments. Remarkably, the rapid growth in access to the Internet and mobile phones across the world has facilitated the adoption of digital payments by vast swathes of populations in developing economies. Visit India, Brazil, or Kenya, and you'll find that customized, cheap, and technologically advanced digital payment services have seen widespread adoption. More advanced economies, such as China, have been pioneers in driving large-scale adoption of digital payment systems (e.g., Alipay, WeChat Pay) in their countries.

In tandem with this move has been the rise of alternate digital assets, popularly known by the umbrella term "crypto." However, this plethora of financial instruments is far from a monolith—"crypto" as an umbrella term includes Blockchain-based, decentralized cryptocurrencies, Stablecoins, and tokenized assets, among many other instruments that have mushroomed in the past decade. From the most mainstream representative, Bitcoin, to wildly fluctuating tokens' Blockchain-based instruments opened the door to a cornucopia of alternate financial instruments that lay outside the reach and regulation of traditional Financial inclusion. While initially seen as a domain of interest for a small group of early adopters, the rapid infusion and channeling of wealth into these new digital assets has forced governments and financial regulators to take notice and take a position. and this.

From the United States and United Arab Emirates' recent enthusiastic embrace of "crypto" to India's clear signaling against their recognition, different countries have marked out their positions on this issue. But yay or nay, these are advances that cannot be ignored and can barely be contained by regulatory will.

The COVID-19 pandemic accelerated these transitions, with technological advances, rapid economic fluctuation, and remote working systems necessitating a broader move toward digitization and digital assets. The growing dominance of private digital payment platforms and decentralized crypto-assets has disrupted the traditional financial system and raised questions about monetary sovereignty. All of this has prompted central banks to explore digital alternatives like CBDCs in order to ensure the accessibility and relevance of public money.

1.2.2 Bringing Financial Services to the Underbanked

A second key driver for central banks and governments to explore rolling out a CBDC has been its potential to promote Financial inclusion, especially in countries where large swaths of the population are unbanked or underbanked. Further, it can potentially simplify the disbursement of welfare funds and subsidies by leveraging technologies such as programmable currencies (which could only be used by authorized providers or to purchase specific items). An important example of this is The Bahamas' Sand Dollar, which was primarily designed to serve the large number of remote islands that lack banking infrastructure.

CBDCs have the potential to make payment systems more efficient, transparent, and competitive. By reducing reliance on private intermediaries, CBDCs lower transaction costs and speed up settlements. From a competition standpoint, they provide an alternative to private-sector payment networks like Visa and MasterCard. Brazil's central bank introduced Pix, an instant payment platform, to make payments faster, cheaper, and more accessible. Pix has a user base of over 160 million as of September 2024. Building on Pix's success, Brazil is piloting Drex, a CBDC project that is aimed at further improving payment system efficiency and fostering competition in the financial sector.

CBDCs can also offer greater transparency in money flows, which central banks can leverage to combat illicit financial activities such as money laundering or counterfeit sales. If so designed, CBDCs can act as tools to enhance oversight and control over capital flows, making illegal activities easier to detect and prevent. This potential for increased transparency is particularly attractive to governments seeking to strengthen financial integrity. Uruguay's e-Peso pilot, for example, included features such as transaction limits and digital records to enhance transparency and traceability.

1.2.3 The Shifting Tectonics of the Global Economic Order

In response to turbulent geopolitical situations across the globe, CBDCs have been emerging as instruments of monetary sovereignty and geopolitical strategy. The digitization of money and payments, previously dominated by private-sector operators and foreign currencies, has raised concerns about national control over payment systems and Monetary policy. Some countries see CBDCs as a means to promote their currency in international payments and challenge the dominance of the U.S. dollar in global finance. By issuing their own digital currencies, central banks aim to maintain control over their monetary systems and reduce dependence on foreign or private payment networks. China's digital yuan is not only intended for domestic use but also as a tool to promote the internationalization of the national currency. By piloting Cross-border payments with Hong Kong and other countries, China aims to reduce reliance on the U.S. dollar and foreign payment networks. On a similar note, the European Central Bank ("the ECB") has fast-tracked its Digital Euro project to counteract pressures from tariff-driven trade disruptions while simultaneously reducing its reliance on U.S.-controlled financial infrastructure.

Within countries as well, political structures play a significant role in the pace and direction of CBDC adoption. Research has shown that governments with more centralized institutional structures have been able to drive the adoption of CBDCs more effectively but have also leveraged them as tools for increased surveillance and control over financial flows. China's Digital Yuan (e-CNY) is integrated with the Social Credit System, and its use is mandatory in cross-border trade settlements. On the other hand, countries with more independent institutional structures tend to proceed with caution, prioritizing Privacy, transparency, and public trust. Additionally, countries with higher levels of perceived corruption and money laundering are more likely to explore CBDCs as tools to increase transparency and fight financial crime.

1.3 Risks and Challenges

As several countries proceed to advanced pilots for CBDCs, challenges in design, execution, and adoption have also begun to emerge. Depending on the economic and political context, these difficulties range from concerns regarding Privacy, trust, and effective use cases to Cybersecurity, operational, and regulatory risks.

1.3.1 Balancing Financial Privacy and Surveillance

Contrary to the anonymous nature of cash transactions, CBDCs provide digital records that can be accessed by central banks and their respective governments. Central banks would be able to monitor individual spending patterns and behaviors, raising concerns about overreach by government authorities. The accumulation of sensitive information, both personal and financial, adds to the risk of data breaches, identity theft, etc. This information is at greater risk when used in the context of cross-border transactions. When the European Central Bank sought public feedback about its digital euro-pilot, Privacy was among the top concerns, with 41% of comments focused on this issue. The ECB President Christine Lagarde acknowledged the fact that the digital euro would not offer complete anonymity.

1.3.2 Disrupting Traditional Banking Systems

Depending on the design, execution, and adoption of their specific CBDCs, central banks could drive major disruptions to the traditional banking infrastructure. If CBDCs offer a safer or more attractive alternative to bank deposits, resulting from government banking and higher liquidity, consumers might end up moving their funds to CBDC wallets, particularly during economic crises (through bank runs). A lower deposit base for commercial banks could be detrimental, impacting bank profit margins and lending. At its most extreme, CBDCs could effectively disintermediate traditional banks by offering Wholesale CBDCs that can subsume interbank transfer functionalities.

A paper published by the IMF modeled the potential for bank Disintermediation following the introduction of CBDCs. The research findings indicate that, in an imperfectly competitive environment, banks tend to increase deposit interest rates following the introduction of a CBDC. This would retain depositors by making traditional deposits more attractive in comparison to the respective CBDC option. This would have a dual effect on the aggregate deposits. Wealthier households would respond to the higher deposit rates by increasing their deposits at the banks (intensive margin). On the other hand, low-income households would shift their funds from banks to CBDCs, attracted by the lower access costs and efficiency offered by CBDCs. The impact on lending is quantitatively small, but broader concerns need to be addressed.

While Monetary policy frameworks are not expected to change in the short term due to CBDCs radically, central banks are proactively tailoring CBDC designs to avoid negative side effects. The prevailing strategy is to start small: limited rollouts, no interest on CBDCs, caps on holdings, and involving banks as intermediaries so that the traditional system and the new digital form grow together. As one Federal Reserve study put it, the effects of a CBDC "depend critically on its design features." With prudent design, early evidence (from The Bahamas, Eastern Caribbean, and Nigeria) suggests that financial stability risks are manageable—these economies have not seen any bank Disintermediation to date, as CBDC uptake remains controlled.

1.3.3 Countering Cybersecurity and Operational Risks

Building upon concerns about financial Privacy through data breaches, CBDC systems are prime targets for hackers, cybercriminals, and the like. CBDC systems possess a concentration of sensitive data, increasing the risk of large-scale data leaks. This could lead to identity theft, fraud, and financial losses.

At the same time, CBDC platforms need to be available at all times. A technical failure or outage could disrupt economic activity, provided CBDCs become mainstream. Central banks need to develop and maintain an incredibly sophisticated infrastructure, inherently requiring large capital investments in hardware, software, and human capital to ensure reliability and scalability. Both the IMF and central banks have acknowledged this challenge since an attack or an outage could undermine public trust in CBDCs and hurt liquidity for the entire country. This is especially challenging for countries that lack both capital and a robust digital infrastructure necessary to tackle these risks.

1.3.4 Navigating Legal and Regulatory Hurdles

Many countries' existing legal structures fail to account for the unique nature of CBDCs. These include aspects like programmability, digital identities, and cross-border use. Countries would need to work on legislation to ensure that CBDCs are classified as Legal tender. Balancing user Privacy versus law enforcement is a challenge that involves navigating the tracking of money laundering, terrorism financing, and other illicit activities while maintaining public trust. The cross-border use of CBDCs makes legal compliance a lot more complicated since different countries may have conflicting regulations with respect to data protection, consumer rights, and financial oversight. The EU's draft law says the digital euro will have Legal tender status, meaning broad acceptance is required, but also recognizes that a period of adoption and provisions for exceptions (like small merchants with no digital connectivity) might be necessary. Nigeria did not explicitly force merchants to accept eNaira in the initial phase, but the government did direct that all government agencies and merchants dealing with the public should not discriminate against eNaira as a payment method. Over time, more forceful mandates could come if adoption stalls—indeed, some reports suggest Nigeria considered making certain state disbursements only via eNaira to drive usage.

1.3.5 Building Financial Literacy

Another major challenge facing the adoption of CBDCs is ensuring that the broad public understands what a CBDC even is. CBDCs are being introduced in populations with low digital and financial literacy. In rural and underserved populations, access to the necessary technology, whether that's smartphones or Internet connectivity, is uneven. Situations like this may exacerbate financial exclusion among these populations. The general public may be unfamiliar with the concepts of digital wallets, programmable money, etc. This unfamiliarity would increase the vulnerability to mistakes and fraud, and users may end up falling victim to scams and phishing attempts. Central banks need to invest in public awareness campaigns to ensure that the user interface is functional and easy to understand.

While understanding the approach of countries toward CBDCs, it is helpful to remember that not all challenges outlined above would apply to any given country. But, depending on the incentive and design selected by a central bank or government, one or more of these challenges are likely to apply. Further, challenges related to Cybersecurity, digital infrastructure, and public trust are likely to impact all countries seeking to develop a CBDC. We provide an overview of these potential risks and challenges to contextualize our observations and arguments throughout this book.

1.4 Stakeholder Perspectives

The journey toward adopting a CBDC involves multiple stakeholders—each with distinct interests, concerns, and expectations. Understanding these perspectives is crucial for the success of any CBDC project, as buy-in from users, financial institutions, and other stakeholders will determine actual usage.

General Public (Consumers): The general public, or consumers, are primarily concerned with how a CBDC will impact their daily lives. For most people, the technical details or policy motivations behind a CBDC matter less than its convenience, cost, and trustworthiness compared to existing payment options. As we have mentioned, the central bank of The Bahamas launched the Sand Dollar to make it easier for residents in remote areas to access financial services. In China, the government has piloted the digital yuan in several cities and has even offered incentives like "red envelope" lotteries to encourage its use. Even so, adoption has been slow, as Retail CBDCs often fail to distinguish themselves from other digital payment services available to users. In some other instances, a lack of trust in the central bank or public institutions drives a reluctance to adopt CBDCs.

Merchants and Businesses: For merchants and businesses, a CBDC is attractive mainly if it can help increase sales, lower transaction costs, and if there is clear customer demand for it. Retailers in Sweden have expressed interest in the e-Krona as a way of maintaining access to digital payments as cash usage declines. However, they have also expressed worries about the costs and logistics of upgrading payment systems to accept a new form of money. The Eastern Caribbean's DCash project initially faced technical challenges, including slow transaction times, which can make merchants hesitant. The merchants who did adopt it found benefits, including reduced cash handling and faster settlements, proving that merchant buy-in can still be achieved if the value proposition is clear.

Commercial Banks: Commercial banks are, in all likelihood, the most sensitive stakeholders in the CBDC conversation, as a digital currency issued by the central bank could disrupt their traditional role as deposit holders and intermediaries in the payment system. Many banks have expressed concerns about losing deposits to CBDCs and the costs involved in updating their infrastructure. In Nigeria, the launch of the eNaira was met with some resistance from commercial banks. These banks were slow in promoting new digital wallets to their customers, which, in turn, contributed to adoption rates that were lower than expectations. European banks have lobbied for limits on how much digital euro individuals can hold out of fear that a CBDC like the proposed digital euro could attract large amounts of funds away from commercial banks and toward the European Central Bank.

Fintech and Payment Service Providers: Fintech companies and payment service providers have a mixed perspective on CBDCs. For some, a CBDC could be seen as competition to their existing payment products, but for others, it represents an opportunity to build new services atop a national digital currency platform. In China, major payment platforms like WeChat Pay and Alipay initially viewed the digital yuan as a potential threat. However, both platforms have since integrated the digital yuan into their apps. Local fintechs in The Bahamas have partnered with the central bank to provide digital wallets and help develop new and innovative financial products, leveraging the Sand Dollar as a foundation for growth.

Central Bank and Government: The central bank and government are also key stakeholders since their reputation and policy objectives are closely tied to the success of a CBDC. Central banks are motivated by goals including Financial inclusion, payment system resilience, and effective Monetary policy, but they also need to manage risks related to Cybersecurity, operational failures, and public trust. The Central Bank of The Bahamas introduced the Sand Dollar to promote Financial inclusion and ensure payment system resilience, particularly after hurricanes disrupted cash supply chains. In Sweden, the Riksbank's push for the e-Krona is a response to the rapid decline in cash use and the need to guarantee that everyone has access to a state-backed means of payment.

International Institutions: International institutions such as the International Monetary Fund (IMF), World Bank, and Bank for International Settlements (BIS) play a crucial advisory and oversight role. These organizations generally support CBDCs for their potential to enhance financial stability, inclusion, and cross-border payment efficiency, but they also caution about operational and regulatory risks. The IMF has provided technical assistance to several countries, including Nigeria, during the eNaira rollout and has published reports on the challenges faced, such as low adoption and the need for better user education. The World Bank has supported the Eastern Caribbean Central Bank with guidance on regulatory frameworks and risk management for its DCash project.

Stakeholder	Key interest/concern
General public	Convenience, cost, trust
Merchants/businesses	Lower fees, integration
Commercial banks	Deposit loss, infrastructure cost
Fintech/PSPs	Competition, platform opportunities
Central Bank/government	Inclusion, resilience, reputation
International institutions	Stability, advice, risk management

1.5 Digital Sovereignty and the Reinvention of Monetary Systems

The emergence of CBDCs marks a pivotal moment in the evolution of money. As nations respond to rapid technological change, declining cash usage, the rise of cryptocurrencies, and intensifying geopolitical competition, CBDCs present a state-backed digital alternative designed to maintain public oversight of monetary systems. Rather than replacing existing forms of money, CBDCs are intended to complement them—supporting goals such as Financial inclusion, operational efficiency, and monetary sovereignty.

An interesting outcome of the differing incentives to adopt CBDCs and the ability choices for CBDCs are shaped by each country's unique priorities and constraints. In The Bahamas, for instance, the emphasis lies on promoting Financial inclusion across remote and underserved areas. In contrast, Sweden focuses on strengthening payment system transparency and competitiveness. Technological decisions—such as adopting centralized versus distributed ledger architectures or enabling offline transactions—are tightly linked to infrastructure capacity and user needs. Political structures also play a decisive role: centralized regimes may deploy CBDCs rapidly through top-down mandates, whereas democracies tend to proceed more cautiously, emphasizing transparency, Privacy safeguards, and public trust.

In this book, we explore the origins, infrastructure, and profound opportunities that CBDCs present for reshaping the future of money and monetary systems in the financial sector.

2

Money: Yesterday, Today, and Tomorrow

Main Messages

- Money evolved from barter systems to commodity currencies like coins and eventually to paper money backed by gold, reflecting changing needs and technologies.
- Financial transactions advanced with debit/credit cards and mobile payments, increasing speed, convenience, and global accessibility while highlighting new security and interoperability challenges.
- Cryptocurrencies and CBDCs offer decentralized, programmable, and inflation-resistant alternatives to fiat money, reshaping how individuals store value and engage with global financial systems.

The rise of Blockchain-based digital assets and various forms of CBDCs present a fundamental shift in the nature of money and how we engage with it. In fact, their rise itself underscores fundamental issues with the current traditional financial systems. Cryptocurrencies, with their decentralized and secure nature,[1] have emerged as a direct response to the inefficiencies, lack of transparency, and security vulnerabilities of traditional banking systems. This shift serves as a powerful reminder that change is not only inevitable

---

[1] Not all cryptocurrencies are decentralized but this point will be discussed later.

but necessary. Yet, as we look to the future, understanding it first requires us to examine the past.

By analyzing historical trends and their connection to the present, we can better prepare for the future and position ourselves to capitalize on emerging opportunities. Before delving into the future of emerging markets, it is essential first to explore the history and evolution of money, a concept that has undergone dramatic transformation over the centuries. In this chapter, we will trace the development of money from the bartering systems of early civilizations to the creation of modern currencies, which have become the primary medium of exchange. Additionally, we will examine the monetary systems of countries that have yet to adopt CBDCs or cryptocurrencies as Legal tender. How do their traditional cash or card payment systems compare to economies that have fully embraced CBDCs and crypto? This contrast will shed light on the potential benefits and drawbacks of these innovations.

We will also give special attention to emerging markets, as they play a critical role in shaping the current global financial landscape. Emerging markets are no longer just participants in the global economy; they are becoming leaders and drivers of innovation. In a remarkable leap forward, many of these markets have transitioned from outdated systems to adopting some of the most advanced technologies in the world. Their rapid progress extends beyond economic growth, revolutionizing political infrastructure, fostering development, and asserting their influence on the global stage.

These markets have become key pillars of the global economy, offering a model for developed nations that now struggle to keep pace with the speed of change. Their embrace of cutting-edge technologies positions them as the next logical step in the evolution of trade and financial markets. These nations are not only developing at an unprecedented rate but also pioneering solutions that could serve as a blueprint for the future of the global economy. Their approach to adopting or resisting CBDCs will undoubtedly influence the future of global finance and may define the next development in the evolution of financial markets and systems.

2.1 From Barter to Digital Exchange: The Global Evolution of Money

To understand how modern financial systems operate, it is essential to trace the origins and evolution of money itself. This section explores the diverse forms money has taken, from barter and coins to "flying cash" and plastic cards, highlighting how shifting technologies, politics, and social needs have continually reshaped their function and meaning.

2.1.1 Defining Money: More Than Just Paper and Coins

At first glance, defining money may seem like a simple question, but a deeper examination reveals its complexity. Across different cultures and societies, people have varying perceptions of what money is—and what it represents. These differences stem from historical, economic, and social factors that shape how value is assigned and exchanged.

At its core, money has always been a means of exchange. More specifically, it refers to items—not necessarily paper bills—that are assigned a specific value, backed by legislative authority, and accepted by both parties in a transaction to facilitate the exchange of goods, commodities, or services. This definition is important because, since its inception, money as a mechanism for exchanging value has undergone numerous transformations. What began as simple barter systems evolved into the use of commodity money, metal coins, and, eventually, the paper currency we rely on today. Understanding this progression provides insight into how different societies have shaped and redefined money over time, setting the stage for its continued evolution.

2.1.2 Barter Economics: The Foundations of Value Exchange

Bartering was the earliest form of value exchange, in which people traded goods or services directly without legal backing, commodity-based standards, or a universal measure of value. In its simplest form, if you owned a goat but needed grain, and I had grain but wanted meat, we would negotiate a trade that both of us found fair—your goat for my grain. This system extended beyond goods-for-goods exchanges and often included trading materials or food for specific services.

Historical records confirm that the barter system was present across major ancient civilizations—the Mesopotamians, ancient Egyptians, Babylonians, and residents of the Indus Valley are examples of ancient communities that traded using the barter system. Examples of goods exchanged included trading beads, animals, grain, and even raw materials—with a range of record-keeping systems indicating sophisticated, at-scale bartering activity without standardized currencies. However, the limitations of the barter system quickly became evident. The biggest challenge was determining what was a fair exchange. Without a universal standard of value, each party relied on their subjective assessment of worth. A goat, for instance, might be highly valuable to one person but less so to another, making negotiations complex and often contentious.

Another significant drawback was the difficulty of storing value. Many of the goods being traded, particularly food and perishable items, could not be preserved for long or divided into smaller units without losing their utility. A goat, for example, could not be split in half without diminishing its usefulness, and an equivalent quantity of grain might spoil before being fully consumed. These practical challenges made barter inefficient for large-scale or long-term trade, highlighting the need for a more reliable and standardized system of value exchange.

2.1.3 The Coin Era: Metal Currencies and the Standardization of Value

Coins have played a central role in the history of money. Dating back as early as 500 B.C., various forms of coins, each with distinct shapes, sizes, and seals, have been used across civilizations as a medium of exchange. While many people associate coins with gold and silver, it's important to note that the earliest coins used as currency differed greatly from the ones we're familiar with today. Although ancient coins were primarily made from silver, their design and function were far more rudimentary compared to the finely minted coins used in modern economies. That said, the ability to mint unique, official insignia of a ruler or government has always been a highly regulated, secure process. At the peak of the Ottoman Empire's reign, the singular official mint was a closely guarded building within the walls of the Topkapi Palace in the heart of Istanbul, the Empire's capital.

However, coins have a significant drawback: once accumulated, they become cumbersome to carry. The weight and bulk of a large number of coins made daily transactions difficult, especially for merchants and business people. This practical issue was especially evident in ancient China, where merchants found it increasingly difficult to transport their wealth from place to place. As a result, they sought a more convenient way to carry money, leading to the innovation of paper currency. This breakthrough marked a pivotal turning point in the evolution of money, laying the foundation for the paper-based tender systems that would later shape the modern financial world. The development of paper currency not only addressed the practical challenges of coinage but also catalyzed the future of global commerce, facilitating faster, more efficient transactions on a larger scale. However, it is worth noting that despite the widespread adoption of paper currencies for centuries, coins continue to serve as Legal tender in many parts of the world, highlighting their enduring effectiveness as a medium of exchange.

2.1.4 Early Paper Currencies: Flying Money on Textiles

Money, or at least the concept of it, has been an integral part of human civilization for millennia. But just how long has it been around? To put it into perspective, as early as the Tang Dynasty (618–907), businessmen in ancient China were already using a form of currency known as Feiqian, which translates to "flying money." However, these Feiqian "bills" were quite different from the paper money we know today. Rather than being printed on the familiar paper materials used for modern banknotes, they were often inscribed on textiles, creating a unique and durable form of currency.

Functioning as bills of exchange, Feiqian represented specific values and were used by government officials and merchants to facilitate trade across long distances. They could be carried from one city to another without the burden of transporting cumbersome coins or precious metals, effectively bypassing the logistical challenges associated with moving physical assets like gold or silver. This innovation made trade more efficient and secure, reducing the risks of theft and loss.

These early forms of "paper money" were revolutionary for their time, serving as a precursor to the widespread adoption of paper currency that would later define global economies. The introduction of Feiqian marks a significant chapter in the evolution of money, highlighting early advancements in financial systems that enabled the seamless transfer of value without reliance on cumbersome, tangible goods.

2.1.5 The Gold Standard: Monetary Stability and Global Decline

Paper money has long served as a medium of exchange, but its widespread use came with significant challenges. Initially, paper bills were exchanged alongside gold and silver, but they lacked a consistent commodity backing to ensure their value. Rampant counterfeiting ensued and undermined confidence in paper currency, and governments occasionally manipulated its value to serve political or economic agendas. These issues eventually led to the creation of the Gold Standard, a system designed to provide stability by directly tying currency to a fixed quantity of gold.

The Gold Standard was first introduced in England during the nineteenth century and soon became a cornerstone of the global financial system. By linking paper money to gold reserves, the system ensured that currency had a tangible and reliable value, as a country's central bank could only issue money proportional to its gold holdings. This framework instilled trust in paper currency, acting as a safeguard against inflation and preventing the over-issuance of paper money. Throughout the late nineteenth and early twentieth centuries, the Gold Standard was widely adopted and seen as a crucial mechanism for controlling inflation and facilitating international trade.

However, the Gold Standard had inherent limitations that would eventually lead to its downfall. One of its most significant weaknesses was its rigidity during economic crises, particularly the Great Depression. In the 1930s, gold's value fluctuated wildly, and countries struggled to maintain their reserves to meet the demands of their economies. The constraints of the Gold Standard prevented governments from adjusting Monetary policy to respond to economic downturns, exacerbating the global financial crisis. As the Depression deepened, the United States, under President Franklin D. Roosevelt, became one of the first nations to abandon the Gold Standard in 1933, allowing for greater flexibility in managing the economy.

Political pressures further accelerated the Gold Standard's collapse. A pivotal moment came during the 1896 U.S. presidential election when William Jennings Bryan delivered his famous "Cross of Gold" speech, denouncing the Gold Standard as harmful to farmers and the working class. He advocated for the adoption of silver as a standard of value to provide greater economic opportunities. Although Bryan lost the election, his speech highlighted growing dissatisfaction with the Gold Standard and contributed to its eventual decline.

The final blow came in 1971 when President Richard Nixon took the United States off the Gold Standard entirely in what became known as the "Nixon Shock." This decision ended the direct convertibility of the U.S. dollar to gold, marking the official transition to a fiat-based monetary system. By severing the currency's link to gold, the U.S. government gained greater flexibility in managing the economy, as it could print money without needing equivalent gold reserves. However, this shift also introduced new challenges, particularly inflation and currency devaluation, which continue to shape financial markets today.

The collapse of the Gold Standard highlighted the need for a more adaptable monetary system, leading to the development of complex financial regulations and economic policies that govern modern economies today.

While the transition to fiat currency has allowed for greater flexibility in managing economic cycles, it has also introduced new risks, including inflation, debt, and global financial stability—issues that remain central to economic discussions today.

2.1.6 Contemporary Forms of Money: Fiat Currencies and Their Limitations

In the modern era, the exchange of value has become increasingly standardized, with continuous advancements aimed at making transactions faster, more efficient, and more accessible. At its most basic level, money is still exchanged primarily through cash payments. While this process may seem straightforward, it is, in reality, highly complex.

One of the main reasons for this complexity is the existence of multiple currencies, each with different values. As a result, transferring value across different currency systems requires accounting for exchange rates and price fluctuations, which introduces economic and financial challenges.

Beyond its function as a medium of exchange, money also serves as a store of value—allowing individuals to sell goods today and later redeem their earnings for future purchases. While money has addressed historical issues of divisibility, its ability to retain value over time remains a challenge. As investor Ray Dalio has noted, "Of the roughly 750 currencies that have existed since 1700, only about 20 percent remain." Moreover, even those that have survived, such as the U.S. dollar, have experienced significant depreciation. The USD, for instance, has lost over 99% of its value since the 1700s due to inflation driven by the continuous expansion of the money supply.

While fiat currencies may appear stable in the short term, history suggests that over long periods, they are prone to significant devaluation. This raises important considerations for individuals and institutions seeking to preserve wealth, highlighting the ongoing evolution of money and the potential need for alternative value storage mechanisms.

2.1.7 Card-Based Transactions: Convenience, Security, and Systemic Challenges

Just as large amounts of coins proved difficult to transport, carrying large sums of paper currency also became impractical. To address this challenge, money had to evolve once again—this time with the help of technology. This evolution led to the introduction of debit and credit cards, which revolutionized financial transactions by making money transfers more convenient and secure.

The impact of debit and credit cards on the exchange of money has been profound. With these cards, moving large amounts of money across long distances is no longer a logistical challenge. Instead of carrying stacks of cash, individuals can slip a card into their pocket or purse and access their funds from any ATM linked to a compatible financial institution. Better yet, by swiping or tapping their card at a cash register, they can make purchases without the need for physical money at all.

Beyond convenience, debit and credit cards offer several advantages over cash. Unlike paper currency, cards are insured, reducing the risk of loss or theft. Credit cards, in particular, provide individuals with access to funds they may not yet have, offering financial flexibility. Additionally, they come with various incentives such as cashback rewards, airport lounge access, loyalty points, and exclusive benefits—features that have made it difficult for advanced economies that have widely adopted card-based transactions to transition away from them.

However, despite these advances, another issue remained: transferring money across borders. While sharing card information might seem like a possible solution, it is neither safe nor practical. Giving someone access to your debit or credit card details exposes you to fraud, identity theft, and unauthorized transactions. Once card information is shared, it can be misused, intercepted by hackers, or even sold on the dark web. Furthermore, card transactions often require authentication through Personal Identification Numbers (PINs), CVV codes (a three- or four-digit number printed on the back of the credit/debit card), or additional security measures, making it difficult for someone else to use your card without encountering these safeguards.

Even if security were not a concern, using a card to transfer funds internationally is impractical. Many cards have restrictions on foreign transactions, and even when permitted, currency conversion fees, processing delays, and potential withdrawal limits can make the process cumbersome and expensive. The alternative—physically traveling to deliver cash—poses its own limitations, including time, cost, and security risks.

2.2 Mobile Payments: Redefining Financial Transactions in the Digital Age

Mobile payments using mobile phones emerged from the need for a seamless, borderless way to transfer money, and they have fundamentally transformed the way financial transactions take place. By eliminating geographical barriers, mobile payment systems enable users to send and receive money across vast distances instantaneously. What once required physical cash, checks, or even card-based transactions can now be completed with just a few taps on a smartphone.

In countries like China, mobile payments have become the dominant method for financial exchanges, not just for peer-to-peer (P2P) transfers but also for person-to-business (P2B) transactions. While many consumers in the United States still reach for their wallets at checkout, mobile payments in China have become second nature. The widespread adoption of mobile payment platforms in China has reshaped daily commerce, making traditional cash transactions increasingly obsolete.

Mobile payments have taken the convenience of financial transactions to an entirely new level, reshaping how people think about and interact with money on a global scale.

2.3 The Future of Money: Cryptocurrencies, CBDCs, and the Next Financial Paradigm

While money and its transfer systems have evolved significantly over time, the financial world remains far from achieving a flawless system. Despite major advancements, persistent challenges such as security risks, supply chain inefficiencies, and record mutability continue to threaten the stability and integrity of financial markets. Additionally, centralized banking institutions still exert control over individuals' access to funds, often imposing withdrawal restrictions and slow processing times, which can create bottlenecks in financial transactions. These limitations are driving a growing shift toward alternative financial models, prompting a reassessment of traditional banking systems.

As concerns over financial security and autonomy grow, more individuals are seeking alternative ways to safeguard their wealth. As discussed in our introduction, this search has contributed to the rise of Cryptocurrency markets, which offer a decentralized alternative to traditional financial systems. While CBDCs have improved divisibility, convenience, and transaction speed, they still inherit the fundamental weaknesses of fiat money, particularly its inability to retain value over time. Though CBDCs function well as a medium of exchange, they remain tethered to national currencies, which are vulnerable to inflation and devaluation.

In contrast, cryptocurrencies like Bitcoin and Ethereum are emerging as an alternative store of value. Unlike fiat currencies, which are susceptible to inflationary pressures, these digital assets are designed to resist depreciation, potentially offering greater long-term stability and purchasing power preservation. While CBDCs will likely continue to serve as essential tools for daily transactions, the increasing adoption of cryptocurrencies challenges the traditional dominance of the U.S. dollar and other national currencies.

As the financial world continues to evolve, the importance of cryptocurrencies and CBDCs cannot be overstated. As we will explore in the upcoming chapters, these innovations represent the next frontier in the evolution of money, with profound implications for how people store wealth, exchange value, and participate in the global economy. In the following section, we'll explore the fundamentals of cryptocurrencies and CBDCs, their roles in the future of finance, and why they are pivotal to reshaping the financial landscape.

2.4 The Rise and Fall of Global Currencies and the Power of Pegging Currencies

Before the U.S. dollar came to dominate global finance, the Spanish dollar, also known as the "piece of eight" or *real de a ocho*, served as the first global currency. It was minted in the Spanish Empire beginning in the late fifteenth century, and it became the dominant medium of exchange across the world, including the Americas, Europe, Asia, and Africa. It was so widely accepted that it remained Legal tender in the United States until 1857.

What made the Spanish dollar unique was its combination of universality and reliability. Each coin contained exactly 371.25 grains of pure silver, consistent at every mint, ensuring trust and ease of exchange. In an age of unreliable and locally varied currencies, the Spanish dollar provided merchants, governments, and travelers a common standard. The coin was so prevalent that it directly inspired the symbol "$" as well as the name of the American dollar.

Its significance extended beyond simple commerce. The Spanish dollar formed the monetary backbone of the colonial world, used in trans-Pacific trade routes, especially between Acapulco and Manila. The coin was often preferred over local currencies, even in far-off regions such as China, where it commanded high trust among merchants. This wide circulation laid the groundwork for understanding how a single monetary standard can achieve global adoption through intrinsic trust and material value.

2.5 Pegging the U.S. Dollar: From Spanish Legacy to American Identity

When the United States established its own monetary system, it did not start from scratch. The U.S. Coinage Act of 1792 defined the dollar as 371.25 grains of pure silver, identical to the Spanish milled dollar. In essence, the U.S. dollar was born as a clone of the Spanish dollar, modeled after and backed by the trust of its credibility and widespread use.

At the time, Spanish dollars were far more common in American commerce than coins minted by the fledgling U.S. government. As a result, the Spanish dollar was not only a foundational influence, it was the dominant currency in practice. This decision to peg the new American dollar to the Spanish one gave early U.S. currency immediate legitimacy both at home and abroad.

This peg set the stage for American monetary sovereignty. By choosing a recognized and credible silver benchmark, the United States avoided monetary chaos and entered the global economy with a currency that was already respected. It also meant that for decades, the U.S. dollar was as much a continuation of the Spanish system as it was a national innovation. This quiet continuity helped America scale its financial credibility even as it sought political independence.

2.6 The Erosion of the Spanish Dollar and the Shift to Gold

Despite its once unassailable status, the Spanish dollar's dominance began to erode in the nineteenth century. A series of historical and structural forces began to undercut its role in the global economy. Latin American independence wars broke apart the Spanish Empire, severing the supply of silver and diminishing confidence in Spanish-minted coins. The resulting political fragmentation made Spanish coinage less reliable and trustworthy in both quality and quantity.

Meanwhile, the British Empire rose to financial prominence and formally adopted the Gold Standard in 1821. This move reoriented global trade around sterling, reducing the demand for silver currencies. Nations that traded with Britain or relied on its capital flows were incentivized to follow suit. As the world drifted toward gold, the intrinsic appeal of silver coins such as the Spanish dollar began to fade.

Economic and technological developments further accelerated this transition. Discoveries of new gold and silver mines led to fluctuating metal prices, undermining the reliability of silver as a store of value. By the time the United States enacted the Gold Standard Act of 1900, it had effectively abandoned the Spanish dollar's legacy. The pivot to gold symbolized a global transition away from a centuries-old silver-based system to one focused on stability, control, and imperial power.

In the twentieth century the U.S. dollar not only filled the vacuum left by the Spanish dollar, but it also exceeded it in reach and influence. After World War II, the Bretton Woods system formalized the dollar's supremacy by pegging it to gold and making it the central reference point for other currencies. This created a monetary order where the U.S. dollar became the global standard for trade, reserves, and financial contracts.

Under this system, central banks held U.S. dollars as a proxy for gold, enabling trade and settlement underpinned by American economic might. The dollar became the new standard of global trade. This moment marked the formal end of Spanish influence in monetary affairs as its former peg transformed into a fiat empire wielding immense leverage. However, this dominance was not immutable. In 1971, President Nixon ended the gold peg, turning the U.S. dollar into a world fiat currency. While it retained global dominance due to U.S. economic power and trust in its institutions, the decoupling introduced new vulnerabilities: inflation, deficits, and monetary manipulation. It also opened the door to deeper questions about long-term monetary trust, questions that would later be revived in the age of digital currencies. Even after decoupling from the peg to gold, up till today the U.S. dollar remains the de facto global currency. Countries around the world including Aruba, Belize, Hong Kong, Saudi Arabia, United Arab Emirates, and others have their currency pegged to the USD. Some countries such as Ecuador, Panama, and BVI use USD solely and do not have their own independent currencies.

However, the story of the Spanish dollar is not merely historical trivia; it is a cautionary tale. The world has seen a dominant currency fall before and no monetary standard is immune to geopolitical shifts, economic upheaval, or technological innovation. Monetary dominance is contingent, not permanent, and the USD must take the necessary steps to preserve its status as a global currency or risk repeating history. Today, the emergence of Central

Bank Digital Currencies (CBDCs), cryptocurrencies, and de-dollarization efforts evoke parallels with the fall of the Spanish dollar. Just as the U.S. dollar once rode on the credibility of the Spanish silver coin, new digital instruments may soon challenge the fiat foundation of the modern financial system. In particular, programmable money with built-in compliance, cross-border functionality, and central bank backing has the potential to reshape what is expected of reserve currencies.

What remains consistent is the need for trust, interoperability, and resilience. The Spanish dollar had these traits in its prime and the U.S. dollar built upon them. History shows that the foundations of monetary power are only as strong as the systems that sustain them and the trust they command globally. The Spanish dollar ruled not by fiat but by weight, quality, and trust. It left behind a legacy embedded in the very structure of modern currencies, especially the U.S. dollar. It proved that physical credibility could become geopolitical strength, and that a single monetary instrument could knit the world together. However, its fall reminds us that currency power is never permanent. The shift from metal to data, from mined to minted, from paper to digital, suggests that the next chapter in monetary evolution is already being written. Similar to the Spanish dollar before it, today's currencies must evolve or risk obsolescence in a digital world.

3

Pain Points in Financial Systems: Financial Inclusion

Main Messages

- Access to financial services like credit, savings, and insurance remains uneven in emerging markets, with over 1.4 billion adults unbanked. Economic size doesn't guarantee access, as infrastructure, cost, and inequality drive exclusion.
- Structural issues like rural inaccessibility, weak digital infrastructure, and underdeveloped agent networks hinder financial access. Informal economies dominate, with SMEs facing a $5.7 trillion financing gap due to limited credit.
- Gender norms, lack of ID, and low financial literacy disproportionately affect women and rural populations. Distrust, fragmented regulations, and weak consumer protection limit adoption of formal and digital financial services.

Financial inclusion means every citizen's right to access vital financial services that can help build and protect your wealth against inflation, including bank accounts, savings, credit, loans, equity, and insurance. The lack of access to financial services is closely linked to poverty, as it limits opportunities for wealth creation, investing, and protecting against crises.

The contribution of Abhi Das to this chapter is gratefully acknowledged.

Table 3.1 Top 10 emerging markets by GDP and unbanked population (2021)

Country name	GDP (2021, in USD)	Population (2021)	% of unbanked population
China	17.8 trillion	1.412 billion	11.29
India	3.1 trillion	1.414 billion	22.47
Brazil	1.6 trillion	209 million	15.96
Russian Federation	1.8 trillion	144 million	10.28
Mexico[a]	1.3 trillion	127 million	51.03
Indonesia	1.18 trillion	276 million	48.24
Turkiye	819 billion	84 million	25.91
Saudi Arabia	874 billion	33 million	25.68
Argentina	486 billion	45 million	28.37
South Africa	420 billion	61 million	14.62

[a] Data for Mexico's unbanked population is from 2022
Source The Global Findex Database, 2021; World Bank Open Data & World Development Indicators (https://www.worldbank.org/en/publication/globalfindex/Data); Accessed June 2025

This can perpetuate cycles of poverty and widen inequality. An empirical study has shown that developing countries that show a steady increase in Financial inclusion show a continuous drop in the poverty rate (Table 3.1).

Financial inclusion is a major issue in emerging markets, where 1.4 billion adults remain unbanked, which represents 38% of adults. Even among the top emerging markets by GDP, Financial inclusion varies dramatically, indicating that economic size doesn't always mean better access to banking. Take China and India, for example. Both have populations over 1.4 billion, but while only 11% of China's population is unbanked, India's unbanked rate is double that at 22%. That's nearly 318 million people without formal financial access in India alone. Mexico, despite being one of Latin America's largest economies, stands out, with over half of its adult population remaining unbanked. Indonesia, with a GDP exceeding $1.1 trillion, shows a very high unbanked rate of 48.24%, translating to over 133 million people. This figure is second only to India in absolute terms. Given the country's geography, this highlights how physical infrastructure limitations and the digital divide continue to hinder access to formal financial systems despite national development gains. Russia and Saudi Arabia, both resource-rich economies, show relatively low unbanked rates (10.28% and 25.68%, respectively) for their regions. However, to a certain extent, the numbers mask inequality: in Russia, rural populations and older demographics remain disproportionately excluded, while in Saudi Arabia, expatriate labor and women historically faced barriers to access, which only recently have started to change. Then you have middle-income countries like Turkey, South Africa, and Argentina, each with their own economic instability or social inequality driving unbanked rates between 15 and 28%. In sub-Saharan Africa, the IMF states that 57% of the population does not have a traditional bank account. In Latin America, approximately 45% of adults in this region do not have bank accounts, which represents approximately 122 million people. These numbers highlight the growing economic prowess of emerging economies, and yet millions of adults are left out of the traditional banking system.

Small to Medium Enterprises (SMEs) also play a major role in emerging markets, and 90% of these businesses operate outside the traditional banking systems, which means 345 million of the 400 million micro-enterprises in emerging markets operate in informal economies. These Small to Medium Enterprises (SMEs) collectively face a $5.7 trillion financing gap. Because SMEs are less likely to be able to obtain bank loans, they must rely on funds from friends and family to launch their enterprises. East Asia accounts for the largest share, 46%, of the total global finance gap and is followed by Europe and Central Asia at 15%. Compared to potential demand, Latin America and the Middle East regions have the highest proportion of the finance gap at 87% and 88%, respectively.

3.1 Structural and Infrastructural Social Barriers

Financial inclusion remains a critical challenge in emerging markets, where structural, economic, and social barriers prevent millions from accessing essential services like banking, credit, and insurance. The key factors driving this gap are the following:

- **Limited physical banking infrastructure** in rural and remote areas makes it difficult for traditional banks to operate cost-effectively. Research by the Consumer Financial Protection Bureau highlights that rural consumers often have to travel long distances to reach bank branches, incurring higher transportation costs and facing logistical challenges. This barrier is compounded by the consolidation of community banks, which has led to a decline in the number of local banking institutions and reduced the availability of relationship-based banking services that are particularly valuable in rural settings. In Africa, many commercial banks are often reluctant to operate in rural areas due to low-income levels, lack of scale economies, and poor infrastructure such as roads and electricity. The absence of financial institutions in these regions not only limits access to banking but also discourages the provision of credit, as banks face difficulties in securing collateral and enforcing contracts. As a result, millions remain excluded from the formal financial system, unable to save securely, access loans, or insure against risks.

- **Poor digital connectivity** and uneven mobile network coverage hinder the adoption of digital financial solutions despite their potential. Digital financial solutions have the potential to bridge access gaps, but their adoption is hampered by poor digital infrastructure in many emerging markets. According to the Consumer Financial Protection Bureau, only 68% of rural households in the United States have home Internet access, compared to much higher rates in urban and suburban areas. The disparity is even more pronounced in many developing countries, where broadband and mobile network coverage remains limited or unreliable. This digital divide means that even when digital banking or mobile money services are available, large segments of the population cannot access them due to a lack of connectivity or digital literacy. The World Bank notes that these infrastructural deficiencies are a major constraint on financial inclusion, as online banking usage is dramatically lower in rural areas compared to metropolitan regions. Without reliable Internet and mobile networks, innovative financial technologies cannot reach the populations that need them most.
- **Underdeveloped financial services networks** (e.g., local intermediaries for cash-in/cash-out services) limit last-mile access, particularly for cash-dependent populations. In many emerging markets, these networks remain underdeveloped or insufficiently scaled. The International Finance Corporation (IFC) reports that 1.6 billion people and 200 million small businesses in emerging markets lack access to formal financial services, in part because agent networks do not extend to the last mile. Microfinance institutions and mobile money operators often struggle to build sustainable agent networks due to high operational costs, regulatory challenges, and limited infrastructure support. In regions where agent networks are weak, people are forced to rely on informal mechanisms or travel long distances to access basic financial services, perpetuating financial exclusion and limiting economic participation.

Economic and Affordability Challenges

- **High costs of formal financial services**, including account maintenance fees and transaction charges, deter low-income households. The expense associated with formal financial services is a significant barrier for low-income households in emerging markets. Account maintenance fees, minimum balance requirements, and transaction charges can be prohibitively expensive relative to the incomes of the poor. According to Demirgüç-Kunt et al. (2018) in the Global Findex Database, nearly 30% of unbanked adults globally cite cost as a primary reason for not having an account. In sub-Saharan Africa, for instance, the World Bank (2022) found that annual fees for basic accounts can exceed 10% of average per capita income for the poorest quintile. These costs are further compounded by indirect expenses such as travel and opportunity costs associated with accessing distant bank branches. For low-income households, the perceived and real costs of formal financial services outweigh the benefits, driving them to rely on informal and often riskier financial mechanisms.
- **Income volatility** in informal economies makes it risky for institutions to offer credit without collateral, leaving 40% of formal SMEs and 345 million informal micro-enterprises underserved. A large proportion of the workforce in emerging markets operates within the informal sector, characterized by irregular and unpredictable income streams. This volatility poses a substantial risk for financial institutions, particularly when offering credit. Without stable income or tangible collateral, lenders are less willing to extend credit, fearing high default rates. According to the International Finance Corporation (IFC), 40% of formal small and medium enterprises (SMEs) and 345 million informal micro-enterprises remain underserved or unserved by the formal financial sector. This credit gap is exacerbated by the lack of credit history and documentation among informal workers, making risk assessment challenging for lenders. Consequently, many entrepreneurs and households are unable to access the capital needed for growth, investment, or even basic consumption smoothing.
- **Savings and credit disparities:** There is a stark contrast in formal savings behavior between emerging and advanced economies. Only 25% of adults in emerging markets save money through formal financial institutions, compared to 58% in advanced economies. This disparity is driven by several factors, including a lack of trust in financial institutions, limited access to convenient savings products, and the aforementioned high costs. The inability to save formally limits households' ability to build financial resilience, invest in education or health, and weather economic shocks.

Similarly, access to formal credit is much lower in emerging markets, restricting opportunities for entrepreneurship and upward mobility. The lack of formal savings and credit options perpetuates cycles of poverty and financial exclusion.

Institutional and Regulatory Hurdles

- **Stringent Know Your Customer (KYC) requirements** exclude those without formal identification or proof of income. The effect on marginalized populations is disproportionate. In emerging markets, 1.1 billion people lack official IDs, and 45% of rural populations cannot meet documentation requirements for basic accounts. Banks often impose supplementary demands like proof of address or tax IDs that act as de facto barriers for low-income households. For example, in sub-Saharan Africa, only 35% of adults can provide the documents needed to open a bank account, forcing reliance on informal financial channels. While innovations like tiered KYC (exempting low-value transactions) and eKYC (Digital identity verification) show promise, regulatory inertia and risk-averse compliance practices limit their adoption.
- **Fragmented regulations** across government agencies create compliance complexities for providers. A 2023 IIF report notes that fragmented cross-border rules force institutions to localize operations, increasing costs by 5–10% of annual revenue. This inefficiency is compounded by geopolitical tensions driving deglobalization, with institutions diverting resources from innovation to redundant compliance tasks. For instance, regulatory divergence costs the global economy over $780 billion annually, disproportionately affecting smaller institutions. The lack of harmonized frameworks also stifles fintech scalability, as seen in Africa's mobile money sector, where conflicting licensing rules hinder cross-border interoperability.
- **Consumer protection gaps** and data Privacy concerns undermine trust in digital platforms. Studies reveal that 42% of digital financial consumers in Southeast Asia face non-transparent contract terms, while 28% experience unauthorized data sharing. Inadequate data governance exacerbates risks: 63% of banks in developing economies lack robust protocols to prevent breaches, leaving sensitive information vulnerable to phishing and ransomware attacks. Regulatory gaps persist, as only 40% of emerging markets have updated consumer protection laws to address AI-driven lending or algorithmic bias. Without stronger oversight, distrust in digital platforms undermines adoption, perpetuating financial exclusion.

Social and Cultural Factors

- **Gender inequality**: Women face a 9-percentage-point gap in account ownership due to mobility restrictions, social norms, and financial literacy barriers. In regions like South Asia and the Middle East, this gap widens to 13–20 percentage points due to mobility restrictions like social norms, which often limit women's ability to travel independently to bank branches or agent networks. Control over resources is another contributor, with up to 58% of married women in heterosexual relationships deferring financial decisions to male partners, even when they are primary earners. Loans or seed capital intended for women's businesses are frequently diverted to household expenses or male-led ventures. Persistent financial literacy gaps, including the fact that women are 30% less likely than men to answer financial literacy questions correctly, often due to lower confidence rather than knowledge deficits. For example, in rural India, women's participation in financial cooperatives is often restricted to unpaid labor, while decision-making roles remain dominated by men.
- **Low financial and digital literacy** limits the effective use of services, even when available. Only 33% of adults globally grasp basic concepts like interest rates and inflation, with rates lower in emerging markets. This gap leads to reliance on risky informal mechanisms, such as moneylenders charging exorbitant fees. Over 40% of adults lack the skills to use mobile banking apps securely, exacerbating exclusion in digitizing economies. In Kenya and Tanzania, financial illiteracy reduces formal savings participation by 25%. Interventions like gamified (mobile training programs show promise but remain scarce in rural areas).
- **Distrust in formal institutions**, driven by historical exclusionary practices (e.g., redlining) and preference for informal networks. In the United States, 60% of Black Americans distrust banks due to centuries of exclusion, subprime lending, and asset confiscation. Similar patterns exist in postcolonial economies, where formal institutions are seen as extractive. 65% of unbanked adults in sub-Saharan Africa rely on community savings groups like *Tontines* due to transparency and cultural familiarity. Data Privacy fears are also a major factor. In Southeast Asia, 28% of digital finance users report unauthorized data sharing, deterring adoption among Privacy-conscious populations.

3.2 Conclusion

Financial exclusion continues to hinder economic development in emerging markets, where over 1.4 billion adults lack access to formal financial services. This exclusion is driven by a combination of structural limitations, high costs, regulatory barriers, and social inequalities. Rural populations, women, and small enterprises are particularly affected, often relying on informal systems that offer limited security or growth opportunities.

Improving Financial inclusion requires coordinated efforts to expand infrastructure, simplify regulations, promote financial literacy, and design services that meet the needs of underserved communities. Inclusion is not just about access, but about enabling full and equitable participation in the financial system. In future chapters, we explore the different approaches countries and institutions have taken to address these challenges.

4

CBDC Systems Engineering

Main Messages

- CBDCs can be built on centralized, decentralized, or distributed ledger systems, with permissioned blockchains and consensus mechanisms like Proof of Authority (PoA) preferred for regulatory oversight.
- CBDCs rely on secure, scalable data storage and leverage smart contracts for automation, AI for fraud detection and optimization, and post-quantum cryptography to future-proof systems.
- CBDCs are significantly more energy-efficient than both traditional banking and proof-of-work cryptocurrencies. Centralized or hybrid architectures minimize consumption, offering a sustainable alternative aligned with global climate and energy goals.

As CBDCs transition from conceptual frameworks to active pilots and regulatory frameworks, attention is shifting from policy theory to the technical infrastructure required to support them. This chapter examines the foundational technologies underpinning CBDCs, offering a comprehensive analysis of the systems engineering involved in deploying sovereign digital currencies that are secure, scalable, and efficient.

The contribution of Gabriel Carvalho to this chapter is gratefully acknowledged.

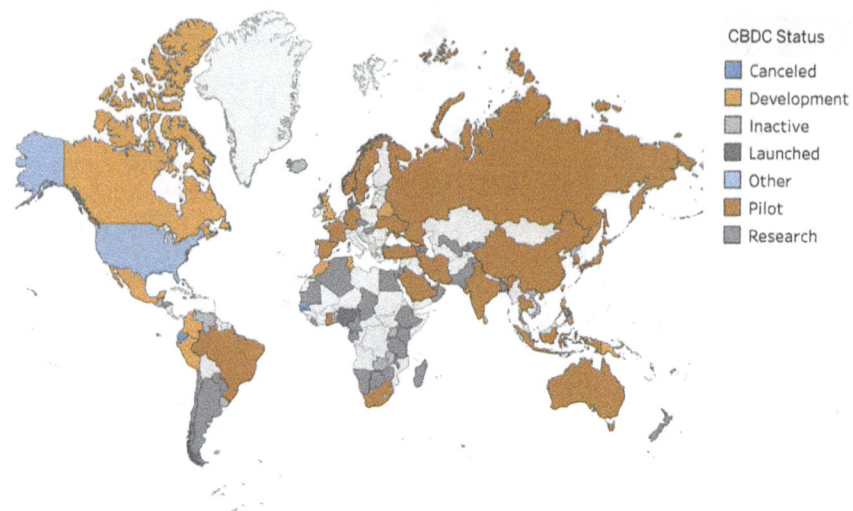

Fig. 4.1 Global CBDC development status as of May 18th, 2025 (*Source* Atlantic Council CBDC Tracker (https://www.atlanticcouncil.org/cbdctracker/); Accessed May 2025)

While global discussions around CBDCs often focus on political, legal, and economic implications, the technological decisions underlying their implementation are equally critical. A CBDC is not merely a digital replacement for a fiat currency—it represents a complex ecosystem of interdependent components, including ledger architectures, data storage solutions, and cryptographic protocols. These design choices have a profound impact on real-world performance, affecting transaction throughput, cybersecurity, financial inclusion, data privacy, and the potential for cross-border settlements.

The global landscape of CBDC development as of mid-2025 is illustrated geographically in Fig. 4.1.

This chapter begins by outlining the core operational models of CBDCs, including centralized, decentralized, and distributed ledger systems. It then assesses the role of blockchain and other distributed ledger technologies (DLT), distinguishing between permissioned and permissionless networks and evaluating consensus mechanisms such as Proof of Work (PoW) and Proof of Authority (PoA). The chapter also explores practical challenges related to data storage, system scalability, redundancy, and offline functionality, drawing on lessons from pilot projects in Brazil, China, Nigeria, and Sweden.

Building on this foundation, the chapter investigates enabling technologies such as smart contracts, originally proposed by Nick Szabo and later implemented in the Ethereum blockchain, AI-driven security measures, and post-quantum cryptographic methods, with a particular focus on their integration into CBDC systems. It concludes with a forward-looking analysis of cross-border interoperability and the evolving global architecture of digital public finance.

Taken together, this chapter offers frameworks for understanding CBDCs not as abstract policy instruments, but as engineered financial systems. By examining the architectural trade-offs and implementation challenges, we understand how central banks can use specific design choices to complement priority use cases and value-based choices on issues such as privacy, anonymity, and degree of centralized control as they roll out their CBDCs.

4.1 Digital Ledger Architecture

At the core of any Central Bank Digital Currency (CBDC) is a digital ledger—a system that records, verifies, and updates all transactions to ensure both operational integrity and transparency. A helpful analogy for understanding this concept is the Library of Congress, which houses over 178 million items. Just as a library requires detailed indexing to manage the borrowing and return of books, a CBDC ledger meticulously logs the "who, what, and when" of every transaction. This systematic recording ensures traceability, accountability, and trust within the currency system.

CBDC ledger systems can be configured as either public systems (permissionless) or private (permissioned) and further differentiated by their architecture: centralized, decentralized, or distributed. Public ledgers, much like an open-access online library catalog, promote transparency and openness but raise concerns about user privacy and data exposure. In contrast, private ledgers limit access to authorized participants, enabling governments and central banks to retain stronger control over data protection, compliance, and system oversight.

Much like large library systems spread across multiple branches, a decentralized ledger architecture allows multiple nodes to maintain and synchronize records. This design enhances resilience and reduces reliance on a single point of failure. While many central banks prefer centralized systems because they are easier to control and manage, these systems can have trouble handling large numbers of transactions. In fast-moving digital economies, centralized systems may not scale well or be resilient enough to meet high demand without slowing down or becoming vulnerable to outages.

To overcome these challenges, many CBDC pilots are experimenting with distributed ledger technology (DLT). In DLT systems, data is shared across a network of nodes and coordinated through structured governance and consensus protocols. This approach enhances system redundancy, fault tolerance, and transparency while still allowing regulatory oversight and institutional control.

For centralized, decentralized, and distributed ledger systems, the following figure illustrates their impact on the following attributes: fault tolerance, scalability, validator authority, transparency, regulatory control, and speed. In this figure, a score closer to 0 (in the center of the figure) for a given attribute indicates a lower positive impact for that attribute. Similarly, for a score closer to 10 (at the edge of the figure) for a given attribute, it indicates a higher positive impact for the same attribute. For example, centralized ledgers offer high regulatory control and validator control and are well suited for speed and scalability. On the other hand, decentralized ledgers offer high transparency and fault tolerance but are not best suited to offer regulatory control and validator authority. Decentralized ledgers might also offer lower performance on speed and scalability compared to centralized ledgers. Finally, distributed ledgers offer a more well-rounded performance, scoring almost uniformly across all attributes.

Central banks and governments can select between these design options based on the outcomes they want to prioritize from introducing CBDCs and the risks they wish to mitigate in the process (Fig. 4.2).

This conceptual radar chart illustrates key trade-offs among centralized, decentralized, and distributed ledger systems across dimensions such as validator authority, transparency, and fault tolerance. The values depicted were assigned subjectively by the author, specifically in the context of central banks exploring CBDCs, and are meant to illustrate general trade-offs rather than serve as empirically validated measures. The chart is intended as a pedagogical tool for readers unfamiliar with CBDC architecture to help visualize key system-level differences. Actual performance and trade-offs vary widely depending on specific technological implementations, consensus mechanisms, and institutional governance models.

One widely adopted form of DLT is blockchain. Blockchains are decentralized, immutable, and capable of processing high transaction volumes. However, traditional public blockchains—with their open validation mechanisms—do not align with the governance needs of sovereign monetary

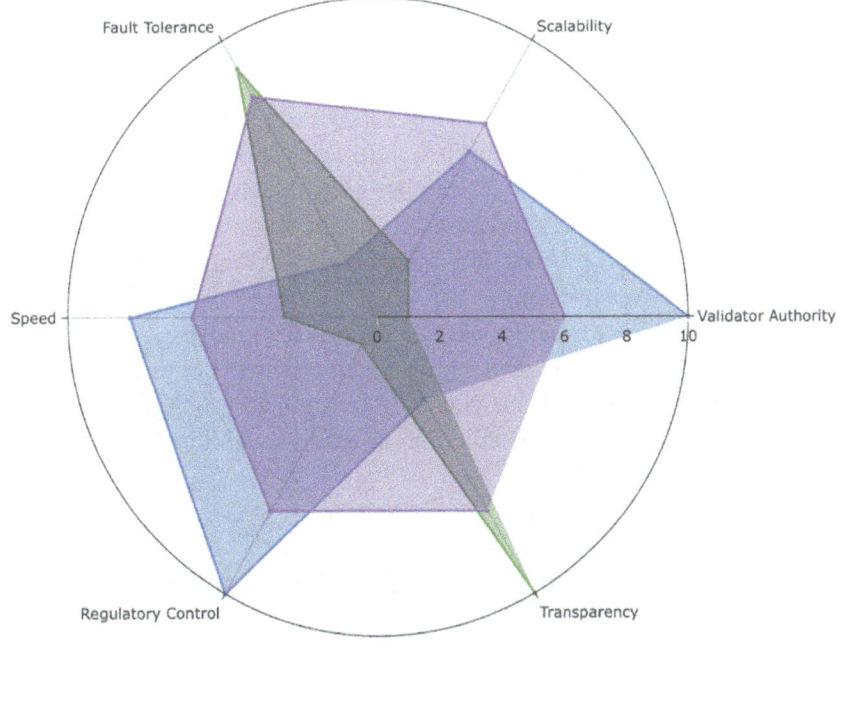

Fig. 4.2 Comparative ledger system attributes in CBDC design (*Source* Designed by Gabriel Carvalho)

systems. To bridge this gap, many CBDC initiatives are adopting permissioned blockchains, where only approved institutions can validate transactions. This model retains the benefits of blockchain—speed, auditability, and security—while allowing central banks to maintain necessary oversight.

Notable examples include Sweden's e-Krona and the European Central Bank's Project Stella. These projects demonstrate that blockchain-based CBDCs can be tailored for both scalability and regulatory compliance, offering a viable blueprint for sovereign digital currency infrastructure.

Ultimately, designing a CBDC ledger system requires navigating complex trade-offs: privacy versus transparency, centralization versus resilience, and control versus openness. Whether a CBDC adopts a centralized or distributed model, the architectural choices will shape not only its technical performance but also the broader financial ecosystem of the issuing nation.

To illustrate how these trade-offs manifest in current and emerging CBDC systems, the following chart maps various digital currencies along the spectrum of transparency and privacy.

In this chart, various ongoing initiatives have been represented on two key attributes: privacy and transparency, which form the two axes in the representation below. As is evident on the upper left quadrant that most initiatives are able to offer medium to high privacy, but might not offer significant transparency. Alternatively, the lower right quadrant depicts initiatives with higher transparency and lower privacy.

Understanding where systems fall on the privacy–transparency spectrum provides essential context for the technical architectures that underpin them. These foundational choices—particularly in how digital ledgers are structured and validated—directly influence the functionality, scalability, and regulatory posture of a CBDC.

4.2 Blockchain Architecture and Validation Frameworks

Blockchain is a type of distributed ledger technology (DLT) that offers capabilities far beyond basic record-keeping. It enables immutable records, multi-party verification, and distributed consensus—features that are especially relevant for central banks developing CBDC infrastructure, and enables CBDCs to execute and settle peer-to-peer transactions. These attributes ensure not only integrity and reliability but also real-time auditability and resilience—critical features for managing sovereign digital currencies.

Central banks are increasingly drawn to blockchain because of its transparency, programmability, and potential for secure coordination across multiple actors. DLT allows real-time synchronization of data between central banks, financial intermediaries, and service providers, enhancing security and operational alignment in complex financial systems involving both public and private participants.

Figure 4.3 provides a simplified view of the CBDC ecosystem, highlighting the central bank's interaction with permissioned validator nodes and end-user wallets.

This diagram illustrates a common two-tier design in which the central bank issues and governs the CBDC while authorized financial institutions, such as commercial banks and payment service providers, operate as validator nodes. These intermediaries distribute CBDC to end users via wallet interfaces and report ledger activity back to the central bank for auditability and

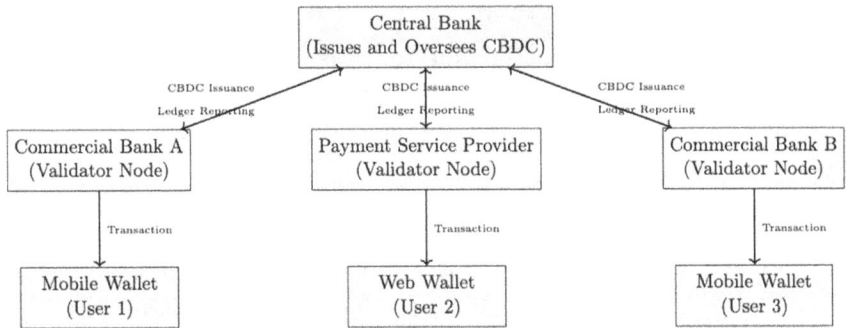

Fig. 4.3 CBDC network architecture in a permissioned distributed ledger setting (*Source* Designed by Gabriel Carvalho)

synchronization. This structure reflects typical design considerations in DLT-based retail CBDC prototypes, though actual implementations may vary in governance, access permissions, and technical design.

Not all blockchain architectures are equally suited for CBDC applications. Public blockchains like Bitcoin and Ethereum emphasize openness and decentralization, but they pose challenges in energy efficiency, regulatory compliance, and transaction finality. These limitations make them less appropriate for sovereign monetary systems. Consequently, most CBDC systems adopt permissioned blockchain frameworks that support higher transaction throughput, lower energy usage, and clearer regulatory oversight—often using consensus mechanisms such as Proof of Authority (PoA). Put simply, PoA is a consensus mechanism where a set of pre-approved, identifiable validators are authorized to create new blocks and validate transactions, relying on their reputation and identity instead of computational work or staked coins. This makes it more suitable for CBDCs, which tend to be governed by central banks or public entities that would prefer having a limited, identifiable set of validators.

The distinction between permissionless and permissioned platforms is foundational. Permissionless blockchains are open to anyone and rely on consensus mechanisms like "Proof of Work" or "Proof of Stake." In this context, the Proof of Work consensus mechanism requires network participants to expend significant computational effort to solve complex puzzles, validating transactions and securing the blockchain. In the "Proof of Stake" consensus mechanism, validators are chosen to create new blocks and confirm transactions based on the amount of cryptocurrency they have staked as collateral, rather than computational power. While both these consensus mechanisms promote decentralized governance, they introduce inefficiencies, unpredictability, and reduced regulatory control—traits that are misaligned with the needs of national monetary authorities. Permissioned platforms, by contrast, restrict transaction validation to vetted institutions such as central banks, licensed financial entities, or approved payment providers. This model is designed to promote trust, efficiency, and compliance from the outset, as validation is limited to vetted and regulated institutions.

One notable example is the mBridge initiative, a cross-border CBDC pilot involving the central banks of China, Hong Kong, Thailand, and the United Arab Emirates. It utilizes a permissioned DLT framework to enable secure, auditable, real-time settlements among regulated financial institutions.

Permissioned systems offer a practical balance between technological innovation and sovereign control. They can retain key blockchain benefits—immutability, auditable transparency for authorized participants, and distributed consensus—while embedding governance frameworks needed for legal and financial accountability. Sweden's e-krona pilot illustrates this approach: it uses R3's Corda platform, where regulated intermediaries distribute tokens issued by the Riksbank. Transactions occur across a decentralized network, but final validation is anchored in a notary node monitored by the central bank, ensuring oversight, policy compliance, and scalability within a controlled environment.

The choice of consensus mechanism plays a crucial role in determining the security, performance, and regulatory alignment of a CBDC system. Public blockchain networks like Bitcoin and Ethereum rely on Proof of Work (PoW) or Proof of Stake (PoS), which involve pseudonymous participants. These mechanisms, while decentralized, are resource-intensive and unsuitable for centrally governed currencies. In contrast, CBDC ecosystems involve known, regulated actors, making Proof of Authority (PoA) a more fitting model. PoA's use of pre-approved validators to authorize transactions enables fast settlement, high throughput, reduced energy consumption, and institutional accountability.

Table 4.1 offers a comparative overview of the most relevant consensus mechanisms considered for CBDC design, emphasizing trade-offs in security, efficiency, throughput, and decentralization. These technical characteristics directly impact the suitability of each mechanism for building sovereign, scalable, and policy-aligned digital currency systems.

This table contrasts leading consensus models across critical performance dimensions, such as transaction throughput, energy efficiency, and decentralization, highlighting how these attributes influence their alignment with the needs of central banks.

Among these, Proof of Authority (PoA) has emerged as a leading candidate for CBDC systems operating in permissioned environments. As discussed

Table 4.1 Comparison of key consensus mechanisms for CBDC design

Consensus mechanism	How it works	Security	Finality (Prob./Det.)	Efficiency	Throughput	Decentralization
Proof of Work (PoW)	Miners compete to solve cryptographic puzzles; energy intensive	High	Probabilistic	Low	Low	High
Proof of Stake (PoS)	Validators are chosen based on staked coins; risk of loss incentivizes honesty	High	Probabilistic/deterministic	High	Low-medium	High (but may concentrate power)
Delegated PoS (DPoS)	Users elect a few delegates to validate transactions on their behalf	High	Deterministic	High	High	Medium
Proof of Authority (PoA)	Only pre-approved, trusted validators can add blocks	Moderate	Deterministic	High	High	Low-medium
Validating Notary Service	A central authority or small consortium validates all transactions	High	Deterministic	High	Medium	Low
Non-Validating Notary Service	A central ledger logs transactions but doesn't validate them independently	Moderate	Deterministic	Very high	High	Low

Source Gabriel Carvalho

earlier in this chapter, under PoA, only pre-approved, identifiable validators—typically central banks or licensed financial institutions—can propose and verify transactions. Because all validators are known entities, PoA supports rapid transaction processing, minimizes energy use, and allows for robust regulatory oversight. These features make it well suited to the compliance requirements of sovereign monetary authorities.

In addition to PoA, several CBDC prototypes are experimenting with hybrid consensus models that incorporate elements from Byzantine Fault Tolerance (BFT). These systems are designed to tolerate a limited number of faulty or offline validators, thereby enhancing resilience without undermining centralized governance. Other experimental designs include rotating validator sets and layered consensus frameworks, which introduce operational flexibility and facilitate scalability, which is particularly important in cross-border CBDC implementations.

Ultimately, consensus design is more than a technical choice; it reflects central banks' broader priorities, including trust, resilience, regulatory alignment, and public legitimacy. The selected model must not only ensure high system performance but also uphold the legal and institutional integrity required of a national digital currency.

Figure 4.4 provides an overview of how the consensus mechanism selection tree functions for CBDCs.

This conceptual decision tree illustrates how key system constraints—such as energy efficiency, validator trust, and latency—can influence the selection of consensus mechanisms in CBDC design. While Proof of Work (PoW) is included for comparative purposes, it is generally not considered viable for sovereign digital currencies due to its energy intensity. Similarly, Proof of Stake (PoS) appears in some experimental or hybrid models but is not widely adopted in retail CBDC deployments. The inclusion of Byzantine Fault Tolerance (BFT) mechanisms reflects their relevance in high-speed, low-latency networks with known validator sets. This visual is intended to contextualize design trade-offs rather than prescribe a specific technical implementation.

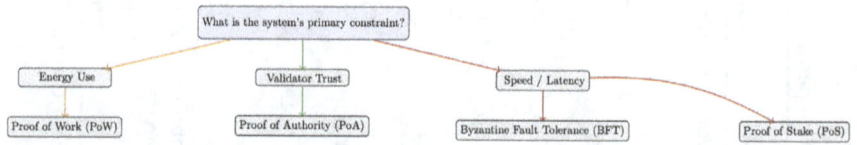

Fig. 4.4 CBDC consensus mechanism selection tree (*Source* Designed by Gabriel Carvalho)

As consensus mechanisms lay the groundwork for how transactions are validated, they also shape the demands placed on another critical layer of CBDC infrastructure: data storage.

4.3   Data Storage and Security

Extending the discussion of ledger architecture, one of the most demanding—and often underestimated—components of CBDC infrastructure is data storage. While the ledger defines how information is structured and authenticated, storage determines a system's ability to support real-time, high-volume economic activity.

CBDCs are not simply digital representations of cash; they are foundational systems for financial interaction that must absorb and process massive volumes of information every second. From groceries and rent to business payments and transit fares, transactions are initiated simultaneously across the economy. Unlike traditional credit cards or legacy banking systems that often batch-process transactions (collecting them over a set period and settling them together at scheduled times), many CBDC models, particularly retail-focused ones, require immediate verification and recording. Whether it's a luxury car purchase or a metro fare, each transaction must be captured in real-time with high accuracy and reliability.

Beyond speed and performance, data storage presents significant scalability and security challenges. Without a robust and scalable storage architecture, even the most sophisticated ledger design can become a bottleneck, exposing the system to risks like transaction delays, data loss, fraud, or even systemic failure.

These technological challenges also raise important questions about governance, privacy, and ethics. The ability to record all financial activity in real-time creates both opportunities and risks. Excessive transparency may compromise individual privacy, while too little may enable illicit activity. Countries have responded to this dilemma in varying ways. For instance, Brazil's DREX system emphasizes both programmability and legal compliance. According to Brazil's Real Digital directive, the system must "observe all principles and rules of privacy and security established in Brazilian legislation, especially the Law on Bank Secrecy and the General Data Protection Law." The Central Bank further states that "solutions for privacy preservation must still be tested… for compliance with legal requirements on information privacy." This underscores a clear effort to balance oversight with personal data protection.

Although no perfect solution has emerged, ongoing pilots and policy frameworks—such as Brazil's DREX—illustrate a global effort to design CBDC systems that are technically effective while upholding democratic values, regulatory mandates, and consumer protections.

These design decisions prompt critical policy questions: How long should transaction data be retained? Under what conditions should it be deleted? And who is ultimately responsible for the costs of building and maintaining the physical and digital infrastructure to support CBDCs at scale?

Ensuring the resilience of CBDC systems requires planning beyond technical reliability. Central banks must anticipate a wide range of risks, from cyberattacks and natural disasters to geopolitical disruptions. Even a brief system outage could jeopardize essential payment functions, particularly in retail CBDC systems. To guard against these risks, some central banks are adopting multi-layered redundancy frameworks, including geo-redundant backups—copies of data stored in physically distinct locations. While common in cloud infrastructures like Amazon Web Services (AWS) or Google Cloud, implementing such strategies in the context of sovereign digital currencies demands real-time synchronization, strict audit trails, and consistent ledgers across distributed replicas.

Cybersecurity is a cornerstone of CBDC development. As a critical financial infrastructure, CBDC systems are likely to attract sophisticated cyber threats from both state actors and criminal organizations. In response, central banks are deploying multiple layers of defense: full-chain encryption, real-time anomaly detection, and AI-based fraud monitoring. Some institutions are also investigating air-gapped backup systems—physically isolated hardware designed for secure, offline data recovery during emergencies. While effective against remote attacks, these systems are slower to deploy and require substantial upkeep.

Beyond digital threats, physical vulnerabilities—such as floods, earthquakes, or political unrest—are also part of the planning equation. In response, several central banks are considering sovereign data resilience strategies, which include underground vaults, dispersed data centers, and even satellite-based backup channels. While many of these remain exploratory, they reflect a growing recognition that CBDC infrastructure must meet continuity-of-government standards, not just enterprise-level reliability.

Data storage and redundancy are not peripheral concerns—they are foundational to CBDC's success. These systems must not only be digital and efficient but also secure, autonomous, and resilient in the face of both technological failures and geopolitical shocks. At its core, CBDC design is about building a robust digital backbone for national monetary systems in a volatile and interconnected world.

4.4 Token-Based Versus Account-Based Models

Another critical aspect of CBDC design involves the method of transaction validation—specifically, whether the system operates on a token-based or account-based model. These two structures have far-reaching implications for user identity, regulatory compliance, privacy, and financial inclusion.

While often described as distinct models, token-based and account-based systems should be understood as ends of a design spectrum rather than mutually exclusive categories. In a token-based model, transaction validity depends on possession of a digital token, akin to how physical cash functions. This structure can enhance privacy and enable greater financial inclusion by reducing reliance on formal identification or Internet access. However, in practice, very few central banks have implemented pure token systems. Most pilots that emulate token-like features—such as offline or near-field communication (NFC) payments—still operate on underlying account-based infrastructure, with some degree of traceability retained. Consequently, while token-based logic may support privacy and inclusion goals, it introduces regulatory challenges, particularly around enforcing anti-money laundering (AML) and counter-terrorism financing (CTF) frameworks.

By contrast, account-based systems tie access and usage of CBDCs to verified identities, often linked to a wallet managed by a financial institution or central bank intermediary. This design makes it easier to embed regulatory compliance, transaction monitoring, and integration with existing financial infrastructure. However, strict identity requirements may pose barriers to access for certain groups, especially in lower-income or digitally underserved populations. This has led many central banks to explore hybrid approaches, combining tiered KYC regimes with optional offline modes to balance inclusion, oversight, and usability. Systems like China's e-CNY and Nigeria's eNaira illustrate this trend, offering token-like functionality within an account-based legal and technical framework.

In contrast, account-based systems require user identification before any transaction can occur. Access to the digital currency is linked to a verified account, typically managed by a commercial bank or a central-bank-affiliated institution. This structure simplifies regulatory compliance and aligns well with existing financial systems. Yet, it may inadvertently exclude vulnerable populations, such as individuals without government-issued IDs, digital literacy, or stable Internet access, especially in developing economies.

To navigate these tensions between privacy and oversight, many central banks are piloting hybrid models. One common approach ties privacy levels to transaction size: low-value transactions may enjoy greater anonymity, while high-value transactions require stronger identity verification. This tiered structure aims to balance user privacy with institutional responsibilities for risk management and compliance.

Offline functionality is another key design consideration. Enabling transactions without Internet access increases system resilience and expands usability in rural or underserved regions. Pilot programs in various countries have experimented with hardware wallets and mobile devices that can complete offline transactions and synchronize later once connectivity is restored.

Some central banks are also implementing dual-layer architectures, in which commercial banks or payment providers deliver user-facing services while the central bank retains control over the ledger and monetary issuance. This structure blends the privacy and flexibility of token-based systems with the regulatory clarity of account-based systems.

In contexts where smartphone or Internet access is limited, USSD-based platforms have been introduced. These allow users to send and receive digital currency using basic mobile phones, thereby extending financial access to populations historically excluded from digital finance.

Ultimately, the choice between token-based and account-based models reflects deeper policy values. Token-based systems prioritize privacy and accessibility, while account-based systems emphasize transparency and institutional accountability. Hybrid designs aim to integrate the strengths of both approaches, enabling secure, inclusive, and adaptable systems suited to the diverse needs of national economies.

4.5 Balancing Privacy, Compliance, and Security

Designing Central Bank Digital Currencies requires constant negotiation between competing priorities. On the one hand, regulators demand transparency and oversight; on the other, citizens and advocacy groups emphasize the need for privacy and data protection. Meanwhile, security must be uncompromising in the face of growing cyber threats.

Figure 4.5 illustrates these tensions and the delicate balance CBDC designers must strike to ensure that no single priority overwhelms the others.

This diagram presents a simplified visual framework to help readers understand the interrelated priorities of privacy, security, and compliance in CBDC system design.

Designing a CBDC involves navigating a complex triad: maintaining transaction integrity, protecting user privacy, and ensuring compliance with regulatory frameworks. Achieving this balance requires integrating encryption protocols, cryptographic authentication, and privacy-enhancing technologies that enable confidentiality alongside transparency.

Most CBDC systems rely on public-key cryptography to secure transactions and verify user identity. In this model, each transaction is digitally signed using a private key and verified through a corresponding public key. This approach not only ensures transaction integrity and non-repudiation but also safeguards user identities in real-time—an essential feature for any high-volume, sovereign digital currency.

To further enhance privacy, several CBDC prototypes have begun experimenting with zero-knowledge proofs (ZKPs)—a cryptographic technique that allows transaction validation without revealing underlying personal or transactional data. This innovation enables private transactions while still permitting regulatory monitoring, offering a framework where confidentiality, auditability, and legal compliance can coexist.

An emerging body of research explores how digital currency infrastructure can embed privacy-by-design principles while still serving the oversight needs of central banks. For instance, Goodell, Al-Nakib, and Tasca (2021) propose a digital architecture based on user custodianship without centralized data aggregation, illustrating how privacy can be preserved without sacrificing accountability.

In addition to cryptographic techniques, modern CBDC architectures are expected to incorporate end-to-end encryption, tamper-resistant hardware

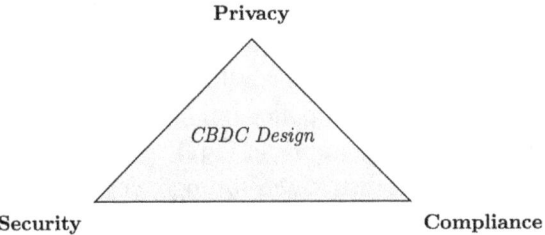

Fig. 4.5 Conceptual triangle illustrating the core trade-offs in CBDC design—privacy, security, and regulatory compliance (*Source* Designed by Gabriel Carvalho)

modules, and post-quantum cryptography—algorithms designed to withstand emerging threats from quantum computing. Together, these components form a robust cybersecurity foundation that protects CBDC systems from fraud, cyberattacks, and unauthorized access.

Ultimately, designing for privacy, compliance, and security is not a matter of choosing one over the others but of carefully integrating all three. CBDCs must be technically resilient, legally accountable, and socially trusted—especially as they evolve into critical infrastructure for national and global financial systems.

4.6 Smart Contracts

A major innovation in the development of Central Bank Digital Currencies (CBDCs) is the integration of smart contracts—software programs that execute transactions or actions automatically once predefined conditions are met. Originally designed for decentralized platforms like Ethereum, smart contracts are now being adapted for use within the oversight-driven environment of central banking. In this context, they offer significant potential to streamline financial processes and enhance public finance through auditability, governance, and accountability.

One promising application is in the realm of tax collection. When integrated with CBDC-based transactions, smart contracts they can automatically calculate and deduct value-added tax (VAT) or sales tax and remit it directly to government treasuries. This creates a more direct and efficient collection process, improving compliance in routine transactions and reducing the scope for underreporting. It can be especially impactful in cash-heavy or informal sectors, where automated deductions at the point of payment minimize administrative burdens and strengthen revenue collection.

Smart contracts can also transform the distribution of government subsidies and welfare benefits. CBDC-based disbursements can be programmed with specific usage conditions, such as expiration dates or spending limits tied to eligible categories like food, housing, or education. This level of programmability increases targeting precision, prevents misuse of funds, and facilitates real-time monitoring of policy implementation.

Figure 4.6 shows how programmable CBDCs can enforce eligibility and spending constraints. Funds distributed through smart contracts can include built-in rules, such as usage limits and time-based expiration, enhancing both accountability and policy impact. For example, a programmable CBDC can provide a monthly stipend to buy groceries at selected government run stores for low-income families as part of a welfare scheme, ensuring that the funds are only used to purchase groceries within a limited time frame.

Beyond public finance, smart contracts may also support monetary policy automation. For instance, stimulus payments could be programmed to encourage spending by including expiration dates or sector-specific constraints. Central banks could also direct liquidity to specific regions or industries experiencing economic distress, thereby improving the responsiveness and precision of macroeconomic interventions.

Cross-border use cases are another area of growing interest. Smart contracts integrated into international CBDC networks could facilitate real-time currency exchange, enforce capital controls, and ensure compliance with varying regulatory regimes. Several pilot projects have already explored how permissioned DLTs and smart contracts can simplify cross-border settlements and reduce friction in international finance.

It is important to distinguish between smart contracts in CBDCs and those used in decentralized finance (DeFi). DeFi contracts—typically deployed on public blockchains like Ethereum—are often immutable, lack centralized oversight, and are more vulnerable to bugs and security breaches. In contrast, CBDC smart contracts are designed to be upgradeable, auditable, and governed by institutional frameworks. They operate in permissioned networks, where all validators are vetted and regulated entities.

Table 4.2 contrasts the design and operational characteristics of smart contracts in decentralized finance with those used in CBDCs. While DeFi emphasizes openness and immutability, CBDC systems prioritize regulatory oversight, upgradability, and institutional trust.

Looking ahead, smart contracts are expected to form the backbone of emerging public digital infrastructure. By embedding conditionality and

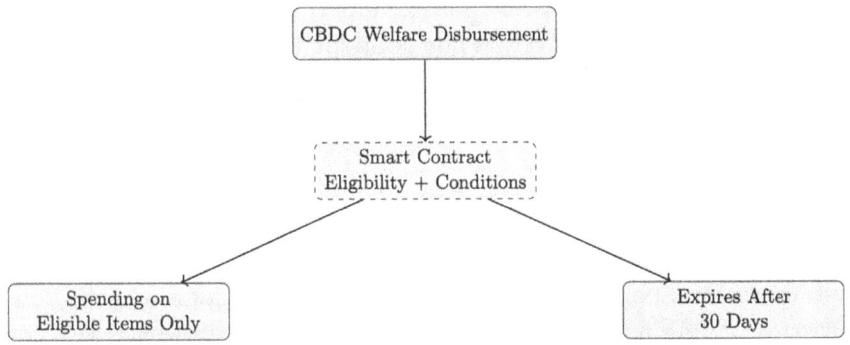

Fig. 4.6 Conceptual model of a CBDC-based welfare disbursement system using smart contracts (*Source* Designed by Gabriel Carvalho)

Table 4.2 Comparison of DeFi and CBDC smart contracts

Feature	DeFi smart contracts (e.g. Ethereum)	CBDC smart contracts
Governance	Decentralized and anonymous participants	Centralized oversight with institutional control
Mutability	Immutable once deployed	Upgradeable under regulator supervision
Auditability	Often limited; dependent on community review	Fully auditable by central authorities
Risk exposure	High: vulnerable to bugs, exploits, and abuse	Reduced: formal validation and sandboxed execution
Execution environment	Open, permissionless networks	Permissioned, regulated environments

Source Designed by Gabriel Carvalho

automation into financial systems, they can enable automated regulatory compliance, data-driven public service delivery, and more responsive government interventions. In this paradigm, money evolves from a passive store of value into a programmable tool of public policy.

CBDCs are evolving from basic transaction platforms to dynamic systems that embed public policy logic directly into financial infrastructure. It reflects the growing role of programmability in shaping the future of money.

4.7 Cross-Border Interoperability

As central banks advance the development of national digital currencies, ensuring that these systems function seamlessly across borders poses both technical and policy challenges. While domestic CBDCs may operate effectively within national frameworks, their potential is limited without the ability to interface with foreign systems. In a global economy dependent on remittances, trade, and international capital flows, cross-border interoperability is essential to avoid fragmentation, inefficiencies, and increased transaction costs.

Achieving interoperability requires coordinated progress along two interrelated dimensions: policy alignment and technical integration. On the policy side, participating jurisdictions must harmonize regulations related to anti-money laundering (AML), counter-terrorism financing (CTF), data privacy, and foreign exchange (FX) controls. On the technical side, CBDCs must be built with interoperable standards that allow communication and transaction execution across diverse ledger infrastructures.

Effective cross-border integration depends on both regulatory coordination (e.g., AML/CTF standards, Foreign exchange (Fx) policies, privacy rules) and technological solutions (e.g., messaging protocols, ledger bridges, oracles).

At the center of technical interoperability is the development of standardized messaging protocols. These systems allow digital currencies to integrate with existing financial infrastructure, including real-time gross settlement (RTGS) systems and international payment networks. Technologies such as ledger bridges support this integration by enabling synchronization between distinct blockchain networks, making atomic settlement of transactions across currencies possible.

Oracles serve as trusted middleware, securely transmitting real-world data to smart contract environments. They verify conditions tied to transactions, help maintain regulatory compliance, and reduce risk exposure. Additionally, open application programming interfaces (APIs) play a pivotal role by providing financial institutions with access to multiple CBDC systems through a unified interface, minimizing the need for duplicative infrastructure or major software overhauls.

However, integrating CBDCs into the global monetary system introduces new complexities for monetary policy. Central banks design their currencies to meet specific domestic goals, such as inflation control or exchange rate stability, and the frictionless movement of programmable digital currencies may influence these objectives. Cross-border use of CBDCs also raise challenges for FX settlements, capital flow surveillance, and systemic risk management.

From an infrastructure perspective, interoperability can be pursued through several architectural models. One approach involves shared platforms, where multiple jurisdictions co-develop and operate a unified ledger system. Another model uses bridged architectures to connect independent national systems while maintaining policy autonomy. A third approach is the upgrading of domestic RTGS infrastructure to natively support CBDC transactions, allowing continuity with minimal disruption.

Ultimately, progress on cross-border interoperability will depend not only on technical innovation but also on international cooperation. Establishing global standards, legal frameworks, and governance structures is just as important as software development. True success lies in creating a financial system where digital value flows globally with the same speed and reliability as information travels across today's Internet.

4.8 Artificial Intelligence and Machine Learning

Artificial intelligence (AI) and machine learning (ML) are emerging as core components in the development and operation of CBDCs. As CBDCs transition from experimental pilots to national-scale implementations, AI and ML offer capabilities that go far beyond automation. These technologies enable systems to learn, adapt, and evolve, supporting real-time transaction processing, financial system stress prediction, and proactive threat detection. Given the massive scale and speed required by digital currency infrastructures, such intelligence is increasingly indispensable.

Artificial intelligence and machine learning transaction data can support fraud detection, cybersecurity, and demand forecasting, enhancing the resilience, compliance, and operational efficiency of CBDC ecosystems.

One of the most critical applications of AI in CBDCs is fraud detection. Traditional banking systems rely heavily on static rule-based checks and manual reviews, which can be slow, inefficient, and prone to oversight. In contrast, machine learning models trained on vast datasets can detect subtle anomalies in user behavior and identify potentially fraudulent transactions. Supervised learning and neural network algorithms analyze patterns in location, transaction frequency, and behavioral history, enabling real-time detection of suspicious activities. These systems can immediately flag, block, or escalate concerns without disrupting legitimate user flows.

Machine learning models assess behavioral risk scores to flag or approve transactions in real-time, ensuring compliance without interrupting transaction flows. AI also strengthens cybersecurity by powering adaptive intrusion detection systems (IDS). These systems continuously monitor network activity for signs of malware, unauthorized access, or distributed denial-of-service (DDoS) attacks. By using anomaly detection and behavioral analytics, AI-driven IDS can adapt to new threat patterns and respond faster than traditional security solutions. This capacity is critical for protecting digital currencies, which are likely targets for cybercrime and geopolitical disruption.

Another key use of AI is in system optimization. Machine learning models can forecast transaction volumes using historical trends and macroeconomic indicators. This allows CBDC systems to allocate computing resources efficiently and prepare for usage spikes, such as during holidays, payroll cycles, or emergency disbursements. More advanced models, such as those based on reinforcement learning, simulate various transaction processing strategies to identify optimal configurations for performance and scalability. These tools help central banks maintain low latency, minimize downtime, and ensure a seamless user experience under changing conditions.

Ultimately, AI and ML are not peripheral to CBDC operations—they are essential to building resilient, secure, and scalable infrastructures. As national economies increasingly rely on digital payment systems, these intelligent technologies will play a defining role in shaping the future of public finance.

4.9 Quantum Computing and the Security of CBDCs

One of the most pressing long-term security challenges facing CBDCs is the emerging threat posed by quantum computing. While no quantum computer has yet demonstrated the capacity to break widely used cryptographic systems, rapid advancements in the field suggest that such capabilities could become feasible within the next two decades. This presents a substantial risk, as most current CBDC architectures rely on public-key cryptographic schemes, such as RSA and Elliptic Curve Cryptography (ECC), that are vulnerable to quantum attacks via Shor's algorithm, which can solve their underlying mathematical problems exponentially faster than classical algorithms.

Figure 4.7 highlights where quantum threats from applying Shor's algorithms can render current CBDC cryptography vulnerable to attack. It also highlights potential sources of cryptographic breakdown.

Shor's algorithm poses a fundamental threat to RSA and ECC, compromising digital signatures, wallet keys, and secure communications.

In response to this looming vulnerability, central banks and cryptographic researchers are actively exploring post-quantum cryptography (PQC). These

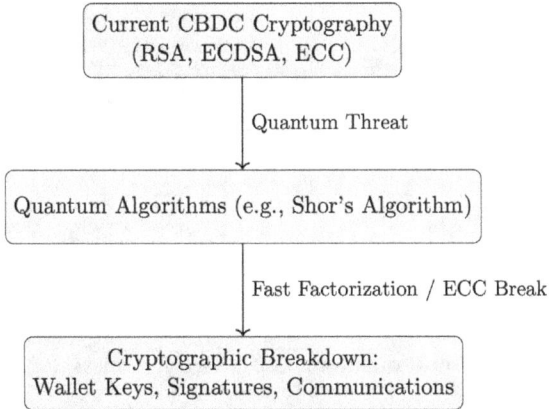

Fig. 4.7 Quantum threat to CBDC systems (*Source* Designed by Gabriel Carvalho)

next-generation algorithms—including CRYSTALS-Dilithium, Falcon, and SPHINCS+—are being developed specifically to resist quantum decryption methods. Many CBDC research initiatives are already testing hybrid approaches that combine traditional cryptography with PQC to ensure both forward security and compatibility with existing systems (Moraes et al., 2024).

In addition to algorithmic defenses, hardware-based solutions are also under consideration. Trusted Execution Environments (TEEs), for instance, can provide secure enclaves for sensitive cryptographic operations. Some CBDC frameworks are exploring distributed ledger infrastructures that natively support PQC, offering both resilience and operational continuity.

Beyond encryption alone, privacy-preserving cryptographic tools such as Multi-Party Computation (MPC) and Oblivious Transfer (OT) are also gaining attention. These mechanisms enable secure data processing across multiple parties without exposing private information, even in adversarial settings, adding another layer of protection to CBDC networks.

Figure 4.8 provides an overview of the constituent elements of the classical CBDC stacks and quantum CBDC security stacks.

While classical systems rely on RSA/ECC and TLS, quantum-resistant models incorporate lattice-based algorithms and, optionally, quantum key distribution (QKD).

Together, these efforts underscore the need for central banks to future-proof digital currency systems against the risks posed by quantum computing. Transitioning toward quantum-resistant infrastructure is not merely a theoretical precaution—it is an essential step toward safeguarding the long-term trust, integrity, and resilience of sovereign digital currencies in a rapidly evolving technological landscape.

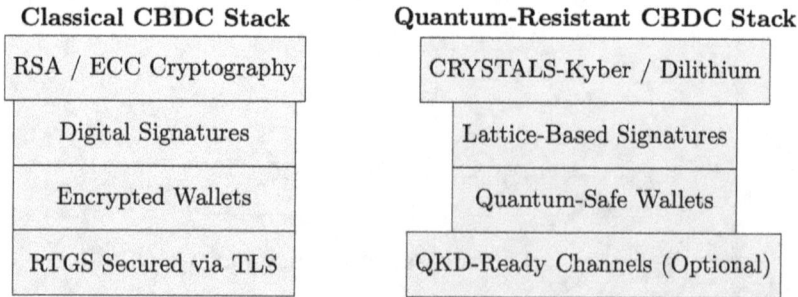

Fig. 4.8 Classical versus post-quantum CBDC security stacks (*Source* Designed by Gabriel Carvalho)

4.10 CBDC Energy Needs and Environmental Impact: A Comparative Analysis of Digital Currency Systems

As central banks worldwide advance CBDC development programs, understanding the energy consumption profiles and environmental impact of these digital currencies has become a critical policy consideration. This analysis examines CBDC energy requirements in the context of traditional banking operations and cryptocurrency networks, providing empirical data to inform sustainable digital currency design decisions.

4.10.1 Current Energy Landscape of Financial Systems

The global financial sector's energy footprint encompasses a complex ecosystem of data centers, physical infrastructure, and transaction processing networks. Traditional banking operations consume approximately 258.85 terawatt-hours (TWh) annually, representing more than 50 times the energy consumption of Bitcoin's proof-of-work network. This substantial energy requirement stems from extensive physical infrastructure, including bank branches, ATMs, data centers, and cash transportation networks that support the conventional banking system (Fig. 4.9).

Traditional banking includes data centers, branches, ATMs, and card networks. Bitcoin's range reflects different estimates; the most recent is 91 TWh, but previous assessments cite up to 167 TWh. CBDC values are based on studies of prototypes like the Swedish e-krona and BIS/ECB research, which consistently find that CBDCs designed with centralized or semi-centralized architectures use less energy than card networks and vastly less than cryptocurrencies.

Contemporary payment networks demonstrate varying degrees of energy efficiency, with significant disparities between different technological approaches. Visa and Mastercard networks each consume approximately 0.00649 kilowatt-hours (kWh) per transaction, substantially lower than cryptocurrency alternatives but still requiring considerable aggregate energy consumption due to transaction volume. The energy profile of cash production and distribution adds additional environmental costs, with each banknote requiring approximately 0.08 kWh during the manufacturing process.

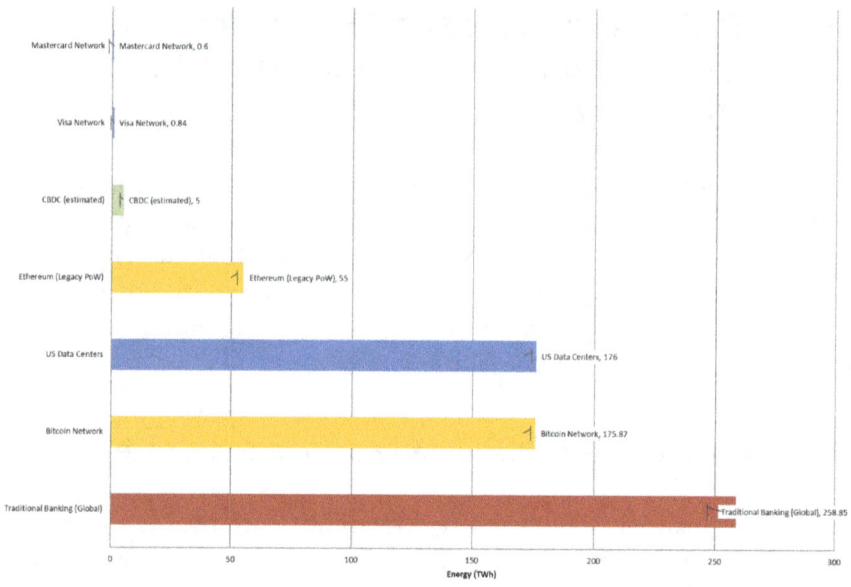

System	Estimated Annual Energy Use (TWh)
Traditional Banking	258.85
Bitcoin (PoW)	91–167.14
Card Networks (Visa)	7.81
CBDC (Centralized)	< Card Networks

Fig. 4.9 Annual energy consumption comparison across financial systems, highlighting CBDC potential for significant energy savings (*Source* Designed by Gabriel Carvalho)

4.10.2 CBDC Energy Consumption Characteristics

Central Bank Digital Currencies present distinct energy consumption patterns that differentiate them from both traditional banking and decentralized cryptocurrency networks. Research indicates that CBDCs designed with centralized or semi-centralized architectures can achieve energy consumption

Table 4.3 Energy consumption comparison across different payment systems per transaction, showing CBDC efficiency relative to traditional methods

Payment system	Energy (kWh/transaction)
Bitcoin (PoW)	118
Ethereum (legacy PoW)	20.3
CBDC (estimated)	0.00649
Visa	0.00649
Mastercard	0.00649
Cash (banknote production)	0.08
Solana (PoS)	0.00017
Ripple	0.000011

Source Designed by Gabriel Carvalho

levels comparable to existing card payment networks, requiring approximately 0.00649 kWh per transaction. This efficiency stems from the elimination of energy-intensive consensus mechanisms like proof-of-work mining that characterize Bitcoin and other first-generation cryptocurrencies.

Table 4.3 compares the energy consumption patterns for different payment systems. As is evident, CBDCs offer better energy consumption patterns compared to Bitcoin or Ether, and are closer in line to consumption patterns of more traditional modes of payment.

Bitcoin's per-transaction energy varies widely due to network activity and block size but is orders of magnitude higher than digital or card payments. CBDC figures are based on central bank pilots and research, showing parity or better efficiency compared to card networks.

The Swedish e-krona pilot project demonstrates that CBDC energy consumption varies significantly based on infrastructure design choices. Centralized CBDC systems exhibit substantially lower energy requirements than decentralized alternatives, with energy consumption closely resembling that of real-time gross settlement (RTGS) systems used in conventional central banking operations. European Central Bank research suggests that CBDCs implementing TARGET Instant Payment Settlement (TIPS) technology could potentially consume less energy than traditional credit card processing systems.

4.10.3 Comparative Analysis: CBDCs Versus Traditional Banking

The energy efficiency advantages of CBDCs become apparent when contrasted with comprehensive traditional banking operations. While conventional banking systems require extensive physical infrastructure, including bank branches, ATMs, and cash transportation networks, CBDCs operate through streamlined digital infrastructure that eliminates many energy-intensive components. Banking data centers represent the largest energy consumption component within traditional systems, accounting for approximately 225.45 TWh annually compared to estimated CBDC consumption of 5 TWh.

CBDCs offer potential energy savings of 253.9 TWh annually compared to traditional banking systems, equivalent to 1.4 times Bitcoin' total annual energy consumption. This dramatic reduction stems from the elimination of physical cash production, reduced need for ATM networks, and streamlined transaction processing infrastructure. The environmental benefits extend beyond direct energy consumption to include reduced carbon emissions, with potential reductions of 126.9 million metric tons of CO_2 annually.

Financial institutions implementing CBDC infrastructure can leverage cloud-based solutions and renewable energy sources more effectively than traditional banking operations. The distributed nature of CBDC systems allows for strategic placement of processing nodes in regions with abundant renewable energy resources, further enhancing environmental performance. This flexibility represents a significant advantage over physical banking infrastructure that requires geographic proximity to customer populations regardless of energy grid characteristics.

4.10.4 Cryptocurrency Energy Consumption Benchmarks

Cryptocurrency networks exhibit extraordinary variation in energy consumption depending on their consensus mechanisms and network architecture. Bitcoin's proof-of-work system consumes approximately 175.87 TWh annually, with individual transactions requiring 118 kWh of energy. This energy intensity stems from the competitive mining process where computational power directly correlates with the probability of earning block rewards. The transition of Ethereum from proof-of-work to proof-of-stake consensus demonstrates the potential for dramatic energy reductions in cryptocurrency systems. Legacy Ethereum consumed approximately 55 TWh annually before its September 2022 transition, while the current proof-of-stake implementation reduces energy consumption by over 99%. This transformation illustrates how consensus mechanism selection fundamentally determines cryptocurrency energy profiles.

Modern proof-of-stake cryptocurrencies like Solana and Ripple achieve remarkable energy efficiency, consuming 0.00017 kWh and 0.000011 kWh per transaction, respectively. These systems demonstrate that cryptocurrency networks can operate with energy consumption levels significantly lower than traditional payment systems while maintaining security and decentralization characteristics. The energy efficiency of proof-of-stake systems provides valuable insights for CBDC design optimization.

4.10.5 Environmental Impact Assessment

The environmental implications of CBDC adoption extend beyond direct energy consumption to encompass broader sustainability considerations. CBDCs eliminate the environmental costs associated with physical currency production, including paper manufacturing, metal mining for coins, and transportation infrastructure. The reduction in physical infrastructure requirements translates to lower resource consumption and reduced carbon emissions across the monetary system lifecycle.

Carbon footprint analysis reveals significant environmental advantages for properly designed CBDC systems. Estimated CBDC emissions of 2.5 million metric tons of CO_2 annually compare favorably to traditional banking emissions of 129.4 million metric tons and Bitcoin emissions of 98.1 million metric tons. These reductions support national and international climate change mitigation objectives while maintaining monetary system functionality.

The geographic flexibility of CBDC infrastructure enables optimization for renewable energy utilization. Unlike traditional banking systems constrained by physical branch locations, CBDC processing can be concentrated in regions with abundant clean energy resources. This strategic placement capability enhances the environmental performance of digital currency systems while supporting broader sustainability initiatives.

4.10.6 Design Considerations for Energy-Efficient CBDCs

Central bank design decisions fundamentally determine CBDC energy consumption profiles and environmental impact. Consensus mechanism selection represents the most critical factor, with permissioned networks avoiding the energy-intensive mining processes required by proof-of-work systems. Implementation of efficient consensus algorithms like practical

Byzantine Fault Tolerance or proof-of-stake variants can achieve security objectives while minimizing computational requirements.

Infrastructure architecture choices significantly influence CBDC energy efficiency. Centralized processing systems typically consume less energy than distributed alternatives, though they may involve trade-offs regarding system resilience and decentralization objectives. Hybrid approaches combining centralized core processing with distributed access networks can balance efficiency and resilience considerations.

Operational optimization strategies can further enhance CBDC's environmental performance. Selection of energy-efficient data center technologies, implementation of renewable energy sourcing, and optimization of transaction processing algorithms contribute to reduced environmental impact. Integration with existing payment infrastructure, where appropriate, can leverage established efficiency gains while supporting CBDC adoption.

4.10.7 Policy Implications and Strategic Considerations

The energy efficiency characteristics of CBDCs present significant policy opportunities for central banks committed to environmental sustainability. The Group of Seven Nations and the European Central Bank have explicitly identified energy efficiency as a fundamental CBDC design principle, reflecting growing awareness of environmental considerations in monetary policy. These commitments create frameworks for implementing environmentally responsible digital currency systems.

CBDC development timelines must account for energy infrastructure evolution and renewable energy deployment. Coordination between central banks and energy authorities can optimize CBDC infrastructure placement to leverage clean energy resources and support grid stability objectives. This coordination becomes particularly important in regions with significant renewable energy deployment and variable generation patterns.

International cooperation on CBDC environmental standards can enhance global sustainability outcomes. Shared methodologies for energy consumption measurement, common sustainability objectives, and coordinated implementation timelines can amplify individual central bank efforts. Such cooperation supports broader international climate change commitments while advancing monetary system modernization.

4.10.8 Implications

Central Bank Digital Currencies present compelling opportunities for reducing the energy consumption and environmental impact of monetary systems while maintaining functionality and security. Properly designed CBDCs can achieve energy consumption levels 51.8 times lower than traditional banking and 35.2 times lower than Bitcoin, representing substantial environmental benefits. These efficiency gains stem from streamlined infrastructure requirements, the elimination of physical currency production, and optimized transaction processing systems.

The technical feasibility of energy-efficient CBDC implementation has been demonstrated through pilot programs and academic research. Swedish e-krona trials and European Central Bank analysis confirm that CBDCs can achieve energy consumption levels comparable to existing card payment networks while providing additional monetary policy capabilities. These findings support central bank confidence in implementing environmentally responsible digital currency systems.

Future CBDC development should prioritize environmental considerations alongside traditional monetary policy objectives. Integration of renewable energy sourcing, optimization of infrastructure placement, and adoption of efficient consensus mechanisms can enhance environmental performance while supporting broader sustainability initiatives. As central banks advance CBDC programs globally, energy efficiency considerations will increasingly influence design decisions and implementation strategies.

4.11 Building Digital Currency Systems That Endure

This chapter has examined the core systems engineering principles underpinning CBDCs and has provided a comprehensive analysis of the technical frameworks, trade-offs, and emerging trends shaping the infrastructure of national digital currencies. Designing a CBDC involves a series of interconnected decisions—ranging from ledger architecture and consensus mechanisms to data storage, privacy safeguards, and network resilience—that reflect not only technical considerations but also broader institutional and regulatory priorities.

The integration of advanced tools such as smart contracts, artificial intelligence, and post-quantum cryptography signals a growing complexity in CBDC systems. These technologies offer significant enhancements in automation, fraud detection, and long-term cryptographic security, but they also demand careful alignment with legal mandates and operational governance frameworks.

Many of these challenges are further amplified when CBDCs are considered in a cross-border context. Participation in the global financial system requires more than technical interoperability; it necessitates policy harmonization, mutual legal recognition, and coordinated oversight among central banks.

A central insight of this chapter is that CBDCs are not merely digital replicas of existing fiat currencies—they are engineered systems that must operate at a national scale while upholding standards of compliance, transparency, and performance. The architectural decisions made—whether permissioned or decentralized, token- or account-based—carry profound implications for the balance between financial inclusion, monetary control, and user privacy.

Part II

The Ins and Outs of CBDC Technology

5

CBDC Launch: e-CNY in China and eNaira in Nigeria

Main Messages

- China's e-CNY reflects its strong digital infrastructure and state-driven innovation, aiming to enhance Financial inclusion, reduce reliance on private platforms, and support global yuan adoption. Despite technical success, private apps like Alipay and WeChat Pay still dominate.
- Nigeria launched the eNaira to boost Financial inclusion and stabilize its currency, but rollout has been hampered by economic instability, institutional mistrust, and infrastructure gaps. Adoption remains low despite policy incentives and government promotion.
- The contrasting experiences of China and Nigeria show that CBDC success depends on public trust, functional infrastructure, and integration with existing systems. Policy design must align with local economic realities for long-term adoption.

As central banks across the globe race to define the future of money, China and Nigeria stand out as early pioneers in the development and deployment of CBDCs. Though vastly different in terms of economic scale, political systems, and digital infrastructure, both countries have embraced CBDCs as

---

The contributions of Puraav Karnavat, Lucea Wright, and Suudarshan Vaidhya under the supervision of Lourdes Casanova are gratefully acknowledged.

tools to modernize monetary systems, enhance Financial inclusion, and assert greater control over their respective financial ecosystems. This chapter offers a comparative exploration of China's e-CNY and Nigeria's eNaira, highlighting how each nation has approached design, implementation, and adoption based on its unique institutional and socioeconomic context. By examining the goals, infrastructure, challenges, and broader implications of these initiatives, we gain insight into how CBDCs are shaping the next phase of global digital finance.

5.1 CBDC Case Study—China

Dr. Mark Mobius and John Ninia embarked on an unforgettable journey to China, accompanied by a close friend from the country. The trip was breathtaking, with landscapes that seemed almost otherworldly. The lush greenery, pristine beaches, and modern infrastructure were so impressive that they could put any other country to shame. What truly left them in awe was the high-speed train that connected Shenzhen to Jingjiang, gliding through the countryside at a blistering 250 km/hr, with the potential to reach an astonishing 350 km/hr. It was clear from the moment they stepped foot in China that this was a place on the rise, captivated by the energy and ambition that permeated the air.

In the small, bustling town of Jingjiang, they wandered through the vibrant local shops, soaking in the sights and sounds of a place where tradition met cutting-edge technology. John decided to get a haircut, figuring it would be a simple errand. But it turned into a small adventure of its own. When it came time to pay, John quickly realized he was stuck; despite his WeChat account being linked to his credit card, foreign cards were simply not accepted. Cash? Forget it. The barbers wouldn't even entertain the idea of taking paper money. As if this wasn't enough, they then made their way to Luckin Coffee for a much-needed pick-me-up. However, they found that ordering there was an entirely different experience. No verbal orders, no paying with cash, and no credit cards at the counter. Everything had to be done through a QR code linked to either WeChat or Alipay. The same challenge awaited them when they tried street food—no vendor would even consider serving them without payment through one of these apps.

Even something as simple as taking a ferry to Hainan Island was an exercise in frustration. The only way to secure a ticket? You guessed it—through WeChat or Alipay. It was a shocking realization that without a local bank account, navigating China's digital payment landscape was nearly impossible for foreigners. What struck them most was the stark contrast between the convenience of these digital systems for locals and the near-impossibility of participating in daily life for those not connected to them. They were left in awe of China's technological advancements but also humbled by how quickly the world around them had evolved—and how challenging it could be to keep up.

As they boarded the metro, it became immediately apparent how seamlessly the local residents moved through the system. With a simple scan of their QR codes on their phones, the gates would swing open effortlessly, allowing them to glide through without a second thought. Mark and John, however, often found themselves pausing at a kiosk to purchase a paper ticket. While the kiosks accepted WeChat and Alipay, they also noticed something new—these machines were beginning to accept e-CNY, China's digital CBDC. It was a quiet yet significant shift toward the future of finance, a glimpse into how China was spearheading the next wave of digital currency adoption. For them, it was a humbling reminder of how quickly the country was advancing and how they were often a step behind in a world that was rapidly embracing digital transformation. This has been a massive leap forward from traditional WeChat and Alipay methods, as e-CNY can be used even if someone's phone is dead or not connected to the Internet. Foreigners can also use and transact in China's e-CNY.

Over the years, China has transformed its economy and established itself as a major player in global markets. As the world's second-largest economy, China is a global economic powerhouse with immense influence on international trade, manufacturing, and technological infrastructure. The country has experienced extensive economic growth in the past several years.

Over the past two decades, China has experienced consistent and substantial economic growth, with steady increases in both overall GDP and GDP per capita. This growth is largely attributed to the market-driven reforms introduced under Deng Xiaoping in the 1990s. A major contributing factor was Xiaoping's Open Door policy, which transitioned China from a state-controlled economy to a market economy focused on export-oriented manufacturing. In 2001, China joined the World Trade Organization (WTO), marking another pivotal moment in its economic trajectory. The country quickly became the world's leading exporter and a major manufacturing hub, attracting significant foreign investment.

China's economic success and rapid industrialization have been supported in large part by its large and growing population, which has provided a vast, low-cost workforce. This demographic advantage helped solidify China's position as a dominant force in the global economy. Historically, a healthy and expanding population has correlated with economic growth. However, in recent years, population growth in China has stagnated, largely due to the long-term effects of the one-child policy (1980–2015) and more recent disruptions from the COVID-19 pandemic. Since 2000, China's population has remained relatively stable, with modest growth tapering off in recent years. This decline in population growth poses challenges for the economy, signaling an aging workforce and a potential shift toward deindustrialization.

Over the past two decades, China has also witnessed a rapid rise in mobile cellular subscriptions, particularly following its accession to the WTO in 2001. As urbanization continues, this growth in mobile connectivity reflects increased consumer purchasing power and broader technological advancements. The surge in mobile penetration signals a significant expansion in digital infrastructure and rapid progress in tech adoption. Leading companies such as Tencent, ByteDance, and Alibaba have played a major role in positioning China as a global technology pioneer, further reinforcing the country's shift from traditional industry toward a more tech-focused economic model. The data reveals that mobile penetration in China has exceeded 100%, indicating that virtually everyone owns a smartphone, and many even own more than one device. Mobile cellular subscriptions have grown exponentially since 2000, reaching near-saturation levels as mobile technology has become deeply embedded in everyday life. Smartphone penetration has also risen steadily over the past decade, with the majority of the population now regularly accessing mobile technology (Fig. 5.1).

China has experienced a remarkable surge in mobile and online banking adoption, now ranking just behind global leaders like Finland and Norway—an indication of the country's rapid advancement in digital Financial inclusion. From 2011 to 2021, the share of individuals aged 15 and older with a bank account increased from approximately 65–80%, highlighting expanded financial access and the integration of more citizens into the formal banking system. During the same period, credit card ownership among this demographic rose sharply, from under 10% to nearly 40%.

China's economic transformation is particularly striking given the short timeframe in which it has established itself as the world's second-largest economy. Over the past 20–30 years, the country has witnessed rapid growth across multiple sectors. However, more recent trends indicate a stagnation in some key indicators, suggesting that China may be entering a new phase in its economic development. The prospects for sustained growth in the coming years will depend on several critical factors, including continued technological innovation, social and political stability, demographic shifts, and the broader geopolitical environment.

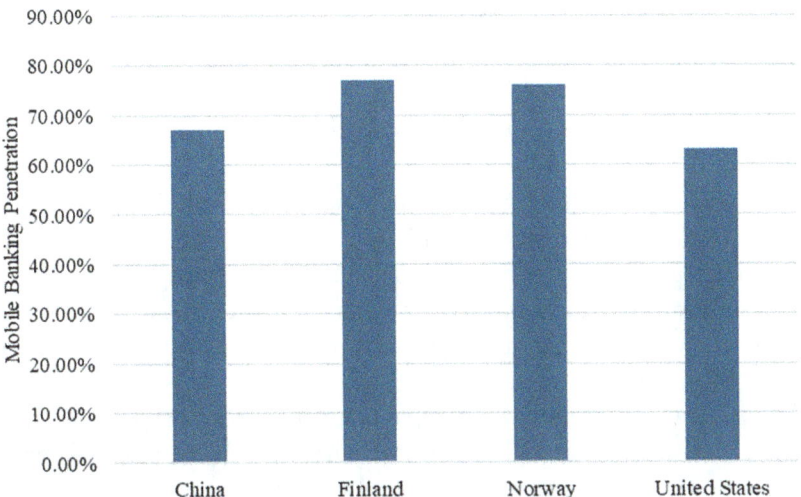

Fig. 5.1 Mobile banking penetration in China compared to other countries (%), 2024 (*Source* Statista Consumer Insights [https://www.statista.com/forecasts/1452621/share-of-online-mobile-banking-users-in-selected-countries-worldwide]; Accessed June 2025)

5.1.1 Mobile Payments

China has rapidly embraced mobile payment technology, with the number of users making mobile payments at least once every six months, growing from 527 million in 2017 to approximately 583 million in 2018. As mobile payments continue to gain traction due to their simplicity and reliability, China is transforming into a predominantly cashless society. But how did this shift to a digital economy happen so quickly?

Unlike in many Western countries, credit cards never gained widespread popularity in China. Their adoption was slow and largely limited to tourist-heavy areas. One major reason for this was the cost: Chinese businesses that accepted credit cards were required to pay a percentage of each transaction to American credit card companies. Additionally, Chinese banks, many of which are state-owned, had little incentive to encourage credit card use, as most consumers had no prior credit history. This created an environment where mobile payment systems, rather than credit cards, became the preferred method for financial transactions.

Without credit cards dominating the payment ecosystem in China, mobile payments were able to gain dominance quickly. The two most prominent mobile payment providers, Alipay and WeChat Pay revolutionized the landscape. Alipay, launched in 2004, marked the beginning of China's transition from cash to digital payments. Before its emergence, UnionPay was the closest alternative to a traditional debit or credit card. However, once Alipay and WeChat Pay entered the market, they quickly became the preferred payment methods, collectively controlling 94% of the mobile payments market by 2018.

Today, even small street vendors in major Chinese cities prefer mobile payments over cash. Virtually everything, from groceries to transportation to tipping street performers, is handled via smartphones using QR codes. This system significantly reduces transaction costs, eliminates the need for physical point-of-sale terminals, and allows merchants to accept payments simply by displaying a printed QR code.

The influence of Chinese mobile payment technology is not confined to domestic markets. Alipay and WeChat Pay have expanded globally, forming partnerships with international banks and financial institutions to integrate their payment systems on a worldwide scale. As mobile payments continue to redefine commerce in China, their growing international presence signals a broader shift toward a fully digital financial future.

What makes WeChat and Alipay better than traditional payment methods? WeChat Pay and Alipay have revolutionized digital transactions by offering mobile wallets that enable low-cost, efficient, and secure payments. Unlike traditional credit and debit card transactions, which often require costly processing fees and specialized hardware, these platforms rely on QR codes for payment transfers. This system is easy to use and requires minimal infrastructure—merchants simply print a QR code, which customers scan within the app to complete a payment. In contrast, businesses in the United States must invest in credit card terminals, which involve processing fees and maintenance costs, making mobile payments a more accessible and cost-effective solution, particularly for small businesses in China.

Beyond cost efficiency, mobile payments significantly reduce transaction time. Many major Retailers, including McDonald's and Starbucks, have integrated self-scanning devices that allow customers to scan QR codes for quick, seamless payments. This eliminates the need for cashiers to process transactions manually, reducing wait times and enhancing the overall customer experience.

While some consumers in the United States worry that mobile payments could expose them to fraud or data theft, mobile payment technology offers enhanced security and Privacy protections. Biometric authentication, such as fingerprint scans and Face ID, is used alongside Apple Pay, WeChat Pay, and Alipay, ensuring that only the device owner can authorize transactions. Additionally, these platforms use Tokenization, which replaces sensitive card information with a randomly generated token, preventing actual card numbers from being stored or shared. When combined with Near Field Communication (NFC) technology—a wireless communication method that allows devices to exchange data over short distances—this greatly reduces the risk of financial data being compromised.

If a fraudulent transaction is attempted, a notification about the transaction would appear on the owner's phone instantly, and 2-factor authentication would prevent the transaction from ever occurring. By contrast, traditional payment methods—such as handing a credit or debit card to a restaurant server or store clerk—pose a greater security risk, as physical cards can be copied or misused. While credit and debit card companies offer fraud protection, mobile payment systems allow users to monitor transactions in real-time and manage outstanding balances more efficiently.

While mobile payment systems provide a faster, safer, and more cost-effective alternative to traditional payment methods and have transformed financial transactions globally, they also come with significant drawbacks, particularly for foreigners and those without access to the local banking infrastructure.

This shift toward e-CNY reflects not only technological innovation but also the government's growing role in shaping the digital financial landscape. As foreign visitors encountered firsthand, China's payment systems are evolving beyond private platforms like WeChat and Alipay to include state-backed alternatives. This evolution is part of a broader strategic vision.

The People's Bank of China (PBOC) oversees the mobile payments ecosystem and has introduced a pilot with the digital yuan (e-CNY) as a state-backed alternative to private payment platforms. As of July 2025, Digital yuan (e-CNY) is the largest CBDC pilot in the world launched in 17 provinces across different sectors. Government involvement focuses on enhancing financial security, preventing fraud, and maintaining oversight over the broader financial system. Table 5.1 highlights key milestones in China's journey from early mobile payment adoption to the development and rollout of its CBDC. These developments illustrate how both market forces and regulatory initiatives have shaped the country's digital financial ecosystem.

Digital payment systems in China, and increasingly in other countries, are generally implemented through three main categories: traditional, contemporary, and specialized methods. These categories reflect the technological progression of payment infrastructures and the growing integration of biometric and Blockchain-based solutions (Table 5.2).

Table 5.1 Timeline of key milestones in the evolution of mobile payments and digital currency in China (2004–2023)

Year	Event
2004	Alipay is introduced as an escrow service for Taobao transactions
2008	Alipay expands its offerings beyond PC transactions to include mobile payments
2011	WeChat Pay, which integrates payments into the social media app WeChat, debuted
2013	Alipay and WeChat Pay implemented QR code payments, resulting in widespread adoption by retailers and customers
2014	Alipay and WeChat Pay integrated QR code payments, driving smartphone use
2015	The Chinese government-issued new laws for third-party payment companies to improve security and supervision
2017	Mobile payments surpassed cash transactions in China
2020	Pilot initiatives for the digital yuan are launched in major Chinese cities
2021	More than 90% of urban inhabitants in China utilize mobile payments for daily purchases
2023	The digital yuan is being integrated into systems such as Alipay and WeChat Pay, enabling smooth hybrid transactions

Table 5.2 Key categories of digital payment methods and their features

Category	Key features	Examples
Traditional	ATM withdrawals, Bank-issued credit/debit cards, ATM withdrawals	UnionPay, POS terminals
Contemporary	QR code payments, super apps, digital yuan	WeChat Pay, Alipay, digital yuan transactions
Specialized	Biometric authentication, blockchain-based financial services	Facial recognition, AI-driven risk analysis, smart contracts

Understanding which digital payment methods dominate everyday use further illustrates adoption trends and consumer preferences. Figure 5.2 presents the most prevalent e-commerce payment methods in China as of 2023.

Despite the sharp increase in digital payment volume—from fewer than 250 million users in 2014 to nearly 1 billion by 2023—the adoption of the e-Yuan remains relatively low. This is largely due to the dominant presence of private digital payment platforms like Alipay and WeChat Pay, which offer Chinese consumers seamless transactions, highly optimized user interfaces, and broad accessibility. As a result, there is currently little incentive for users

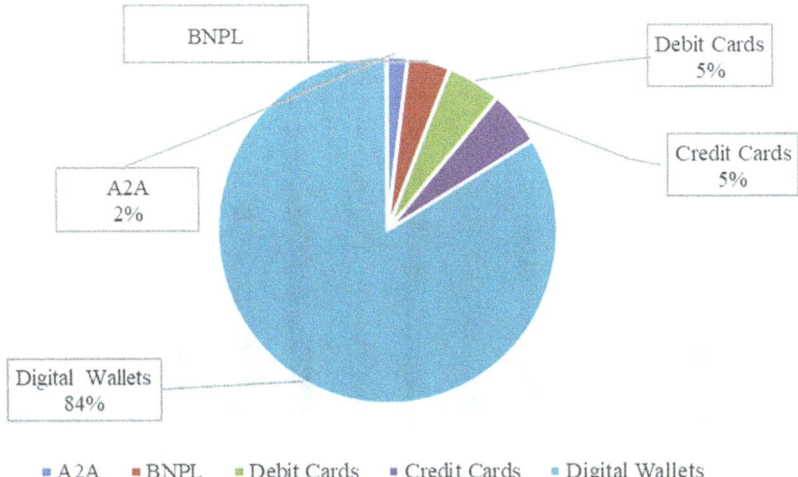

Fig. 5.2 E-commerce payment methods in China (in %), 2023 (*Source* EMI research team based on data from Statista)

to transition to the e-Yuan. The rest Buy Now Pay Later (BNPL), A2A (asked to answer), or debit/credit cards are small players.

For the e-Yuan to gain broader adoption, it must offer clear advantages that existing platforms do not. Furthermore, as a CBDC, the e-Yuan faces skepticism among users concerned about Privacy and data security. Without a compelling value proposition or increased trust, many consumers remain hesitant to shift from their current digital payment habits.

Nevertheless, things are subject to change depending on the growth of remittances through digital payments in China from 2017 to the present and the predicted forecasts of its growth until 2029. The size of the digital remittance market in China is growing substantially. Assuming this growth rate continues, the market is projected to reach $19.47 billion in transaction volume by 2029.

Mobile payments, made specifically via mobile devices like smartphones or tablets, have become a dominant force in China's digital economy, rapidly outpacing traditional forms of payment such as credit and debit cards. Mobile payment methods are not only growing in overall transaction value but are also being used across a wide range of everyday transactions.

Figure 5.3 tracks the annual growth of mobile payment transactions, digital remittances, and digital commerce in China over more than a decade.

Fig. 5.3 Digital payments transaction values (in billions) (*Source* Statista Market Insights, 2025 [https://www.statista.com/outlook/fmo/payments/digital-payments/worldwide?currency=USD]; Accessed June 2025)

Mobile POS payments, digital commerce, and remittances are growing rapidly, highlighting the increasing role of mobile infrastructure in China's financial system. Mobile payments have overtaken credit cards across nearly all sectors, signaling a transformation in both consumer preference and infrastructure design.

5.1.2 China's e-CNY: A Strategic CBDC at the Nexus of Innovation and Global Ambition

China's development of a CBDC, known as the e-CNY, reflects both domestic policy priorities and strategic global ambitions. Through its digital currency initiative, China is transforming its monetary system by advancing innovation in policy design, technical infrastructure, distribution models, and patterns of adoption.

The CBDC, known as the e-CNY, is closely aligned with the country's broader objective of becoming a global leader in technology. The goals of the CBDC initiative include:

- Financial inclusion
- Monetary policy and government financial control

- Reducing the reliance on popular private payment platforms
- Promoting the international use of the yuan
- Advancing China's geopolitical position

Retail CBDC is designed for everyday use and is the digital equivalent of cash. Its application spans peer-to-peer and peer-to-merchant transactions, reinforcing its role in daily consumer activity. Unlike private platforms such as Alipay and WeChat Pay, Retail CBDC does not impose additional transaction fees on consumers. However, the adoption of the Retail CBDC has been limited. In response, the Chinese government has integrated the e-CNY into existing private payment platforms to boost usage. Despite rapid urbanization and industrialization over the past four decades, a significant portion of China's population continues to reside in rural and agrarian areas. As of 2024, approximately 33.84% of the total population resides in rural areas. Recognizing this, the Retail CBDC offers offline transaction capabilities, enabling individuals in regions with limited Internet access to participate in digital commerce. In this way, Retail CBDC supports broader goals of accessibility and Financial inclusion.

Wholesale CBDC is designed for use by large financial institutions, corporations, and commercial banks conducting high-value transactions and settlements. It is not intended for everyday consumers. Wholesale CBDC enables efficient, secure, and transparent transactions within the financial system, helping to mitigate systemic risk. This form of CBDC plays a strategic role in modernizing China's financial infrastructure, replacing legacy systems with digital alternatives that align with the country's ambitions to become a technological superpower. It also supports the internationalization of the yuan, promoting its use in global transactions and reinforcing China's economic presence on the world stage.

Cross-border CBDC integrates features of both Retail and Wholesale models, with its primary goal being the facilitation of international transactions. A key objective is to reduce global dependence on the SWIFT network and diminish the dominance of the U.S. dollar in international trade. Cross-border CBDC is central to China's vision of expanding the global reach of the yuan and bolstering its position in international markets. This form of CBDC is also integral to Project mBridge, a Blockchain-based platform developed by the People's Republic of China to support cross-border CBDC transactions (see Chapter 8). Moreover, cross-border CBDC aligns with the broader goals of the Belt and Road Initiative (BRI)—a global infrastructure development strategy launched in 2013 to strengthen China's economic ties with partner countries. Through the development and implementation of CBDC, China aims to deepen its global economic connectivity and enhance its influence in international financial systems.

China's e-CNY is distributed using an indirect, two-tier system. This model maintains centralized control at the central bank level while leveraging the existing infrastructure and networks of commercial banks and private payment platforms to deliver digital currency to end users (Table 5.3).

First Tier: The People's Bank of China (PBOC) is the sole issuer of the digital yuan and maintains a centralized ledger to ensure monetary stability. Rather than distributing the e-CNY directly to individuals, the PBOC distributes it to commercial banks and payment service providers such as Alipay and WeChat Pay.

Second Tier: These institutions then distribute the digital yuan to businesses and individuals through digital wallets, mobile apps, and other payment systems. In this structure, banks and payment platforms act as intermediaries, facilitating the delivery of the digital currency to end users.

The e-CNY operates on a hybrid, centralized Blockchain system within the two-tier distribution model. This design balances centralized monetary oversight with the scalability and infrastructure of commercial banks. Table 5.4 outlines the key reasons behind China's technological approach, emphasizing its benefits in terms of efficiency, control, and financial system stability:

In June 2021, 20.87 million personal wallets and 3.51 million corporate wallets were opened, with the total transaction value reaching $5.39 billion. By early 2022, over 260 million wallets had been opened. By June 2023, total

Table 5.3 Indirect distribution of e-CNY via the two-tier system

Central Bank People's Bank of China
- Issues e-CNY to commercial banks and financial institutions
- Has centralized control

↓

Commercial Bank and Payment Platforms
- Commercial banks and Private payment platforms like Alipay and WeChat Pay give e-CNY to users/consumers
- Manage digital wallets and facilitating transactions

Table 5.4 Key design factors underlying China's CBDC technology model

Design factor	Description
Scalability and efficiency	Commercial banks currently have the necessary infrastructure and client base to distribute the digital yuan
Monetary control	Centralized control over currency supply while banks handle daily user interactions
Financial stability	Allows current financial institutions to remain relevant instead of cutting out banks where individuals directly hold accounts with the central bank

transactions using the e-CNY had reached nearly $1 trillion. As of July 2025, China officially included the e-CNY in its currency circulation calculations which is about USD 986 billion.

In terms of international expansion, the e-CNY was integrated with Hong Kong's Faster Payments System (FPS) in September 2023, and two months later, Standard Chartered China became one of the first foreign banks to trial the digital yuan.

Since its launch, the e-CNY has demonstrated both notable achievements and ongoing challenges. The following examines key measures of success and areas where the initiative has yet to meet its goals.

Level of Adoption: As of June 2024, e-CNY has achieved a transaction volume of 7 trillion yuan, supported by a user base of 261 million individuals—an impressive indicator of its growing presence. However, despite this substantial usage, adoption still lags behind dominant private platforms. For comparison, Alipay processes approximately $17 trillion annually, highlighting the considerable distance e-CNY must cover to reach comparable levels of adoption.

Frequency of Transaction: The current e-CNY infrastructure supports 10,000 transactions per second (TPS), with plans to scale up to 300,000 TPS. In contrast, Alipay can already process up to 544,000 TPS, underscoring the need to enhance the e-CNY system's scalability and technological competitiveness.

Accessibility of Services: Through the integration of existing platforms such as Alipay and WeChat Pay, e-CNY has successfully expanded its reach to a broader population. Additionally, government initiatives, including the distribution of salaries and subsidies via digital yuan wallets, have supported the implementation and adoption of e-CNY across many communities.

Security and Oversight: A key strength of the e-CNY lies in its advanced security protocols, including digital certificates and digital signatures that safeguard user data and transaction integrity. Moreover, the centralized framework allows the People's Bank of China (PBOC) to effectively monitor and regulate the system, enhancing overall security and trust in the digital currency.

Currency Stability: Unlike decentralized cryptocurrencies, the e-CNY is fixed 1:1 to China's domestic currency, ensuring price stability and shielding it from the volatility commonly associated with digital assets like Bitcoin or Ethereum.

These outcomes reflect both the promise and the constraints of China's mobile payments. Understanding how the e-CNY has been operationalized through its infrastructure, legal frameworks, and public engagement strategies sheds light on the state's evolving approach to digital finance.

Technology infrastructure: The e-CNY supports Near Field Communication (NFC) technology, enabling offline transactions without requiring Internet connectivity. With encrypted storage and robust security protocols, the system ensures both secure data handling and operational reliability.

Legislation: In conjunction with the rollout of the e-CNY, China has introduced strict regulatory frameworks to govern its use and to prevent illicit activities. Simultaneously, the government has implemented tight controls on private cryptocurrencies to preserve monetary authority and promote the broader adoption of the digital yuan.

Marketing strategy: To boost public adoption, local governments have employed strategies such as lotteries and subsidies distributed through digital yuan wallets. By partnering with major platforms like Alipay and WeChat Pay, the government has leveraged their extensive user bases to increase visibility and ease of access. Additionally, international expansion efforts, including cross-border payment pilots with Hong Kong's Faster Payments System, aim to strengthen the digital yuan's role in international trade and tourism, enhancing its global profile.

5.2 CBDC Case Study—Nigeria

Nigeria, rich in natural resources, is among Africa's leading economies, serving as a beacon of progress for the continent. The country demonstrates strong potential for continued growth, with trade flows and global interactions playing an integral role in its increasingly robust world standing. However, as shown by Fig. 5.4, recent events have hindered Nigerian development, impacting the evolution of the country's financial landscape.

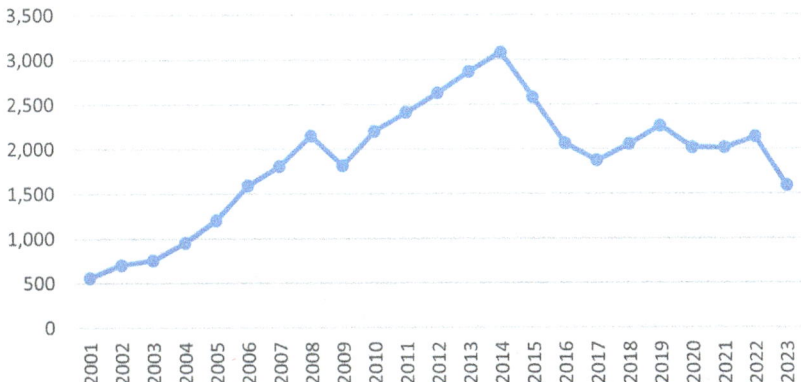

Fig. 5.4 GDP per capita in current U.S. dollars of Nigeria, 2001–23 (*Source* World Bank, 2025 [https://data.worldbank.org/indicator/NY.GDP.PCAP.CD?locations=NG]; Accessed June 2025)

Understanding Nigeria's economic and political circumstances provides context for the recent changes. On the economic front, Nigeria has been facing a highly unstable macroeconomy, as well as currency headwinds. Inflation reached 29.9% in January 2024, and the naira went to its all-time lowest value against the USD in February 2024. Deepening inflation has been driven by a cost-of-living crisis, failed food harvests, and a falling exchange rate caused by economic shocks.

Poorly executed economic reform has much to do with the precarious nature of the economy. Fuel subsidies in place since the 1970s were abruptly removed in May of 2023, resulting in a more than 200% increase in gas prices. At the same time, the relaxation of currency controls has led to a devaluation of the naira. At present, the economy is troubled by a triad of factors—conflicting actions between the government and monetary authority, a combination of monetary and structural issues, and the existence of parallel markets due to unfavorable interventionist measures.

Monetary policy, in the form of considerable interest rate hikes, has somewhat stabilized the free-falling currency. Nevertheless, declining oil revenues have slowed dollar inflows into Nigeria, increasing the role of the black market in providing access to the dollar. Meanwhile, the central bank has partially cleared the foreign exchange backlog to the tune of $2.5 billion, while the government has authorized the release of certain foods from central reserves in an effort to address shortages and contain rampant inflation.

These economic woes are compounded by political instability. Widespread protests have led to an outbreak of violence in certain parts of the country. Farming communities have been forced to flee from conflict zones, all while labor unions sharply criticize the government's food distribution and policy initiatives. Evidently, the present regime's efforts to move toward a more market-led framework have not come without difficulties for many Nigerian citizens.

It is also important to consider Nigeria's recent measures to move toward a technology-centric economy through digital payments and the development of CBDC. With the central bank's goal of a "cashless economy" in mind, several policies, such as limiting cash accessibility from POS merchants and banks, the introduction of the eNaira, and others, have been formulated. However, the rapid movement toward digital finance has shown some unideal outcomes, in part due to Nigeria's distinct sociopolitical features.

5.2.1 Digital Payments

In Nigeria, players in digital payments include the government, the monetary authority, the Central Bank of Nigeria, consumers, businesses, and financial institutions. New modalities of companies with intersections between domains are also quickly arising. For instance, Nigerian fintechs, including many providing modern payment services, such as Flutterwave and Paystack, raised over $1 billion in investment in 2022 alone.

The Central Bank of Nigeria recently launched the Nigeria Payments System Vision 2025, which involves the various stakeholders in a two-sided paradigm of cooperation and competition. The central bank serves as a regulator and oversees two levels: payment infrastructure on clearing and settlement and Payment Service Providers (PSPs), which perform the function of transaction processing. PSPs are involved in various channels and products for individuals, corporations, and the government. There are different types of PSPs, with domains such as cards and payments, mobile money operators, switching and processing, payment solution services (PSS), payment terminal service aggregators, and payments service holding. A large number of players operate in payment solution services with varying specializations. Within the paradigm, cooperation between stakeholders ensures a degree of standardization in foundational layers, as well as effective regulation to ensure the soundness of technical structure and processes. Meanwhile, competition ensures that firms in the sector are competitive, increasing innovation and allowing the end users to get the best possible digital financial services (Table 5.5).

Implementation has faced certain hurdles. For instance, over 40% of potential users have encountered problems with the KYC process. Fraud is also a major concern, given the tendency in Nigeria to bypass official systems.

Table 5.5 Timeline of key milestones in the evolution of mobile payments and digital currency in Nigeria (2007–2025)

Year	Event
2007	Payments System Vision (PSV) 2020 is launched by the Central Bank of Nigeria, signaling fintech's role in economic growth
2011	The "cashless economy" policy is introduced to reduce transactions and systems based on physical cash
2012	The NFIS (National Financial inclusion Strategy) is launched with the goals of reducing the adult financial exclusion rate and expanding the formal financial sector
2013	The PSV 2020 has a second release featuring improved risk management in payment structures
2014	The concept of Bank Verification Number (BVN) is introduced to boost security through identification
2016	SunTrust Bank Limited begins operations with a "branchless strategy"; many more digital banks and fintech platforms, such as Paga and Remita, emerge
2019	Value of mobile money transactions reaches 5.10 trillion naira, and interbank instant e-payments reach 105.2 trillion naira
2021	The Central Bank of Nigeria bans financial institutions from participating in Cryptocurrency transactions
2021	Nigeria becomes the first country in Africa to launch CBDC, with eNaira projected to boost GDP by $29 billion in its first ten years
2024	Nigeria's most popular mobile wallet company, PalmPay, partners with Jumia, the largest e-commerce company in Africa, with direct integration of digital payments
2025	Outlook by Visa reveals positive momentum in Nigeria, with 83% of surveyed businesses viewing digital payment investment as a crucial aspect for growth

In fact, attempted fraudulent mobile transactions increased by 20% in 2023. Further, systemic flaws hinder the implementation of digital payments in Nigeria. Basic elements of technical infrastructure, including electricity and Internet connectivity, are not widespread. Only about 40% of Nigerians possess Internet access. Moreover, digital payments fail to resonate with the Nigerian population. Only 36% of adults are considered to be financially literate, while a history of mistrust in authority, including the central bank, exacerbates the public's disconnect with modern digital finance.

Still, Nigeria's efforts to digitalize finance have led to some positive outcomes. According to research by McKinsey, around 36% of Nigerians now have access to digital financial services, a figure which sat at just 10% only five years ago. There has been an acceleration in the use of alternative digital methods, with PoS transactions valued at 807.16 billion naira in January 2023, a 40.7% YoY increase. The total value of cashless transactions was 39.58 trillion naira in January 2023, representing 45.41% growth over the last year. There have been substantial shifts from traditional channels, such as ATMs, to modern means, including online transfers through mobile applications. As of 2022, ATM transactions had a value of 32 trillion naira compared to 783.6 trillion naira for online transfers.

The rollout of digital payments in Nigeria underscores a broader challenge for other countries with low trust in authority and large informal economic sectors. In Nigeria, where Micro-, Small, and Medium-sized Enterprises (MSMEs) and small-scale startups dominate, firms generally rely on functional business exchanges rather than personal trust or institutional enforcement. However, in the case of digital payment systems, strict enforcement has shown to be effective. Now, nearly half (46.2%) of informal business holders' transactions are conducted through cards and digital transfers. This demonstrates the potential for countries with similar environments to circumvent institutional difficulties via high-handed enforcement in order to implement modern digital payment services.

An important reason for increasing the usage of digital payments in Nigeria is limiting the number of illicit cash transactions. Yet, digital payment implementation has done little to deter criminal and terrorist activity. For instance, many Nigerian terrorist groups have chosen to demand ransoms in the form of material goods rather than cash, thereby bypassing the intended deterrent of recently enforced digital payment policies.

Digital payments are also recognized for their potential to improve the efficiency of public services. For example, the Central Bank of Nigeria has launched a new payment solution for Ministries, Departments, and Agencies (MDAs) while adopting digital management of documents. Such technologies are projected to improve payment turnaround time by 70% and have positive implications for government transparency within the financial sector.

The main sectors for digital payments include e-commerce and online banking, for which transactions increased by 50% during the COVID-19 pandemic. As of 2023, there are more than 30 million mobile wallet users in Nigeria, with the number of mobile payments consistently increasing in recent years. Such growth is driven primarily by the younger population, particularly those aged 18–34, considering their relatively high levels of technological literacy and a heightened desire to adapt to changing technology.

It is also important to note regional disparities which affect digital payment usage. The northern areas of Nigeria are underdeveloped in terms of technological capabilities. Mobile penetration rates are low relative to the rest of the country, and cash-based agricultural trade remains a cornerstone of the economy. In contrast, the southwest region, which includes urban centers

Abuja and Lagos, represents more than 50% of mobile data subscriptions and a greater number of cashless exchanges when compared with other regions of Nigeria. As such, the southwest region has experienced a much faster uptake of digital payments.

Finally, it is crucial to understand that digital payment usage is heavily dependent on both parties in a given transaction. For example, if a citizen intends to use digital payment, yet an institution or corporation insists upon using cash, the system fails. There have been many such instances in Nigeria as digital payments progressively roll out. In some cases, citizens reliant on digital payments could not admit family members into hospitals because of the hospitals' insistence on cash. Such disjunction is also visible between various financial stakeholders. For instance, citizens may struggle to withdraw cash from certain financial institutions as the Nigerian economy slowly adjusts to a digital payment system. This reveals an important insight into how on-the-ground realities work—a government policy of removing cash and enforcing digital payments has serious ramifications for the economy's many stakeholders, especially in the beginning stages of technology adoption.

5.2.2 Nigeria's eNaira: A CBDC Caught Between Ambition, Public Resistance, and Policy Reinvention

Nigeria's purpose for launching a CBDC more or less falls in line with that of any other country exploring the new technology. One of the primary objectives is that of Financial inclusion. In 2020, the Financial inclusion rate was 64.1% in Nigeria. Looking at specific subfields of the financial system, payment penetration was at 45%, credit was at 3%, and formal services were at 50.5%. With an ambitious aim of 95% inclusion by 2024, it is clear that Nigeria sees CBDC as an integral part of its Financial inclusion strategy.

Additionally, the naira is particularly weak compared to the U.S. dollar. This has been posited as a reason for the push toward CBDC. With the Central Bank of Nigeria having greater control over the Monetary policy of a centrally issued digital currency, many project a strengthening of the naira against the dollar. Another goal on related lines pertains to intra-African trade and international investment. Currently, Africa faces a currency illiquidity problem due to a significant number (41) of currencies on the continent. Therefore, CBDC can help pave the way for improved liquidity and efficacy of regional and global transactions.

Other objectives include the eased flow of remittances from the diaspora, as there are currently high costs for Nigerian citizens transacting overseas. Policy measures such as streamlined welfare payments and improved efficiency in domestic payment systems are also the main imperatives. Additionally, due to the size of the informal sector, the government aspires to increase the transparency and traceability of the sector's functioning. CBDC can help expand the tax base and formalize certain informal economic activities, allowing for greater government revenue and tightened regulation.

Implementation has primarily revolved around Retail CBDC. However, there are plans to integrate Wholesale CBDC as well, with the Central Bank of Nigeria announcing that the eNaira would be embedded into the Nigeria Inter-Bank Settlement System (NIBSS), facilitating transfers between financial institutions.

Emphasis has been placed on Retail CBDC due to the nature of Nigeria's financial landscape. Considering Nigeria's position as an emerging market, Retail CBDC serves as a social good, acting as a financial instrument for the mass populace. On the other hand, Wholesale CBDC pertains to transactions between financial institutions. For example, in Project Jura, the central banks of France and Switzerland demonstrated the possibility of foreign currency clearing through Wholesale CBDC. Wholesale CBDC strategies, meanwhile, have been pursued mainly by developed countries. Canada, for instance, is experimenting with domestic interbank settlement via DLT and a notary node consensus model, having successes in LSMs (Liquidity Saving Mechanisms) and settlement scalability. This CBDC dynamic is echoed by Adeolu Fadele, the program manager of eNaira in Nigeria:

> Most of the emerging economies are focusing on the Retail CBDCs because there are opportunities to leapfrog some infrastructural challenges, and CBDCs can help us with that.

But Nigeria is also moving forward with applications concerning Wholesale and cross-border CBDC. A Stablecoin pegged to eNaira is currently under development. Meanwhile, globally, the BIS expects nine Wholesale CBDCs to go live by 2030. Therefore, some attention is expected to shift toward non-Retail CBDC as well.

As with most emerging markets exploring CBDCs, Nigeria has opted for an intermediated distribution model. This means the CBDC is not directly disseminated by the central bank but is instead distributed by intermediaries, including banks and other financial institutions.

Such a method of dissemination stems from the main rationale behind CBDC being that of a competitive payment system and efficient financial transactions within and outside borders. Hence, a hybrid and two-tiered model is followed, wherein the Central Bank of Nigeria is responsible for the production, issuance, storage, and distribution of eNaira to financial institutions and International Money Transfer Operators (IMTOs). Then, the institutions hold responsibility for issuing eNaira to citizens, companies, and other entities.

The model described also functions well within the existing financial landscape of Nigeria. Because the CBDC model is complementary to cash, different mediums of exchange can coexist within the Nigerian economy. The model also allows for the preservation of the Central Bank of Nigeria's wider operating model, all while supporting market mechanisms that promote innovation and competition.

On the user side, citizens can access CBDC via a wallet found in a mobile application called eNaira Speed Wallet. This system features a Digital Currency Management System (DCMS) to facilitate transactions, which was developed by the Central Bank of Nigeria in collaboration with Barbados-based Bitt Inc. The underlying technology is based on Blockchain and DLT, with transaction network Hyperledger Fabric. In late 2023, technological features were upgraded, with the addition of Near Field Communication (NFC) enabling contactless payments.

As previously mentioned, Nigeria faces a lack of Internet access for large segments of the population, as well as a generally unstable electricity supply, both of which act as barriers to the usage of eNaira. Furthermore, due to nascent technology systems, Cybersecurity risk is heightened, a common concern held across a number of African central banks.

These challenges are being addressed by a combination of innovative solutions. For instance, USSD technology has been utilized to counter Internet accessibility issues. Further, in March 2024, the Central Bank of Nigeria signed a MoU with Gluwa, a firm specializing in Blockchain, to improve adoption by improving the functionality of eNaira.

The eNaira was launched in September 2021. At the same time, roughly 18 billion naira has been issued in the form of CBDC. As of May 2023, 98.5% of the issued CBDC wallets had never been used. Evidently, the Nigerian population has been slow to adopt the Retail CBDC into regular use.

Despite a quick initial boom, a gradual tapering off in usage occurred. On the technical front, implementation was quite successful, as there was no outage during the first year of operation. This was not the case with certain CBDC launches in the Caribbean. As of November 2021, there were about 860,000 Retail eNaira wallets, and the average weekly value of eNaira transactions was 923 million naira. In 2023, there was some improvement, with the value of transactions increasing by 63%. However, despite the technical success, the eNaira has failed to become a widespread form of payment thus far.

According to consumers, operational issues persist with the eNaira. For example, a dual CBDC wallet requirement for both the sender and recipient in a money transfer reduces on-the-ground effectiveness. Nevertheless, there has been a steady rise in the amount of eNaira in circulation, from 9 billion nairas in July 2023 to 14 billion nairas in March 2024. In March 2024, the eNaira made up 0.36% of total currency in circulation, compared to just 0.02% in October 2021. The Central Bank of Nigeria has expanded its 2024–25 policy guidelines for trade and exchange by allowing eNaira payments into government accounts and enabling government wings to perform beneficiary and vendor payments through their eNaira wallets. This suggests the potential for eNaira to continue to grow despite an underwhelming initial launch and persisting operational difficulties.

Currently, less than 0.5% of Nigeria's population has adopted CBDC, whereas the proportion of Nigerians using Cryptocurrency is significantly higher. To boost CBDC adoption, the government has tried numerous incentivization measures. Policies like restrictions on the usage of cash and cash withdrawal limits were imposed, which led to public backlash. To spur utilization, the regulations for CBDC access were loosened, and discount options for payments, such as taxi fares, were also proposed.

Following these measures, central bank governor Godwin Emefiele stated that adoption rose to 6%. However, the IMF reports otherwise, while Emefiele himself has been arrested on charges of corruption. Acceptance of CBDC still has not been significantly influenced as a result of deeper systemic issues. Enabling public trust and understanding of CBDC, along with supporting various stakeholders, will be key in ensuring the successful diffusion of CBDC in the future.

As of October 2024, an estimated 33% of Nigerians invest in Cryptocurrency, making Nigeria the second-largest country in the world in terms of Cryptocurrency adoption. Nigerian citizens strongly prefer Cryptocurrency over CBDC for a variety of reasons, including a general attitude of opposition toward the government and sub-par economic conditions. The poverty-stricken public has fallen victim to a number of Cryptocurrency schemes, including those promoted by celebrities Ramon Abbas and David Adeleke. Furthermore, the naira's extreme volatility as of late has given greater reason for citizens to opt for Cryptocurrency.

In Nigeria, Cryptocurrency is particularly popular in foreign exchange transactions and within criminal networks. Cryptocurrency's implication in criminal activity in the country is so strong that government fears of Cryptocurrency's role in financing terrorism led to the detainment of a Binance executive in 2024. While the government previously rejected cryptocurrencies outright, there has been a shift to somewhat of a middle ground, with licenses being given to certain trading platforms, including Quidax Technologies and Busha Digital, in September 2024. Additionally, new regulations have been developed for the taxation of Cryptocurrency exchanges, leveraging them as a driver of government revenues and causing Nigerian authorities to look more favorably upon the technology.

There have been some risks associated with the deployment of CBDC. One key consideration is the existence of parallel markets in Nigeria, which can hinder the utilization of CBDC within key channels. For example, physical transmission of forex in Nigeria's borders, as well as the use of third-party relationships in cities such as Lagos to perform parallel forex transactions, are common, thereby inhibiting CBDC usage.

A second risk is that of monetary instability. In October 2023, the exchange rate had risen to 774 naira against the USD, with a black market exchange rate of 1035 naira against the USD. Inflation was high, and an increase in fuel prices compounded the crisis, causing the Central Bank of Nigeria to carry out five interest rate hikes in 2024 alone. Such instability has been common in Nigeria in recent years.

Legislation banning Nigerian financial institutions from dealing in cryptocurrencies was enacted in February 2021. Since then, policies have been established to implement CBDC as a mainstream mechanism. For instance, the requirement of a bank account for using CBDC was waived in August 2022, a major step when considering that roughly 36% of Nigeria's adult population is unbanked. Further, in December 2022, cash withdrawals were restricted to $1123 for corporations and $225 for individuals weekly. Such limits ensure the eNaira's long-term viability as a vehicle for payments, preventing unwanted competition against bank deposits.

Additionally, the creation of identity verification through mobile numbers and bank verification numbers allows for higher regulatory oversight and heightened security against illegal transactions, increasing the viability of mainstream CBDC usage. A currency redesign was also undertaken in November 2022 for reasons of monetary stability and curbing shadow crime. This action aimed to help spur the transition to eNaira as a mainstream form of payment but was largely unsuccessful due to failures in digital financial infrastructure.

Marketing has centered around a distinct positioning strategy for CBDC policy. The prevailing paradigm of CBDC's role as a social good is present, with eNaira being touted as the next step forward in Nigeria's path to development. Yet, there remain certain marketing elements that make the push toward CBDC in Nigeria unique.

For instance, CBDC is branded as an initiative driven by a benevolent social planner in the form of the national government. In the words of deputy governor of the Central Bank of Nigeria Kingsley Obiora, "All the eNaira needs is a little push from the government." While centralized power has historically been perceived negatively by the public due to a political environment characterized by a general distrust of authority, Nigeria now seeks to emphasize CBDC's strength as the product of a trustworthy national government.

It is necessary to note that CBDC marketing has been influenced by important political forces in recent years, including changes in government leadership. The president changed in May 2023, which caused a reversion to a more orthodox Monetary policy. Meanwhile, the former governor of the Central Bank of Nigeria, Godwin Emefiele, a leading proponent of CBDC, was detained on multiple criminal charges, including corruption, damaging government efforts to promote the rollout of the eNaira.

5.2.3 Looking Ahead: Lessons from CBDC Launches in China and Nigeria

The cases of China's e-CNY and Nigeria's eNaira reveal the complex interplay between technological ambition, financial infrastructure, and the sociopolitical context in shaping the future of money. Both countries approached the launch of CBDCs with bold policy goals, ranging from enhancing Financial inclusion and modernizing payment systems to asserting greater monetary control and geopolitical relevance. Yet their paths diverge sharply in terms of scale, adoption, and public trust.

China has leveraged its advanced digital infrastructure and state capacity to pilot and expand the e-CNY with impressive speed, though it still contends with entrenched private-sector dominance and adoption hurdles. Nigeria, meanwhile, has introduced the eNaira amid economic instability and institutional mistrust, facing challenges that stem less from technical limitations and more from structural and social frictions.

What these cases underscore is that CBDC success cannot be measured by rollout speed alone. Adoption hinges on user trust, institutional coherence, supportive regulation, and value-added functionality relative to existing alternatives. As more countries move from pilot to policy, China and Nigeria serve as instructive, if contrasting, models. Their experiences offer critical insights for global policymakers navigating the promise and pitfalls of sovereign digital currencies in an increasingly cashless world.

6

Mobile Payments: Pix in Brazil and UPI in India

Main Messages

- Brazil's Pix has revolutionized digital payments through real-time, fee-free transactions, reaching over 10 billion annual uses. Drex, Brazil's CBDC, builds on Pix's infrastructure with programmable features aimed at inclusion and monetary sovereignty.
- Pix and Drex reflect a strategic public–private model to digitize finance, reduce inequality, and assert national control.
- India's UPI is a real-time, interoperable payment system driving mass adoption through public–private collaboration. It underpins the country's Financial inclusion strategy, with platforms like PhonePe and Google Pay leading adoption.

In recent years, mobile payments have become a driving force in the global transition toward digital finance, reshaping how individuals and institutions interact with money. Brazil and India, two of the world's most populous and digitally ambitious economies, have developed robust payment infrastructures through Pix and Unified Payments Interface (UPI), respectively. These systems reflect not only technological innovation but also broader efforts to

---

The contributions of Advik Gupta, Gabriel Carvalho, students at Cornell University and Suudarshan Vaidhya, researcher at the Emerging Markets Institute at Cornell University under the supervision of Lourdes Casanova are gratefully acknowledged.

enhance Financial inclusion, modernize Monetary policy, and assert digital sovereignty. This chapter examines the evolution of mobile payments in both countries, the public–private partnerships that underpin their success, and the growing role of CBDCs in shaping the future of financial ecosystems.

John and Mark were walking down Copacabana Beach on Carnival weekend, surrounded by the lively rhythm of samba and the buzzing energy of the crowd taking over the street. The beach was filled with color, people adorned in costumes, vibrant floats rolling by, and vendors selling everything from beach towels to jewelry.

As they strolled along, Mark's attention was caught by a vendor with a cooler full of limes and a collection of rum bottles. The air smelled of fresh lime and sugar as the vendor sliced up a few limes and began mashing them in a glass with sugar under the hot sun. He was preparing caipirinhas, the famous Brazilian cocktail. Mark was parched, and the idea of a refreshing caipirinha sounded perfect for the hot day.

"Caipirinha?" Mark asked, leaning over to the vendor, who responded in rapid and enthusiastic Portuguese. "Sim, yes," Mark responded, although he didn't understand much of what was said. The vendor pointed to the drink, then back at Mark, and repeated the word "Pix" while pointing to a small QR code on a piece of laminated paper lying on the beach towel in front of him.

Mark raised an eyebrow, unsure of what was happening, but the vendor smiled and gently nudged his phone toward Mark. There, displayed on the phone screen, was a QR code with the word "Pix" in bold letters. Mark pulled out his phone, quickly scanning the code as the vendor continued to work, crushing the limes, adding sugar, and pouring in the rum.

As the fresh and ice-cold caipirinha was handed over, Mark's attention was directed more to the effortless payment transaction rather than the refreshing drink. He couldn't help but marvel at how effortlessly the transaction had occurred. No cash, no credit card, nor a swipe. Just a quick scan, and the payment was made. The vendor smiled, nudging over the drink with an "Obrigado!" and a nod, signaling that everything was taken care of.

John, watching the whole exchange, was equally impressed. "That was fast," he said while pulling out his phone to order one for himself. The vendor was moving seamlessly between preparing the drinks and processing the payments.

The two of them continued walking down the beach, each with a caipirinha in hand, watching as other beachgoers were doing the same—scanning QR codes for drinks, snacks, and souvenirs. As they walked past another vendor selling hats, Mark saw that the same system was in place: a simple

QR code to pay right on the vendor's stand. "This is everywhere now," Mark said. "It's not just the big businesses; Pix is part of everyday life here. It's like cashless transactions are inescapable."

John nodded, taking a sip of his drink.

As they continued to soak in the lively atmosphere of the beach, with the sound of samba and laughter filling the air, it became clear to them both: Brazil had truly embraced digital payments, and Pix had become the backbone of it all. Whether for a simple caipirinha, a souvenir from the beach, or an Açaí Bowl at a sit-down restaurant, the future of payments had arrived, and it was fast, easy, and everywhere.

6.1 CBDC Case Study—Brazil

Brazil's evolving digital economy offers a compelling case study of how mobile infrastructure, fintech innovation, and public policy converge to reshape financial access. The socioeconomic context, digital behavior, and technological landscape surrounding Brazil's CBDC, along with the rapid rise of real-time payment systems like Pix, reveal the country's potential to lead inclusive digital finance across Latin America.

Brazil, the largest economy in Latin America and the ninth largest globally, continues to demonstrate significant economic growth despite persistent social and economic inequalities. In 2023, Brazil's nominal GDP stood at $2.17 trillion, with projections estimating an increase to $2.31 trillion by 2025, reflecting a steady growth trajectory. This progress is expected to also raise the nominal GDP per capita, signaling moderate improvements in living standards.

Despite this positive outlook, income inequality remains a major challenge, impeding both Financial inclusion and economic mobility. Brazil's Gini coefficient, currently at 52.9, reflects one of the highest levels of income disparity in Latin America, significantly shaping consumption patterns and limiting access to financial services. This inequality is compounded by inflationary pressures and currency volatility, which further erode consumer purchasing power and discourage savings.

Brazil's economic structure reveals a dual financial system. While affluent individuals benefit from sophisticated financial products, lower-income groups often rely on informal financial services, exacerbated by limited access to traditional banking. The consistently high Gini coefficient underscores the systemic wealth imbalance, creating structural barriers to social and economic mobility.

While Brazil continues to experience steady economic growth, income inequality remains a critical obstacle to inclusive financial development. A growing middle class is driving the adoption of digital payment systems, yet financial illiteracy and limited banking infrastructure keep lower-income populations on the periphery of this transformation. The CBDC, known as Drex, represents a strategic opportunity to bridge these divides by offering accessible digital financial services to underserved groups.

Brazil ranks among the most digitally connected nations in Latin America, driven by high mobile and Internet penetration. In 2023, the country recorded 213 million mobile cellular subscriptions and an Internet penetration rate of 86.6%, supported by robust urban digital infrastructure.

While digital connectivity is strong, projections indicate a slight decline in mobile cellular subscriptions, with forecasts suggesting 102.66 subscriptions per 100 individuals by 2025, pointing to market saturation and a plateau in growth.

Smartphone adoption in Brazil has laid the foundation for widespread mobile banking use. As of Q4 2024, 73% of all bank account holders in the country regularly use mobile devices to conduct financial transactions, a figure that highlights Brazil's readiness for a fully digital financial ecosystem. This shift is strongly supported by the growth of mobile Internet access nationwide.

Figure 6.1 shows the rapid growth in mobile Internet users. This trajectory reflects the deepening reach of digital connectivity across urban and rural areas alike, enabling greater access to financial tools and services via smartphones.

Building on this digital infrastructure, Brazil has seen a parallel growth in digital finance. Figure 6.2 illustrates the upward trend in user adoption across four key categories: digital payments, net banking, digital investments, and digital assets. Digital payments have driven the majority of growth, while neobanking (what is this?) and investment platforms are steadily gaining traction. The increasing diversification of Brazil's digital finance landscape reflects a population that is not only connected but also increasingly engaged in a range of financial activities beyond basic transactions.

As digital finance expands across Brazil, social media and mobile connectivity have played a crucial role in shaping user behavior and financial engagement. Brazilian's digital habits, especially on social platforms, have influenced the adoption of financial technologies. Brazil ranks among the world's most active countries in social media engagement, with 66.3% of the population active on platforms such as WhatsApp, Instagram, and Facebook. This widespread engagement has contributed to rising digital financial

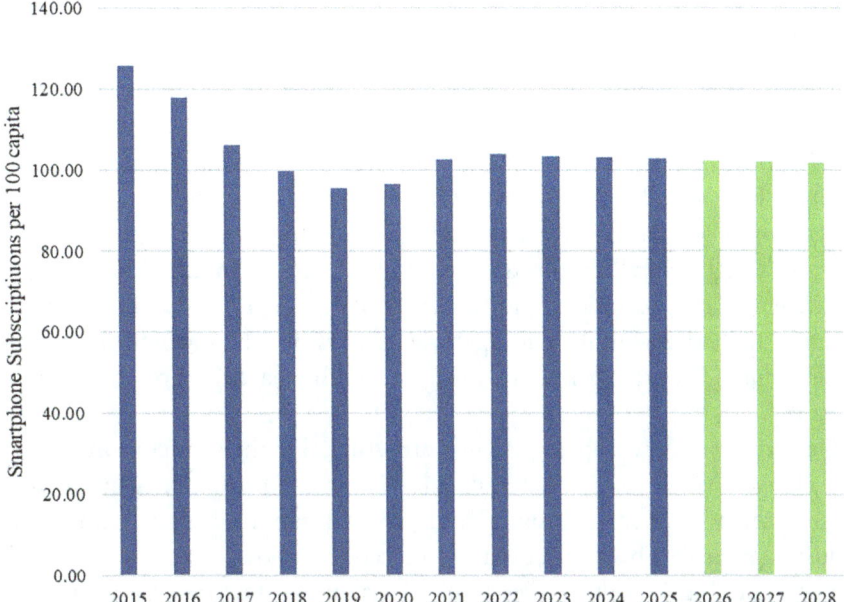

Fig. 6.1 The number of mobile cellular subscriptions in Brazil from 2015 to 2028 (per 100 capita) (*Source* Statista Market Insights [https://www.statista.com/]; Accessed June 2025)

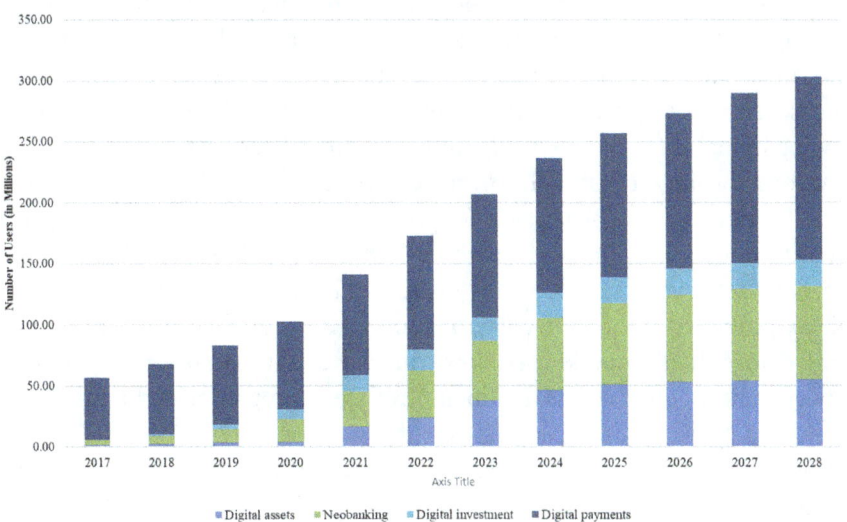

Fig. 6.2 The graph shows the growth in digital payments, net banking, and digital investments, emphasizing the rise of digital finance over the years (*Source* Statista Market Insights [https://www.statista.com/]; Accessed June 2025)

literacy and accelerated the adoption of mobile banking and digital payment platforms.

Despite high national levels of mobile and Internet connectivity, a significant digital divide persists between urban and rural areas. Urban regions benefit from advanced broadband infrastructure, while rural broadband coverage lags at 81%. This disparity limits financial accessibility and hinders the adoption of digital payment systems in remote communities.

Brazil's high overall connectivity provides a strong foundation for digital payment system adoption and the rollout of CBDC (Drex). However, bridging the urban–rural digital gap remains essential to achieving comprehensive Financial inclusion and ensuring equitable participation in the digital economy.

Despite Brazil's strong digital infrastructure, Financial inclusion remains a challenge. As of 2021, 16.4% of adults remained unbanked, particularly in rural areas with limited digital and physical banking infrastructure. This exclusion is driven by a combination of economic disparities, low financial literacy, and high banking fees, which discourage low-income households from engaging with formal financial services.

In Brazil, credit card usage is a cornerstone of the country's robust payments market, which is valued at an impressive $402 billion. As one of the largest and most diverse markets in Latin America, Brazil's credit card landscape is fueled by a combination of traditional banking institutions and innovative, tech-driven companies. The market is dominated by a few key players, each of which has strategically expanded its offerings to tap into the growing demand for seamless, digital-first financial services.

Among the largest players in Brazil's credit card market is Itaú, which holds a 24.3% share of the space. As a legacy institution, Itaú has leveraged its extensive branch network and customer base to expand into the digital world. The bank has embraced the rise of mobile banking platforms and digital wallets, providing customers with the tools to manage their finances on their smartphones. Itaú's mobile app allows for easy credit card payments, account management, and even personal loan offerings, ensuring that the institution stays competitive in an increasingly cashless society.

Nubank, however, has become one of the most disruptive forces in the Brazilian financial sector. With a market share of 12.9%, the digital-first bank has revolutionized the traditional banking model. Founded with a mission to provide simple and accessible financial products, Nubank has captured the attention of Brazil's tech-savvy youth demographic. By offering a fully online platform with no physical branches, Nubank appeals to a generation that values convenience, transparency, and low fees. Its credit cards, which come with no annual fee and an intuitive mobile app, have gained a significant following among young professionals and digital natives, propelling the bank to become one of the country's most valuable fintech companies.

Bradesco, another dominant player with a market share of 12.5%, is also strategically enhancing its digital presence. As one of Brazil's largest and oldest financial institutions, Bradesco has invested heavily in digital innovation to ensure it remains relevant in a rapidly changing market. The bank offers a wide range of credit card products tailored to different customer needs, from rewards programs to credit cards for small businesses. Bradesco's digital wallets and mobile banking platforms are well-integrated with its traditional banking services, allowing customers to easily track their spending, make payments, and manage their credit cards directly from their phones.

One of the most notable trends in Brazil's credit card ecosystem is the rise of digital wallets and mobile banking platforms. As smartphone usage continues to surge, particularly among younger generations, Brazilian consumers increasingly prefer to manage their finances on mobile apps rather than in-person visits to the bank. This shift has been amplified by the pandemic, which accelerated digital adoption across various sectors. The ease of paying with a mobile wallet or making credit card payments through apps has made these platforms indispensable tools for everyday transactions.

Nubank's success, in particular, showcases the shift in Brazil's financial landscape, where digital-first offerings are becoming increasingly popular. Unlike traditional banks, which often require in-person visits or lengthy paperwork, Nubank's approach allows customers to sign up, access credit, and manage their finances entirely from their mobile phones. This focus on technology has resonated with Brazil's younger population, which is more accustomed to handling all aspects of their lives through apps.

The rise of credit card usage in Brazil is not just about financial convenience—it's also about creating a more inclusive financial system. Digital-first players like Nubank are pushing the boundaries of traditional banking, offering products to underserved segments of the population, particularly those who may not have access to brick-and-mortar banks. Nubank's ability to issue credit cards with no annual fees and low interest rates has opened up financial access to many Brazilians who were previously excluded from the traditional banking system.

In conclusion, Brazil's credit card market is defined by a competitive mix of legacy institutions and digital-first innovators. Itaú, Nubank, and Bradesco dominate the market, each with their unique strategies for reaching the country's diverse population. As digital wallets and mobile banking platforms continue to gain traction, it's clear that the future of credit card usage in

Brazil will be shaped by these digital innovations, with fintech companies like Nubank leading the charge in creating a more accessible and inclusive financial ecosystem.

6.1.1 Digital Payments

Brazil's digital payments ecosystem has experienced a dramatic shift in recent years, with Pix emerging as the dominant player in the market. Launched by the Central Bank of Brazil in 2020, Pix is a real-time payment system that allows individuals and businesses to make instantaneous transfers, 24/7, with no associated fees. By 2024, Pix has reached a remarkable 98% share of the e-commerce payment transactions in Brazil, solidifying its position as the primary payment method. This overwhelming dominance is a clear reflection of its efficiency, accessibility, and growing adoption among both consumers and merchants.

The success of Pix can be attributed to several factors. First, its integration with existing mobile banking apps and ease of use have made it a preferred choice for Brazilians, particularly in a market where mobile phone penetration is exceptionally high. With, as of 2023, over 256 million mobile connections in Brazil and a population of only 213 million, there are approximately 1.2 phones in Brazil per person. This implies virtually everyone in Brazil owns at least one phone, and many own more than one. The ability to send and receive payments directly from mobile phones has fostered rapid adoption of Pix across various demographic groups. It allows anyone in Brazil, regardless of their socioeconomic status, to have access and the ability to process payments for personal or business use. Furthermore, Pix's real-time capabilities and the absence of transaction fees make it an attractive option for consumers and businesses alike, especially compared to traditional bank transfers or credit card payments, which can come with additional costs or delays.

In contrast, other payment systems like PayPal, Mercado Pago, and PicPay are significantly outpaced by Pix. PayPal, one of the global leaders in digital payments, accounts for just 24% of e-commerce transactions in Brazil. While still a major player, it has struggled to capture the same level of market penetration as Pix, especially given the local nature of Brazil's payment preferences. Mercado Pago, the digital wallet linked to the popular e-commerce platform Mercado Livre, holds 17% of the market share. It remains a strong competitor, particularly for users of Mercado Livre, but its reach is still limited in comparison to Pix's universal adoption across platforms. PicPay, another prominent digital wallet in Brazil, has secured 13% of the e-commerce payment market. Though it enjoys a large user base, it is still far behind Pix in terms of overall transaction volume.

The success of Pix can also be seen in its role in Financial inclusion. As a free service available to everyone with a bank account, it has allowed unbanked and underbanked populations to participate in the digital economy. Its widespread usage is not only limited to e-commerce but extends to various other sectors, such as utilities, government payments, and peer-to-peer transfers.

Looking ahead, Pix's dominance is expected to continue growing, particularly as the system integrates more innovative features, including QR code payments and expanded international capabilities. The Central Bank's vision for Pix is to enhance its utility and competitiveness further, positioning it as a global leader in real-time payments. As Brazil continues to lead the way in digital payments in Latin America, Pix's growth could set the stage for other emerging markets to adopt similar systems, thereby accelerating the global shift toward digital financial transactions.

While PayPal, Mercado Pago, and PicPay still hold important shares of the Brazilian market, Pix's current share of 98% of e-commerce payment transactions illustrates its unparalleled success and widespread adoption. This shift underscores the growing importance of real-time, fee-free digital payment systems and signals a larger transformation in Brazil's digital economy (Fig. 6.3).

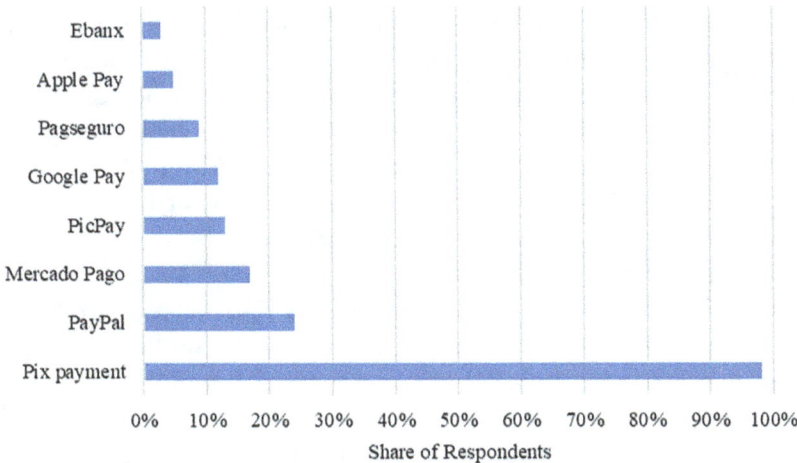

Fig. 6.3 Biggest e-commerce payment brands in Brazil as of December 2024 (the use of multiple platforms is common) (*Source* Statista Market Insights [https://www.statista.com/]; Accessed June 2025)

The success of Pix highlights a fundamental shift in consumer behavior toward real-time, mobile-first payment systems. The rise of digital-first banks like Nubank reflects evolving consumer preferences for flexible and mobile financial services. At the same time, Brazil's sizable unbanked population presents a significant opportunity for inclusive digital transformation.

Together, Pix and Drex represent potential tools to extend financial services to underserved populations, addressing long-standing gaps in access, affordability, and usability in Brazil's financial system.

6.1.2 Mobile Payments in Brazil: Pix

Brazil's mobile payments sector reflects the country's broader push toward digital Financial inclusion. Widespread smartphone use, supportive regulation, and Pix have redefined how individuals and businesses conduct everyday transactions, making mobile finance a key pillar of Brazil's digital economy.

Over the past decade, Brazil's digital payments landscape has undergone a profound transformation driven by regulatory reforms and technological innovation. The foundation for this shift was laid with the enactment of the Payment System Law (Law 12,865) in 2013, which established a comprehensive legal framework for electronic payments. Crucially, the law facilitated interoperability among financial institutions, enabling the integration of innovative payment solutions and laying the groundwork for future advancements—most remarkably, the launch of Pix in 2020.

Developed by the Central Bank of Brazil (Banco Central do Brasil, BCB), Pix is a real-time payment platform designed to promote Financial inclusion, enhance payment system efficiency, and reduce transaction costs. Unlike traditional payment systems, Pix operates 24/7, enabling instantaneous transactions through QR codes, mobile apps, and aliases such as phone numbers or email addresses. Its open infrastructure model enables participation from all regulated financial institutions, fostering both interoperability and healthy market competition.

Since its launch, Pix has reached several major milestones (Table 6.1).

Building on the regulatory and adoption milestones outlined above, Pix's transaction volume has surged over time, both in Brazilian reals and U.S. dollars. Figure 6.4 illustrates the rapid acceleration of Pix transactions from 2020 to 2023, reflecting its growing dominance in Brazil's digital payments ecosystem.

The sharp rise in transaction volumes underscores not only Pix's popularity but also its operational effectiveness. Understanding what enabled such rapid scaling is essential to evaluating its broader impact.

Table 6.1 Timeline of key milestones in the evolution of pix in Brazil (2020–2024)

Year	Event
2020	Launched with a zero-cost model for individuals, Pix rapidly gained popularity among consumers and merchants
2021	The introduction of Open Finance regulations required financial institutions to share consumer data, spurring innovation and increased competition
2024	Pix processed 10 billion transactions annually, contributing to a significant decline in cash usage in Retail—from 36% to 19%

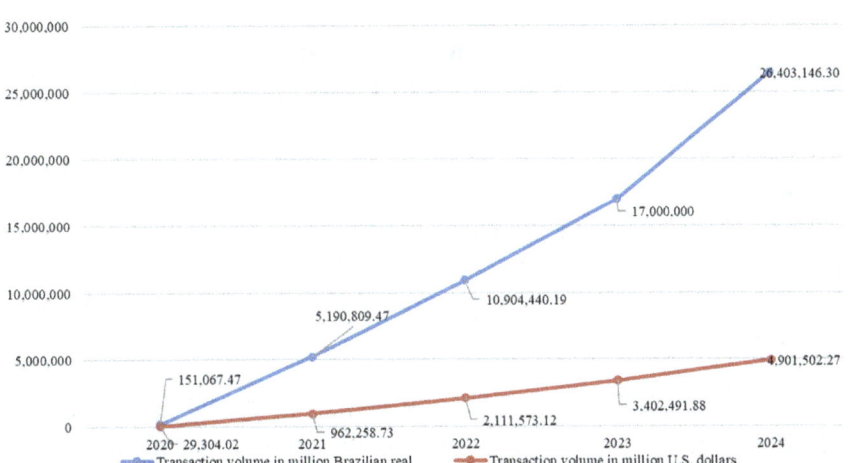

Fig. 6.4 Value of real-time payments in Brazil with local scheme Pix from 2020 to 2024 (in million Brazilian real, and estimates in U.S. dollars) (*Source* Statista Market Insights [https://www.statista.com/]; Accessed June 2025)

The rapid adoption of Pix can be attributed to several interrelated factors:

- **Cost-effectiveness:** Individuals enjoy zero-cost transactions, while businesses face minimal fees, making the system financially accessible.
- **Real-time functionality:** Users benefit from instant payments via multiple channels, including QR codes, aliases, and mobile applications.
- **Government-backed infrastructure:** The system is supported by the Central Bank of Brazil, which ensures mandatory participation of all regulated institutions, promoting consistency and inclusivity.
- **Open and interoperable architecture:** This allows seamless collaboration between public infrastructure and private innovation, enhancing competition and driving adoption.

Pix has dramatically reshaped Brazil's digital payments landscape, helping to close Financial inclusion gaps while setting a global benchmark for modern, real-time digital payment systems.

The success of Pix exemplifies a strategic public–private partnership: The Central Bank of Brazil provides robust public infrastructure while private-sector players drive innovation and consumer-focused solutions. This synergy has produced a vibrant, inclusive, and competitive digital finance ecosystem, offering a compelling model for other nations aiming to expand financial access through digital transformation.

The Central Bank of Brazil (BCB) plays a pivotal role in shaping the country's digital payments ecosystem through regulatory authority and public infrastructure support. Its responsibilities include:

- Providing public infrastructure that ensures interoperability among financial entities.
- Mandating participation from all regulated financial institutions, creating an inclusive payments ecosystem.
- Regulating transaction fees, ensuring cost efficiency, and broad consumer adoption.

On the private side, fintech companies and digital-first banks have leveraged Pix's infrastructure to scale user adoption and enhance digital financial experiences. The most influential players include:

- **Nubank:** Leading digital-first bank focusing on credit expansion through digital wallets and loyalty programs.
- **Mercado Pago:** Integrates mobile payments with e-commerce, capitalizing on Brazil's growing online shopping market.
- **PicPay:** Innovates with social payment features, targeting tech-savvy consumers.

Major traditional banks such as Itaú and Bradesco have integrated Pix into their operations to retain customer loyalty and remain competitive in the face of fintech disruption. However, it is fintech firms that are driving the most significant growth, leveraging agile platforms and intuitive interfaces to engage Brazil's digitally connected consumer base.

The result is a strategic public–private synergy that has dramatically accelerated the adoption of digital payments in Brazil. By combining robust public infrastructure with private-sector innovation, Brazil has cultivated a dynamic and inclusive financial ecosystem that supports both economic growth and broader Financial inclusion.

Pix has fundamentally reshaped Brazil's digital payment landscape, becoming the nation's most widely used platform within just a few years. By 2024, it accounted for 41% of all financial transactions, outpacing traditional credit card usage and driving a major decline in reliance on cash. Its widespread adoption stems from a zero-cost model for consumers, real-time functionality, and seamless integration into both peer-to-peer and commercial payment contexts.

Key adoption metrics further illustrate Pix's profound impact:

- Over 10 billion transactions will be processed annually by 2024
- 20% of all digital transactions conducted via mobile payments
- Retail cash usage fell from 36% to 19%

These figures reflect not just the efficiency of Pix's infrastructure but also its role in accelerating Brazil's shift toward a cashless, inclusive, and digitally empowered economy. While credit card volumes rose by 33% post-pandemic, Pix's no-fee, mobile-first model has proven more accessible and adaptable to user preferences. With mobile payments now comprising a growing share of digital transactions, Pix has not only surpassed credit cards in volume but also catalyzed Brazil's broader transition to a cashless, inclusive digital economy.

Pix's widespread adoption signals a broader move away from conventional banking models toward digital-first, cost-effective solutions, contributing meaningfully to Brazil's journey toward a cashless economy.

The Central Bank of Brazil (BCB) launched Pix with three core strategic objectives:

1. **Financial inclusion:** Extend digital payment access to Brazil's 30 million unbanked individuals, offering a low-barrier entry point into the formal financial system.
2. **Cost Reduction:** Eliminate transaction fees for individuals, contributing to annual savings of $1.2 billion in banking costs.
3. **Fraud Mitigation:** Leverage AI-driven authentication, GSMA Open Gateway APIs, and other advanced technologies to enhance security and minimize fraud risks.

While Pix has achieved substantial success and strategic impact, several persistent challenges may hinder its continued growth and scalability.

Digital inclusion remains a significant hurdle. Only 58% of rural areas in Brazil have access to broadband coverage, creating a stark digital divide that limits Pix adoption in remote and underserved communities. Without targeted investment in digital infrastructure, large segments of the population risk being left behind in Brazil's transition to a digital economy.

Cybersecurity threats are also on the rise. As digital transactions become more widespread, so too do incidents of cyber fraud and security breaches. This escalating risk underscores the need for stronger authentication protocols, improved data protection frameworks, and real-time fraud detection systems to safeguard user trust and the integrity of the payment system.

Regulatory complexity further complicates the landscape. Navigating Brazil's evolving data Privacy and Cybersecurity regulations presents ongoing challenges for both fintech firms and traditional financial institutions. Striking a balance between regulatory compliance and continued innovation is essential to maintaining the agility and user-friendliness that have fueled Pix's rapid adoption.

While the government's proactive regulatory approach has played a critical role in facilitating Pix's adoption, addressing these infrastructural, security, and regulatory challenges will be essential to sustaining the momentum of digital payments and ensuring their reach across all segments of Brazilian society.

6.1.3 Drex: Brazil's Programmable CBDC for Inclusion and Digital Sovereignty

Launched by the Central Bank of Brazil in 2023, Drex is a CBDC initiative designed to advance Financial inclusion, improve Monetary policy efficiency, and promote digital sovereignty to enhance Brazil's economic competitiveness. The initiative targets Brazil's 30 million unbanked citizens by offering smartphone-accessible digital financial services. Key features include programmable microloans and digital savings accounts aimed at empowering underserved populations. From a policy standpoint, Drex strengthens the central bank's control over the money supply, enabling real-time interest rate adjustments to support more effective inflation management and Monetary policy transmission.

Drex also seeks to reduce Brazil's reliance on foreign payment systems, asserting national digital sovereignty through the use of DLT (explain DLT) in cross-border transactions. In doing so, Drex reflects Brazil's broader ambition to lead in the global digital economy by building a secure, efficient, and inclusive financial infrastructure.

In comparison, other country's CBDC designs reflect their specific strategic priorities. China's Digital Yuan focuses on reducing dependence on private third-party platforms and enhancing state control over data and financial flows. Nigeria's eNaira places Financial inclusion at the forefront, aiming to integrate unbanked populations into the formal financial system. Brazil's Drex, by contrast, distinguishes itself through its emphasis on Smart contracts and Tokenization, positioning it as a programmable digital currency tailored to the demands of an increasingly digital and diversified economy.

Importantly, Drex balances its twin goals of Financial inclusion and economic sovereignty by leveraging Brazil's strong digital infrastructure and robust regulatory environment. As such, it represents a forward-looking approach to CBDC design, one that aligns social equity with technological innovation and macroeconomic resilience.

Drex operates on a hybrid Retail–Wholesale architecture that integrates Hyperledger Besu (explain) and DLT to support both consumer transactions and interbank settlements. On the Retail layer, Drex utilizes tokenized deposits issued by commercial banks to enable programmable financial products such as microloans and digital savings accounts. These transactions are executed via Smart contracts, ensuring automation, compliance, and auditability. The Wholesale layer facilitates interbank settlements using atomic transactions to minimize counterparty risk. It also supports the issuance and exchange of tokenized securities, such as government bonds, thereby improving market liquidity and reducing transaction costs.

The underlying technology stack is designed for scalability, Privacy, and interoperability. Hyperledger Besu serves as the foundational Blockchain infrastructure, offering flexibility and integration with existing systems. Zero-knowledge proofs (ZKPs) are employed to enable anonymous transactions while maintaining compliance with regulatory frameworks. Additionally, the use of Smart contracts and Tokenization allows Drex to support programmable money and decentralized finance (DeFi) applications. Collectively, this architecture ensures a secure, Privacy-preserving, and highly scalable platform that can seamlessly integrate into Brazil's broader digital financial ecosystem.

Drex followed a phased rollout strategy (2023–2025), allowing for incremental testing of its infrastructure, compliance, and real-world use cases.

1. Phase 1 (2023–2024):

   - Conducted core infrastructure testing with 70 financial institutions, including Visa, Santander, and Microsoft
   - Simulated transactions for tax compliance, property transfers, and Wholesale settlements

2. Phase 2 (2024–2025):

   - Expansion into thematic pilots, focusing on DeFi integration, tokenized carbon credits, and cross-border remittances
   - Includes 13 thematic pilots exploring Financial inclusion, trade finance, and Digital identity verification

3. Full-Scale Deployment (2025):

   - Nationwide launch with expanded Retail and Wholesale functionalities
   - Collaboration with the Brazilian Securities Commission (CVM) to regulate tokenized securities and DeFi platforms

This gradual rollout allows the BCB to minimize systemic risks while positioning Brazil as a global leader in CBDC development.

Despite its forward-looking architecture, Drex faces a number of implementation and operational challenges that could impact its long-term success. One of the most pressing concerns is Privacy: balancing transactional anonymity with the need for regulatory transparency remains a complex issue, especially as Drex integrates programmable and traceable financial instruments. Closely related is the risk of Disintermediation, as tokenized deposits issued through the Drex platform may divert customer funds away from traditional banks, potentially destabilizing existing financial institutions and reducing their role in the credit ecosystem.

Regulatory complexity also presents a significant barrier. The governance of tokenized assets and the need for compliance with rules established by the Brazilian Securities and Exchange Commission (CVM) introduces legal and operational burdens that must be navigated carefully. In parallel, the increasing digitization of financial activity raises Cybersecurity concerns. A greater volume of online transactions expands the surface area for potential cyberattacks, making robust security infrastructure essential to safeguard user data and preserve confidence in the system.

Lastly, Drex's value stability is inherently tied to the Brazilian Real (BRL), which is prone to volatility in global currency markets. This connection exposes Drex to broader macroeconomic risks, particularly during times of fiscal or political uncertainty.

Addressing these challenges will require strong public–private collaboration, comprehensive regulatory clarity, and continuous investment in Privacy and Cybersecurity infrastructure to maintain public trust and enable Drex to scale securely and equitably.

6.2 CBDC Case Study—India

India has emerged as one of the fastest-growing major economies in the world, positioning itself as a leading voice of the Global South and a critical factor in shaping global development discourse. With a nominal GDP exceeding $3.7 trillion and a population of nearly 1.4 billion, India represents both a vast domestic market and a laboratory for digital public infrastructure at scale.

The country has averaged an impressive GDP growth rate of 8% over the past four years. This sustained economic expansion is underpinned by a powerful confluence of demographic strength, technological advancement, and institutional reforms. A defining element of India's growth story is its demographic dividend: more than 65% of the population is under the age of 35, contributing to a dynamic labor force and sustained consumer demand.

Between 2007 and 2020, India's population increased by nearly 17%, fueling urbanization, income mobility, and demand for financial services. Technological adoption has also advanced rapidly. Mobile cellular subscriptions climbed from approximately 800 million in 2010 to nearly 1.2 billion today, illustrating the ubiquity of digital connectivity across urban and rural regions. Smartphone penetration and mobile Internet access have opened new pathways for entrepreneurship, employment, and digital payments.

India's Financial inclusion journey has mirrored its broader digital transformation. The share of adults (aged 15 and above) with bank accounts grew from just over 50% in 2014 to roughly 80% by 2021. This expansion has enabled the emergence of a vibrant middle class and increased participation in the formal economy. Paired with targeted public initiatives, such as the Pradhan Mantri Jan Dhan Yojana (PMJDY), Aadhaar Digital identity, and UPI, India has laid the groundwork for a robust digital financial ecosystem (Fig. 6.5).

Credit card adoption and digital payments continue to rise, driven by both private-sector innovation and public infrastructure. Together, these developments have created fertile ground for the introduction of a CBDC that builds on India's digital public goods and extends the reach of formal financial services.

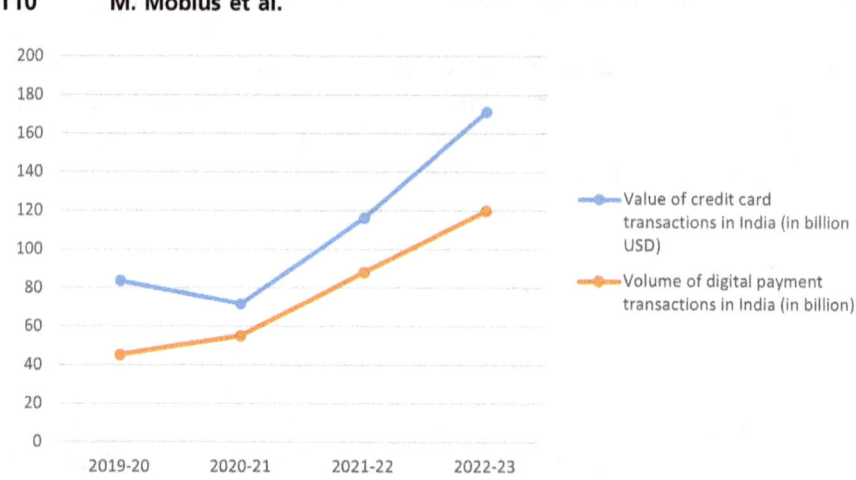

Fig. 6.5 Credit card and digital payment trends in India, 2019–2023 (*Source* Statista Market Insights [https://www.statista.com/]; Accessed June 2025)

6.2.1 Mobile Payments

India's digital payments ecosystem has undergone a remarkable transformation, powered by a collaborative framework between public infrastructure and private-sector innovation. Central to this ecosystem is the UPI, a real-time payment system developed by the National Payments Corporation of India (NPCI), a public-sector entity backed by the Reserve Bank of India (RBI). UPI facilitates seamless, instant payments across platforms and institutions, underpinning the country's rapid shift to digital finance.

Dominating the space are two major players, Google Pay and PhonePe, which together process the majority of UPI-based transactions. As shown in Fig. 6.6, these platforms have gained significant market share through their intuitive design, robust functionality, and deep integration with banking systems.

India's digital payments ecosystem is built on a collaborative framework between public-sector infrastructure and private-sector innovation. At its core lies the UPI, developed by the NPCI, a public-sector entity established by the RBI.

The ecosystem is composed of diverse participants across several domains:

- **Banks**: Both public and private banks play critical roles. Public institutions such as the State Bank of India, Central Bank of India, and Indian Bank operate alongside major private banks like HDFC Bank, Axis Bank, and ICICI Bank.

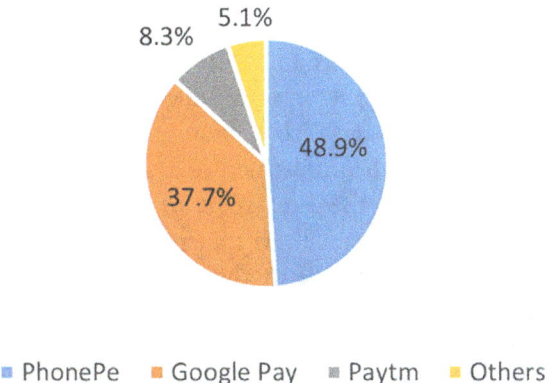

Fig. 6.6 Market share of payment apps in India's UPI, share of transaction volume processed via these payment apps in April 2024 (*Source* Statista Market Insights [https://www.statista.com/]; Accessed June 2025)

- **Third-party apps and fintech firms**: Companies such as PhonePe, Paytm, and Razorpay serve as the primary user-facing interfaces, facilitating everyday transactions.
- **Ancillary financial service platforms**: Players like Cred and Upstox extend the ecosystem's value by offering investment tools, credit scoring, and rewards systems.
- **Stakeholders**: Government ministries, regulatory bodies, and consumers themselves are deeply embedded in the system's operation and evolution.
- **Investors**: Global investment firms, including SoftBank and Sequoia Capital, have fueled rapid innovation and scale through strategic funding.

Together, these actors form a dynamic and interdependent ecosystem that underpins India's digital payment revolution.

India's digital payments architecture is structured across three interdependent layers. The first includes public institutions like the RBI and relevant ministries, which provide regulatory governance and foundational infrastructure. The second layer comprises operational financial entities, such as banks and payment service providers, that integrate and scale the platform. The third consists of private-sector innovators that deliver digital products and services directly to consumers and merchants.

This collaborative, multi-layered framework has not only fostered widespread adoption but has also enabled a steady evolution of digital payments in India. The progression of this ecosystem, from early electronic banking services to sophisticated real-time payment platforms, can be traced through a series of key milestones that reflect India's broader push toward financial modernization and inclusion (Table 6.2).

India's digital payments ecosystem has developed along a distinct and deliberate path. In its early stages, core financial services underwent digital transformation, establishing the infrastructure necessary for widespread adoption. This was followed by the expansion of use cases, extending from peer-to-peer transfers to sectors such as transportation, Retail, and utilities, integrating digital payments into the rhythms of daily life. More recently, the system has been mobilized to support broader national objectives. Government services, including welfare disbursements, toll collection, and bill

Table 6.2 Timeline of key milestones in the evolution of UPI in India (2003–2024)

Year	Event
2003	The company BillDesk began their payment aggregator service for merchants
2004	Launch of the first-ever e-wallet, called Oxigen Wallet
2005	The popular service National Electronic Funds Transfer (NEFT) was started for interbank transfers
2010	Immediate Payment Service (IMPS), for instant money transfers, was launched
2010	Aadhaar Enabled Payment System (AEPS) was started for interoperable bank payments through authentication of identity
2012	RuPay card was conceptualized by NPCI as India's indigenous card system
2012	National Automated Clearing House (NACH), a facility to support interbank transactions that are high volume, low value, and repetitive, is offered to banks for both debit and credit
2014	A USSD-based mobile banking service, named *99#, for offline fund transfer, balance enquiry, etc.
2016	UPI was launched by Raghuram Rajan, governor of RBI at that time, to facilitate interbank transactions through mobile phones
2016	National Electronic Toll Collection (NETC) FASTag, a passive RFID tag on vehicles for automatic toll payment deduction at checkpoints on highways
2017	Bharat BillPay, an ecosystem for all bill payments like electricity, gas, and education, was developed by NPCI
2018	Widespread adoption of RuPay cards, with the highest number of cards issued and second-highest in terms of volume and value on e-commerce platforms and PoS machines
2019	National Common Mobility Card (NCMC), an interoperable transport card for different types of public transport, as well as parking charges and toll taxes
2021	e-RUPI, a digital voucher-based payments model for the transfer of welfare payments even without a bank account, was launched by NPCI
2024	Cross-border UPI transactions are enabled with countries like Nepal and Singapore through bilateral agreements

payments, are now embedded with digital payment capabilities, positioning the platform as a vehicle for inclusive development and public service delivery.

India's digital payments infrastructure encompasses a wide array of mechanisms that reflect the country's transition from conventional banking services to advanced, tech-driven financial tools. These methods span from traditional instruments like credit cards and Internet banking to contemporary platforms such as mobile wallets and biometric authentication systems. Specialized solutions, including toll collection and automated clearing houses, further extend the ecosystem's reach into sector-specific applications. Table 6.3 outlines the diverse modes of digital payment implementation currently active in India.

Following this progression of institutional milestones and technological innovations, a natural question arises: which digital payment methods are most widely adopted today? To answer this, we can examine the transaction volumes across various platforms, which offer a snapshot of user preferences and the functional reach of different digital instruments (Fig. 6.7).

The implementation of digital payments in India gained significant momentum during the COVID-19 pandemic, which accelerated the demand for secure, contactless financial technologies. The development and widespread adoption of these systems are anchored in three foundational pillars:

- **Accessibility** refers to the system's ability to reach users across socioeconomic strata, regardless of their digital literacy. This design approach has expanded financial access among rural populations, small businesses, and traditionally underserved communities.

Table 6.3 Key categories and methods of digital payment implementation in India

Traditional	Contemporary	Specialized
Credit and debit cards	Mobile banking	National Electronic Toll Collection (NETC)
National Electronic Funds Transfer (NEFT)	Unstructured Supplementary Service Data (USSD)	National Automated Clearing House (NACH)
Immediate Payment Service (IMPS)	Aadhaar Enabled Payment System (AEPS)	
Internet banking	Bharat Interface for Money (BHIM) Aadhaar	
Real-time gross settlement (RTGS)	BHIM UPI	
	Closed loop wallet	
	Prepaid Payment Instrument (PPI)	

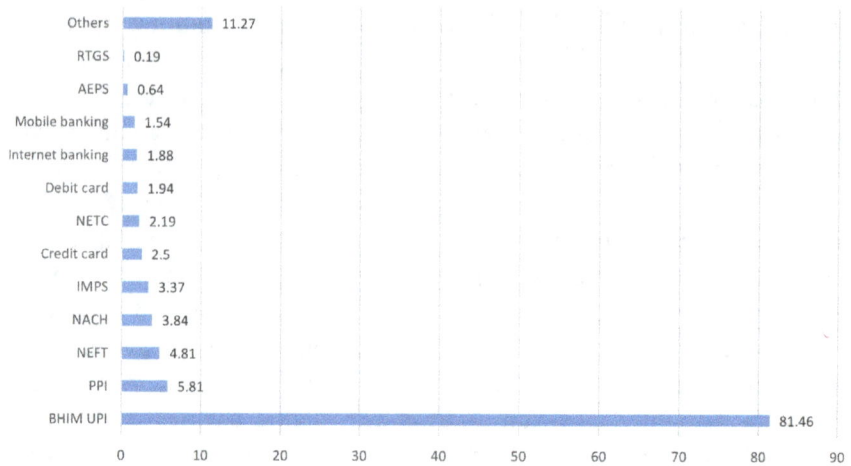

Fig. 6.7 Volume of digital transactions in India in FY24, by mode (in billions) (*Source* Statista Market Insights [https://www.statista.com/]; Accessed June 2025)

- **Interoperability** enables users to link and manage multiple bank accounts through a single interface, while facilitating seamless integration between private financial institutions and public infrastructure. This ensures consistent and efficient transaction experiences across platforms.
- **Availability** is supported by regulatory oversight that ensures equitable access to digital payment services. By limiting the dominance of private profit motives, the government has cultivated a cooperative ecosystem that encourages participation from a diverse range of stakeholders.

The UPI embodies these three principles through its open architecture, which allows for the integration of varied financial tools and services. Its modular, API-based infrastructure enables flexible, user-centric solutions tailored to the everyday financial needs of Indian citizens.

India's digital payment ecosystem has witnessed a sharp rise in usage, reflecting two intertwined trends: widespread adoption and growing consumer trust. Not only are more individuals and businesses engaging with digital payment platforms, but the frequency and value of transactions have also increased, indicating deeper integration into everyday financial behavior.

Digital payment activity in India can be broadly classified into three segments: Business-to-Business (B2B), Business-to-Consumer (B2C), and Peer-to-Peer (P2P). Among these, Retail transactions dominate, highlighting the central role of individual consumers and small merchants in driving digital financial flows (Fig. 6.8).

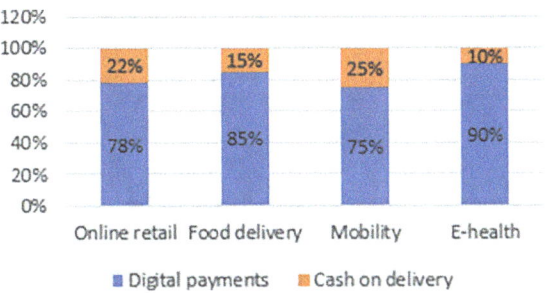

Fig. 6.8 Transaction value across sectors in India in FY23, by payment method (%) (*Source* Statista Market Insights [https://www.statista.com/]; Accessed June 2025)

Among digital payment methods, UPI leads in both volume and versatility. It is heavily utilized across online Retail, food delivery, mobility services, and e-health sectors that represent the vanguard of India's digital commerce transformation. This expansion has not only digitized traditional sectors but also created entirely new modes of economic interaction.

India has also experienced significant shifts in cross-border remittances. Between 2015 and 2021, the average cost of sending $200 fell from $12 to approximately $10. This decrease reflects growing competition, primarily driven by fintech entrants and improvements in infrastructure and operational efficiency. By 2023, fintech firms charged an average of 4.2% per remittance, compared to 5.4% by Money Transfer Operators (MTOs) and 11.5% by traditional banks.

As cross-border CBDC projects gain traction, these systems are expected to further reduce remittance costs. Globally, average remittance fees remain at 6.18%, exceeding the United Nations Sustainable Development Goal (SDG) target of 3%. Combining UPI with a future interoperable CBDC architecture offers a promising strategy to lower transaction costs and increase remittance volumes. Research shows that a 1% reduction in remittance fees can result in a 1.6% increase in remittance flows.

Mobile payments have become an increasingly popular mode of transaction, spanning a variety of everyday scenarios (Fig. 6.9).

Survey data highlights the prominence of mobile payments in trade and commerce while also revealing emerging applications in sectors such as health services and international transfers. Transaction values vary by use case, reflecting the growing complexity and diversification of mobile financial behavior.

The success of India's mobile payments infrastructure, particularly UPI, has laid the groundwork for a future CBDC. Its scalability, interoperability, and demonstrated user value offer a robust foundation for further innovation.

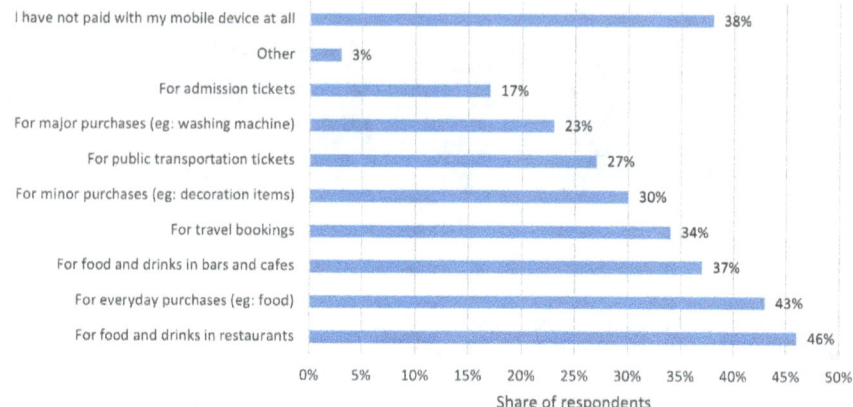

Fig. 6.9 Mobile payments usage by situation in India, 2024 (% of respondents). India, four waves from April 2023 to March 2024, 4032 respondents, 18–54 years (*Source* Statista Market Insights [https://www.statista.com/]; Accessed June 2025)

As India advances toward a digital rupee, these platforms provide a proven model for meeting consumer needs and accelerating financial modernization at scale.

6.2.2 CBDCs in India

The goals of a CBDC in India are multifaceted and centered on advancing social good across several dimensions. As of July 2025, the digital rupee is the second-largest CBDC pilot in the world with about USD 123 million in circulation. Key objectives include:

- Financial inclusion
- Combating money laundering
- Promoting a cashless economy
- Fostering innovation in payment systems
- Simplifying the settlement of government securities

In emerging markets and developing economies (EMDEs), such as India, the goals of CBDC tend to focus more on Monetary policy, domestic payment efficiency, and Financial inclusion. In contrast, advanced economies (AEs) often prioritize payment safety and cross-border payment efficiency in their CBDC initiatives.

India's approach to CBDC encompasses three categories, Retail, Wholesale, and cross-border, each designed to address distinct use cases within the broader monetary ecosystem.

Retail CBDC is intended for day-to-day use by individuals, households, and businesses, supporting both peer-to-peer (P2P) and peer-to-merchant (P2M) transactions. Functioning as a digital equivalent of physical cash, Retail CBDC is envisioned to reduce the inefficiencies associated with paper currency, including printing, logistics, and security risks. Issued directly by the RBI, it provides a level of trust and monetary stability that privately issued digital currencies, such as cryptocurrencies and Stablecoins, cannot offer. The Retail CBDC is designed as a token-based system, where the digital token acts as a bearer instrument, with ownership established by possession rather than identity verification.

Wholesale CBDC, by contrast, is tailored for the financial sector, particularly banks and large institutional actors. It facilitates high-value transfers, interbank settlements, and securities transactions, operating as a digital representation of central bank reserves. Structured as an account-based model, it maintains precise transaction records and ownership balances, enhancing the transparency and efficiency of India's domestic monetary operations.

Cross-border CBDC integrates features of both Retail and Wholesale models, enabling international transactions for individuals, businesses, and financial institutions. India currently participates as an observer in Project mBridge, a multinational initiative led by the Bank for International Settlements (BIS), including China, Hong Kong, Thailand, and the United Arab Emirates (see Chapter 8). The project seeks to build a decentralized platform for instant, transparent cross-border settlements using CBDCs, significantly improving the efficiency of global financial flows.

India's cross-border efforts are further reinforced by its growing role in global digital payments. The UPI is now integrated with platforms in over seven countries, including Singapore, where it is linked with PayNow to facilitate real-time remittances. India is also a member of Project Nexus, which aims to establish interoperable cross-border payment systems across ASEAN countries such as Malaysia, the Philippines, and Thailand. Bilateral agreements with countries like the UAE, Sri Lanka, and Singapore underscore India's strategy of expanding its digital payments infrastructure globally.

Simultaneously, India is conducting cross-border CBDC trials with the UAE, with future collaborations planned with the United States and the European Union, particularly targeting trade and remittance corridors.

India also plays a prominent role within the BRICS consortium, where digital financial integration is gaining strategic importance. The BRICS Interbank Cooperation Mechanism, involving institutions such as India's Exim Bank, seeks to deepen collaboration on financing urban development and infrastructure. One of the coalition's key ambitions is the promotion of national currencies in international trade, reducing dependency on the U.S. dollar.

Initiatives like the BRICS Cross-border payments Initiative (BCBPI), or BRICS Pay, are also being explored by India. This system would allow member nations to transact in local currencies through an independent, multilateral payment framework. More ambitiously, discussions around a common BRICS currency have also emerged, raising the prospect of a new geopolitical force in global finance capable of challenging dollar dominance.

A key design consideration in India's CBDC architecture is the degree of centralization in issuance and transaction processing. A centralized issuance model managed through a centrally administered database reinforces public trust in the RBI as the monetary authority. However, this approach also raises concerns around single points of failure, increased operational demands on the central infrastructure, and the potential for undue influence from private intermediaries.

Conversely, a more decentralized architecture can improve system resilience and reduce costs, yet it may dilute the central bank's oversight and control over Monetary policy tools. India's evolving CBDC framework seeks to balance these trade-offs, integrating select features of decentralization within a system anchored by centralized trust. The goal is to maintain regulatory integrity while enabling innovation and operational efficiency.

India's CBDC is built on a Blockchain-inspired architecture that incorporates DLT, yet with important variations tailored to national policy goals. Two fundamental models shape the system's technological underpinnings: token-based and account-based. Retail CBDC operates on a token-based model, where ownership resides with the holder and authenticity is verified directly. In contrast, Wholesale CBDC is account-based, with balances and transactions recorded by the RBI and validated by designated intermediaries.

The RBI has pursued a Value-Focused Thinking (VFT) framework to guide technology deployment, aligning infrastructure choices with socioeconomic priorities. This has enabled targeted pilots that demonstrate CBD C's utility across diverse sectors:

- In 2024, the State Bank of India launched a pilot in Odisha and Andhra Pradesh using programmable CBDC to disburse agricultural subsidies, eliminating the need for land title verification.
- IndusInd Bank tested programmable CBDC for carbon credit allocation in Rajasthan, highlighting applications in green finance.
- CBDC-based agricultural loans are being explored in several states, providing tenant farmers with conditional, purpose-driven digital disbursements.
- Under the Subhadra Yojana initiative in Odisha, 12,000 women received government transfers in digital rupees, enabling direct access to funds and reducing administrative overhead.

India is also integrating CBDC into its broader sustainability agenda. Plans are underway to incorporate programmable features into sovereign green bonds and deposits, allowing for transparent, traceable, and outcome-linked environmental financing.

A defining feature of India's CBDC is its offline functionality. By supporting transactions without Internet connectivity, the system extends digital financial access to remote and underserved regions. This capability has the potential to significantly enhance rural inclusion, reinforcing CBDC's role as a bridge between digital innovation and economic empowerment.

India's CBDC implementation strategy has followed a more reactive trajectory compared to the country's earlier digital payment innovations, which evolved organically through public–private collaboration. While the UPI gained momentum through rapid voluntary uptake, the CBDC rollout has been characterized by a more top-down approach, presenting notable execution challenges in its early phases.

As of March 2024, the Wholesale CBDC pilot remained limited in scale, with total holdings amounting to just $0.0093 million (put that in thousands). In contrast, the Retail CBDC has demonstrated comparatively greater activity, reaching $27 million in total holdings and averaging one million daily transactions by the end of 2023. However, these figures warrant closer scrutiny. Much of the observed traction has been the result of institutional mandates rather than organic user demand.

For instance, the RBI has directed participating banks to actively promote Retail CBDC use among customers and has encouraged adoption by requiring certain public-sector institutions to disburse employee salaries in digital rupees. These measures, while effective in boosting short-term usage, reflect a compliance-driven model rather than a market-led or user-centric adoption pathway.

The current phase of India's CBDC implementation highlights a transitional period, one in which foundational infrastructure is being established, but broad-based public engagement remains limited. Sustained success will depend on moving beyond directive-based participation toward building trust, utility, and long-term value in the eyes of both consumers and institutions. By examining levels of adoption, accessibility, safety, and innovative applications, it becomes clear where progress has been made and where critical barriers remain.

Level of Adoption: India's CBDC initiative has produced a mixed set of outcomes, revealing both early promise and persistent limitations. The Retail pilot, launched in December 2022, reached over 5 million users and involved 16 participating banks by October 2024. However, one of the key obstacles to broader adoption has been the lack of a distinct value proposition when compared to existing systems like the UPI. For most users, the transaction experience between UPI and the digital rupee appears nearly identical, with the fundamental difference lying in the backend architecture. UPI moves funds via traditional bank accounts, while CBDC transactions are conducted through digitally issued tokens.

To drive meaningful adoption, India will need to implement targeted strategies that clearly differentiate CBDC use cases and encourage behavioral change among users. Progress on the Wholesale front has been more strategic. The RBI is exploring CBDC's role in call money settlement and evaluating its potential in tokenizing securities and money market instruments, such as Certificates of Deposit (CDs) and Commercial Papers (CPs). For Retail use, enhancing interoperability, for instance, through the integration of CBDC wallets with UPI QR codes, could streamline usability and accelerate adoption.

Accessibility of Services: Operational challenges continue to affect CBDC usability. In the Retail segment, transactions are currently limited to specific denominations, creating friction for small-value payments that require multiple denominations. Wholesale usage also faces structural inefficiencies, with trades settled individually rather than through batch netting, limiting scalability for institutional users.

Security concerns persist as well. India's two-tier issuance model, underpinned by public-key cryptography, introduces vulnerabilities at various stages of the transaction lifecycle. Additionally, the traceability of CBDC transactions has raised questions around Privacy, particularly in contrast to the anonymity of cash, a concern acknowledged by RBI officials.

Despite these limitations, CBDC has demonstrated potential in targeted use cases. Its programmable capabilities can help ensure proper fund utilization in sectors vulnerable to fraud, such as welfare distribution and subsidies. Pilot programs like the United Lending Interface (ULI) have shown how CBDC can support credit disbursement to underserved sectors such as agriculture and MSMEs. Moreover, the granular data generated through CBDC transactions offers policymakers valuable insights into income and spending patterns, supporting more precise economic planning.

Safety: India has prioritized monetary sovereignty and systemic stability in its CBDC design. To preserve the role of commercial banks as financial intermediaries, the digital rupee is non-interest-bearing. This measure helps prevent large-scale deposit shifts from traditional banks to CBDC wallets, mitigating risks to liquidity and credit intermediation. By maintaining the core functions of money within the central bank's purview, India aims to anchor its CBDC within a sovereign and resilient framework.

Currency Volatility: One of the primary advantages of Wholesale CBDC lies in its ability to reduce settlement risk and improve transaction efficiency, factors that can help dampen currency volatility in both domestic and cross-border financial markets. By facilitating government securities trading without the need for clearing corporations, Wholesale CBDC streamlines interbank settlement and supports more stable liquidity conditions.

Another innovative application is the use of CBDC for emergency financial relief, or "helicopter money." Unlike physical cash, digital currency allows for real-time, secure distribution of aid during natural disasters or economic crises, enhancing the government's ability to respond rapidly and equitably in high-risk situations.

While technical infrastructure and pilot programs have laid the groundwork, broader adoption hinges on policy clarity and public trust. India's legislative and marketing strategies offer insight into how the government is shaping the narrative, regulatory environment, and incentives around CBDC use.

Legislation: The Indian government has adopted a nuanced legislative approach toward the development of CBDC. A key driver has been the goal of strengthening domestic Monetary policy tools while discouraging reliance on decentralized private virtual currencies. Although cryptocurrencies are not banned in India and can legally be traded, they are not recognized as Legal tender and are burdened with high taxation: 30% on trading profits and a Tax Deducted at Source (TDS) on transactions above INR 50,000. These disincentives signal the government's preference for sovereign digital solutions.

Simultaneously, the Indian government has actively embraced Blockchain technology for public-sector applications, including land registration, legal documentation, and e-governance. The Ministry of Electronics and Information Technology's release of a National Strategy for Blockchain in 2021 illustrates this commitment to digital innovation. On the CBDC front, the RBI has steered the policy dialogue through instruments such as its 2022 concept note on CBDC and the inclusion of the Digital Rupee in the Union Budget 2022–23. Together, these moves underscore a coordinated policy approach that favors centralized digital currency systems while maintaining regulatory oversight over private crypto-assets.

Marketing Strategy: India's CBDC marketing strategy is built around positioning the digital rupee as a practical and empowering solution to everyday financial needs. Framed as a tool for efficiency, inclusion, and innovation, the narrative emphasizes CBDC's role in improving governance and reducing friction in financial transactions.

The communication strategy targets multiple stakeholders:

- For businesses, CBDC is presented as a growth enabler for fintech innovation and seamless financial service delivery.
- For the government, it offers administrative efficiency, reducing bureaucratic layers and opportunities for corruption.
- For citizens, CBDC is portrayed as a safe, accessible, and inclusive instrument aligned with the broader goal of digital financial empowerment.

Strategically, India aims to deploy CBDC in sectors such as agriculture, IT, and MSMEs, where programmable and traceable transactions can enhance service delivery and accountability. With an emphasis on cross-border functionality and technological interoperability, India's approach to CBDC promotion is broad-based and future-oriented.

6.2.3 Divergent Models, Shared Ambitions

Pix and UPI represent two of the most successful digital payment innovations in the Global South, each emerging from distinct institutional contexts yet converging on shared goals of Financial inclusion, efficiency, and sovereignty. Brazil's Pix, led by the central bank, demonstrates the power of real-time payments when integrated directly into public financial infrastructure. India's UPI, in contrast, showcases a layered public–private partnership model that leverages regulatory oversight alongside fintech dynamism.

Despite differences in design and implementation, both systems have redefined payment behavior at scale. Pix has rapidly reduced Brazil's reliance on cash and improved access for underserved populations. UPI has enabled a competitive digital finance ecosystem with broad-based adoption and global interoperability ambitions. In both cases, mobile payments have laid critical groundwork for the deployment of CBDCs, Drex, and the digital rupee, signaling an evolution from transactional platforms to programmable digital economies.

Together, Pix and UPI illustrate how mobile payment infrastructure, when rooted in local needs and supported by enabling governance, can transform national financial systems and shape the global future of digital currency.

7

Experimenting with CBDCs: Ghana, Peru, The Bahamas, Zimbabwe, Kenya, and the Eurozone

Main Messages

- Ghana's eCedi project takes an inclusive, phased approach, emphasizing offline access and Financial inclusion.
- Peru's CBDC efforts focus on bridging rural–urban financial gaps through digital wallets and public–private partnerships. Its pilot with Bitel and UPI-style infrastructure aims to expand financial access.
- The Bahamas launched the world's first Retail CBDC, the Sand Dollar, to improve inclusion and disaster resilience. Despite strong infrastructure and policy support, adoption remains limited due to user habits and trust issues.
- Zimbabwe's gold-backed ZiG aims to restore currency stability amid hyperinflation and economic volatility. However, it faces low public trust, rapid depreciation, and rejection by the informal economy.
- Kenya, with its highly developed mobile money system, has taken a wait-and-see stance on CBDCs. The Central Bank prioritized upgrading existing infrastructure over introducing a digital currency.
- The digital euro aims to modernize payments, enhance sovereignty, and reduce reliance on non-EU payment systems. Currently in its preparation phase, it faces regulatory hurdles and public skepticism.

The contributions of Abhi Das, Ofosuah Frimpong and Jacob Chizunza are gratefully acknowledged.

Central banks across the globe are grappling with the implications of digitalization, and many have turned to CBDCs as potential tools for enhancing Financial inclusion, improving payment efficiency, and modernizing monetary systems. This chapter explores the experimental approaches to CBDCs undertaken by three distinct economies, Peru, Zimbabwe, and The Bahamas, and other global experiments in Kenya and the Eurozone.

Ghana, one of West Africa's most stable and rapidly digitizing economies, has emerged as a regional leader in both technological innovation and financial modernization. With a population of over 34 million and a growing urban middle class, the country has made significant strides in mobile connectivity, digital entrepreneurship, and fintech adoption. Its capital, Accra, has become a hub for startups and digital finance, while rural areas have benefited from expanding telecom infrastructure and mobile money platforms. In this broader context of national digital ambition, the Bank of Ghana's eCedi project represents a natural next step: an effort to build a central bank digital currency that can serve as both a complement to cash and a catalyst for greater Financial inclusion. Ghana's approach to CBDC development aims to bridge geographic and socioeconomic divides.

Peru, a rapidly developing South American nation, is leveraging its CBDC initiative to bridge long-standing gaps in Financial inclusion, particularly in rural regions where formal banking remains scarce despite rising smartphone and Internet penetration. With support from telecom providers and foreign expertise, including a partnership with India's NPCI to replicate UPI-style infrastructure, Peru's central bank has launched pilot efforts focused on Retail use and digital wallets. The government aims to reduce cash reliance and restore trust in formal financial services through a hybrid public–private deployment model.

In contrast, The Bahamas has assumed the mantle of CBDC pioneer with the launch of the world's first fully deployed Retail CBDC, the Sand Dollar, in 2020. Two decades of payment system modernization efforts culminated in the Sand Dollar's creation, designed to bridge service gaps across a geographically dispersed population spread over hundreds of islands. The goals were to improve disaster resilience and bring Financial inclusion to underserved communities. Despite strong regulatory backing and substantial technological investment, adoption remains limited, highlighting the practical challenges of digitalization.

Meanwhile, Zimbabwe presents a markedly different case. Its introduction of the Zimbabwe Gold-Backed Digital Token (ZiG) in 2024 was driven not by inclusion or convenience but by an urgent need for currency stabilization in the face of chronic inflation and economic volatility. Although backed by physical gold and integrated into tax and payment systems, the ZiG has struggled to gain acceptance, particularly among the informal economy that dominates Zimbabwe's society. A lack of trust, limited usability, and poor macroeconomic conditions continue to undermine its long-term viability.

These four distinct countries are advancing digital payment systems in response to their unique national challenges, ranging from limited banking access and high cash dependency to inflation and monetary instability. While the pace and design of their transitions differ, each case reflects how local economic conditions, infrastructure gaps, and institutional priorities shape the evolution of digital finance. Together, these efforts illustrate how broader digital payment ecosystems are being built-in tandem with strategies for Financial inclusion and modernization.

7.1 Ghana's eCedi Project

Ghana's eCedi initiative offers a rich case study of a central bank digital currency project in an emerging economy context. The Bank of Ghana (BoG) was among the first in Africa to announce concrete steps toward a CBDC, and it has since proceeded methodically through design, implementation, and pilot phases. In this section, we delve into the eCedi's journey: the motivations and design principles laid out by the BoG, the execution of pilot programs (including outcomes and findings), and the current status and future plans for the eCedi. We will also consider how Ghana's experience compares to Nigeria's eNaira, given the regional proximity and similar timelines of their CBDC efforts. Project Genesis and Design: The idea of a digital cedi (eCedi) was formally announced by BoG Governor Dr. Ernest Addison in 2021, positioning Ghana as a frontrunner in Africa's CBDC race. The eCedi was framed as part of the "Digital Ghana Agenda," a broader governmental push to digitize services and boost the digital economy. Key goals articulated were to "complement the Ghanaian cedi and serve as a digital alternative to physical cash," furthering the country's cash-lite agenda and Financial inclusion objectives. Notably, BoG emphasized from the outset that the eCedi would not replace cash but circulate alongside it, giving people more choices in how to transact. To develop the eCedi, the BoG partnered with international technology firm Giesecke+Devrient (G+D) in 2021 for a pilot implementation. G+D provided its Filia CBDC solution adapted to Ghana's needs. The choice of G+D, a company with a long history in currency and security printing, signaled BoG's priority on reliability and security. The pilot plan was structured in three phases: design, implementation (system setup), and pilot testing. During the design phase, BoG consulted stakeholders and invited feedback—the eCedi Design Paper was published in 2022, outlining the concept and soliciting public comments. This transparent approach aimed to ensure the project would "meet the needs and aspirations of Ghanaians."

From the design paper and subsequent communications, some core design decisions for eCedi included:

- It would be a Retail CBDC, available for use by individuals and businesses for everyday transactions in both online (connected) and offline modes.
- Distribution would follow a two-tier model: the BoG issues eCedi to regulated financial institutions (banks, possibly payment service providers), which then distribute it to users. Users would hold eCedi in digital wallets (likely a mobile app and/or hardware wallets) provided by these intermediaries.
- Financial inclusion features were central. The credit system was to support those without smartphones—possibly via SMS or through smart cards—and without formal bank accounts. The aim was to allow anyone, including in remote areas, to transact in eCedi, even offline.
- Offline functionality was a must-have in the design, as highlighted earlier. G+D's technology-enabled consecutive offline payments; BoG wanted to test this to ensure rural connectivity issues would not impede adoption.
- The eCedi would be non-interest bearing (like cash) and, in pilot, was issued at par with physical cedi (1 eCedi = 1 GHS). BoG capped holdings and transactions during the pilot to manage risk, though exact figures weren't public; one could infer they mirrored mobile money limits.
- On the legal side, BoG signaled that necessary legislative reviews would be done. While not explicitly stated, it's likely BoG would seek to amend the Currency Act to recognize use as Legal tender in the event of a full launch.

Pilot Execution and Results: Ghana's eCedi pilot took place in 2022–2023 in a few selected areas. According to the "eCedi Pilot Report" released by BoG in October 2024, the testing involved urban, semi-urban, and rural communities: specifically, Accra (the capital, representing an urban setting with good connectivity), Tarkwa (a smaller town), and Sefwi Asafo (a rural community chosen for the offline test).

The pilot was conducted with real participants—consumers and merchants—though in controlled numbers. Key results reported include:

- **Transaction Volume and Value:** Over the pilot period, a total of more than 96,000 eCedi transactions were recorded, amounting to GHS 473 million in value. This high total value, relative to the number of transactions, suggests that some sizable payments (likely between financial institutions or larger merchants) were part of the test, not just microtransactions. It indicates the system was tested for both Retail small payments and larger transfers.
- **Participation:** 2750 people participated in the online (connected) pilot across Accra and Tarkwa, using eCedi for peer-to-peer transfers, person-to-business payments (like buying goods), business-to-person (like refunds or payroll), and bill payments. Another 173 people participated in the offline pilot in Sefwi Asafo. These numbers, while small relative to Ghana's population, are typical for a pilot study aimed at qualitative insights rather than big adoption.
- **Performance of Offline Transactions:** Offline usage was successful but remained a tiny portion of total activity—only 0.004% of the value and 0.475% of the count of transactions were offline. This is expected since offline was confined to one rural area and presumably low-value Retail payments. Importantly, no double-spending or reconciliation issues were reported when those offline transactions were eventually synced, demonstrating that the solution (smart cards holding eCedi) worked as intended. The pilot thus validated that eCedi could facilitate transactions in an off-grid scenario, which was a major objective.
- **User Experience and Acceptance:** The BoG gathered user feedback on using the eCedi. The pilot report highlighted that uptake in rural areas will require substantial education and trust-building, as cash was deeply entrenched. In Sefwi Asafo, many participants still preferred cash for most transactions, citing habit and also the fact that local businesses widely accept cash and mobile money but were just being introduced to eCedi. In Tarkwa (peri-urban), mobile money was very popular, so eCedi had to be positioned relative to that. Users generally liked the speed of eCedi transactions and that it didn't incur fees like some mobile money transfers do. However, some reported concerns about what happens if the phone battery dies or if there are technical glitches—underscoring the need for robust support.
- **Security and Technical Findings:** The pilot evaluated security (no major breaches were reported publicly). It also looked at the impact on existing payment systems. Since the pilot was small, it did not disrupt anything, but BoG analysts examined how eCedi transactions might affect monetary aggregates or payment flows if scaled up. They concluded that clear

frameworks would be needed if eCedi goes live to manage liquidity—for example, how banks convert large amounts of cash to eCedi and vice versa without affecting the money supply. In the pilot, conversion was tightly managed by BoG (they issued a fixed pool of eCedi to the participant banks for the test).

- **Policy Insights:** One strong emphasis in the pilot report was that objectives need to be clear. BoG noted that "the result of the field pilot indicates the importance of establishing clear objectives for a CBDC." This implies that during the pilot, there may have been some ambiguity among users or even stakeholders on whether eCedi is meant to replace mobile money or whether it's mainly for offline use cases, etc. So, BoG likely learned that in a production rollout, communication must clearly define the value proposition of eCedi to different groups (e.g., to banks, to fintechs, to users).

Comparing eCedi with Nigeria's eNaira: It is instructive to compare Ghana's and Nigeria's approaches, as they are both large West African economies with significant mobile money usage and similar aims for CBDC, yet their outcomes diverged in speed and scale. Nigeria launched eNaira in October 2021 nationwide in one go, a rather bold move. Ghana instead took a cautious pilot approach from late 2021 to 2023. Nigeria's approach gave it the "first mover" title in Africa but also meant many initial challenges (technical issues with the app, low adoption due to limited stakeholder engagement) played out in the public eye. Ghana's gradual approach allowed BoG to iterate behind the scenes and avoid some pitfalls. For example, Nigeria initially required a bank account to sign up for eNaira, which limited inclusion; they later removed that requirement (allowing just a national ID-linked phone number for the basic tier). Ghana, from the start, planned for non-bank account holders to use eCedi (leveraging telco mobile money accounts or other KYC light methods), possibly learning from Nigeria's early restriction. Another difference is stakeholder buy-in: Ghana actively engaged fintechs via the hackathon and was reportedly working closely with mobile money operators (like MTN's Mobile Money, which has huge penetration in Ghana) to see how eCedi could interface. Nigeria's launch was more bank-centric and had less initial involvement from the telcos or fintech startups, some of whom might even view eNaira as competition to their services. The outcome is that by the end of 2022, Nigeria had very low usage metrics, whereas Ghana, in its pilot, got positive feedback and even international recognition—the Bank of Ghana won an award in 2024 for "Innovation in Digital Currency Design for Financial inclusion," highlighting its offline eCedi work. This doesn't mean Ghana's eCedi will automatically be a success, but BoG's careful strategy has won praise for focusing on real needs like offline capability and user co-creation.

Current Status and Next Steps: As of late 2024, Ghana has not yet launched the eCedi for public use beyond pilots. However, officials have hinted at timelines. A report in early 2025 suggested that BoG is preparing for a possible rollout of eCedi by the end of 2025. This suggests that 2024–2025 is being used to refine the technology (perhaps upgrading systems based on pilot feedback), strengthen the regulatory framework, and build wider ecosystem readiness. The BoG Governor has reaffirmed the commitment to a digital currency, stressing that Ghana wants to maintain leadership in fintech innovation in Africa and not be left behind as the world moves toward CBDCs.

Key focus areas for Ghana moving forward likely include:

- **Legal Framework:** Drafting or amending laws to give eCedi Legal tender status and delineate BoG's powers and responsibilities formally. This may go to Parliament for debate.
- **Infrastructure Scale-up:** Ensuring that the technology can scale from a pilot of a few thousand users to potentially millions. This might involve more partnerships or even a phased national rollout (perhaps starting with government payments in one region, etc.).
- **Public–Private Collaboration:** Deepening integration plans with banks, fintech, and mobile operators so that eCedi can be loaded and used as easily as mobile money is today. Possibly, wallets might be integrated into existing mobile money apps to leverage their user base.
- **Education and Marketing:** Rolling out nationwide awareness campaigns to educate Ghanaians on what eCedi is, how to use it, and its benefits. The pilot report's stress on clear objectives implies BoG knows a strong narrative is needed to drive voluntary adoption.
- **Continued Pilot/Testing:** It would not be surprising if BoG conducts additional targeted pilots—for example, trying cross-border remittances with eCedi (a Ghanian abroad sending eCedi home) or connecting eCedi with government e-services—before the full launch.

7.2 Peru: Bridging Rural Gaps Through Gradual Digital Inclusion

To understand Peru's CBDC effort in context, it is important to examine the country's broader economic and digital landscape. Peru has been a rapidly developing nation in South America, with a nominal GDP of approximately $267 billion and a GDP per capita of around $6455. The population stands at roughly 45 million, with mobile cellular subscription rates reaching 120% in 2022, largely due to multiple device ownership. Smartphone penetration has also increased significantly, rising from 66% in 2016 to 88% in 2021 across both rural and urban areas.

Despite strong economic growth over recent decades, Financial inclusion, particularly among rural populations, remains a challenge. Over 30% of Peru's adult population is unbanked, limiting access to traditional financial services. Credit card usage remains low, reaching just under 13% in 2021. The country's financial sector is led by institutions such as Banco de Crédito del Perú, Interbank, BBVA, and Scotiabank Peru.

Peru remains highly dependent on cash, especially in rural areas that have only recently gained improved cellular connectivity. Many Peruvians rely on informal financial systems due to mistrust of traditional banking, high account maintenance fees, and a lack of nearby bank branches (Fig. 7.1). While Internet usage has risen sharply, approaching 80% in 2023, the number of commercial bank branches per 100,000 adults has remained stagnant over the past two decades.

In response to these gaps, the Peruvian Central Bank has sought to leverage digital payment systems and CBDCs to expand financial access. While cash remains central to everyday transactions in Peru—particularly in informal markets and rural areas—digital payments have expanded rapidly. Services like PagoEfectivo support cash-based online commerce, while hybrid platforms such as BIM aim to bring mobile payments to the unbanked. Mobile wallets like Yape and Plin, launched by major Peruvian banks, along with the growing use of QR codes, represent significant milestones in Peru's shift toward a more digitized financial ecosystem.

International partnerships have played a key role. In June 2024, the Central Reserve Bank of Peru (BCRP) partnered with NPCI International to introduce a UPI-style real-time payment system modeled after India's success. This initiative is expected to significantly improve transaction efficiency and expand financial access. India anticipates two UPI-based launches in Africa and South America by early 2027.

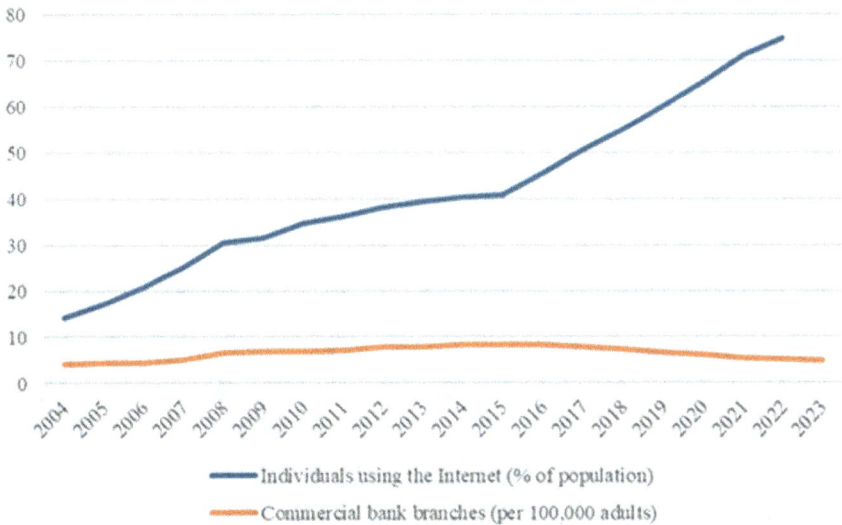

Fig. 7.1 Individuals using the Internet (% of population) vs commercial bank branches (per 100,000 adults) (*Source* World Bank, World Development Indicators [https://data.worldbank.org/indicator]; Accessed November 2024)

Although mobile payments now account for a growing share of transactions, cash still dominates. However, the total transaction value in Peru has risen steadily over the past decade, with mobile payments comprising nearly 24% of all transactions by 2024 (Fig. 7.2). Remittances, a key component of the economy, have increasingly moved to digital channels, reducing costs and improving efficiency for cross-border flows.

Peru has also experienced growth in Buy Now, Pay Later offerings. Programs like Cuotéalo from Banco de Crédito del Perú and Divídelo from Interbank reflect this trend. At the same time, financial literacy initiatives such as Finanzas en el Cole and non-profits like Fundación Capital have helped promote better money management and digital payment adoption. Partnerships among banks, telecom companies, and fintech startups are expanding rural access to services through agent banking and mobile platforms.

Peru's approach to CBDC has been relatively measured. Still, in the early stages of research and development, the BCRP laid out its vision in a March 2023 white paper. The central objective is Financial inclusion, building on the momentum of digital wallets and mobile payments. Other goals include improving the efficiency and security of domestic payment systems, reducing the costs of cash management, and fostering innovation and competition in the payment ecosystem. At a macro level, the Central Reserve Bank of Peru

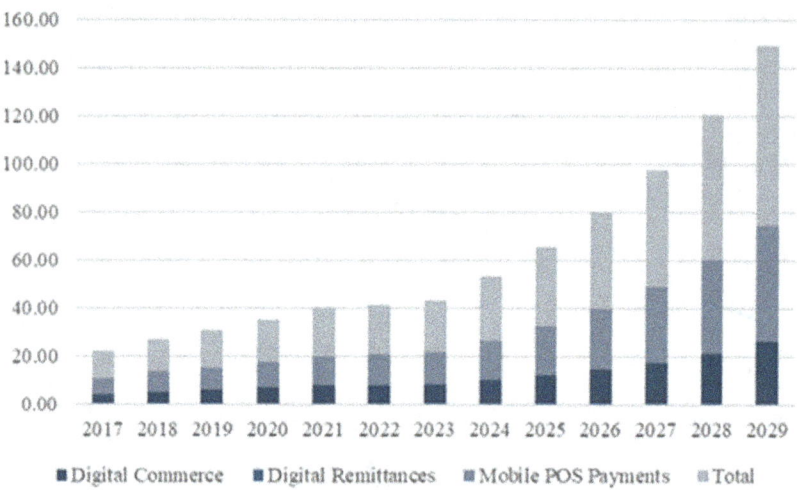

Fig. 7.2 Transaction value by market in billions ($) (*Source* Statista Market Insights [https://www.statista.com/]; Accessed November 2024)

sees a potential CBDC as a tool to improve the transmission of monetary policy, enhance public confidence in the Peruvian sol, and gradually reduce reliance on the U.S. dollar in domestic transactions.

The CBDC under development is Retail-focused, intended for everyday transactions between individuals and businesses. Cross-border and Wholesale applications are not immediate priorities, though the BCRP is monitoring international initiatives like mBridge, which supports real-time cross-border transactions among multiple central banks.

To deploy the CBDC, the BCRP plans to delegate implementation to private-sector financial institutions, payment service providers, and mobile operators. This would allow the central bank to maintain transaction oversight while leveraging private infrastructure. The CBDC will be token-based and deployed through either a centralized database or a Blockchain-based DLT platform.

Progress accelerated in July 2024 when the BCRP awarded its first development contract to Viettel S.A.C. (Bitel) Peru, citing the company's strong rural presence (2.5 million rural users) and its existing digital wallet, BiPay. The pilot is expected to last one year, with the option to extend. Under the agreement, the BCRP manages core infrastructure, while Bitel oversees user-facing services, including Know Your Customer processes, wallet integration, account registration, and payments.

Bitel must first deposit funds into a CBDC account at the BCRP before distributing digital currency to agents and users. People can load CBDC into their wallets via cash deposits or direct transfers and use it for payments to individuals, businesses, and utilities. When Bitel converts CBDC back into bank money, it withdraws funds from the CBDC system, ensuring monetary balance.

The International Monetary Fund (IMF) has supported the research process, identifying high transaction fees and a lack of trust in digital systems as key barriers to adoption. Another challenge is ensuring offline transaction capability in rural areas with weak Internet connectivity. Bitel's proposed solution involves enabling basic transactions through mobile phones over its extensive 3G network. Security features include encrypted messaging, IP-layer protection, transaction speed verification, and usage limits.

To promote regulatory stability and security, the BCRP has introduced a series of legal and compliance requirements for private-sector partners. While current central bank laws permit CBDC issuance, regulatory alignment is underway to ensure operational compliance. Bitel is required to maintain a reserve balance at the BCRP that is at least 2% greater than the total CBDC held by users. It must also secure a PEN 500,000 ($130,000) financial guarantee from a highly rated bank. The BCRP will receive anonymized transaction data in near real-time and will monitor balances twice daily through a secure, encrypted network.

Recognizing that trust and usability are critical for adoption, the BCRP has outlined targeted engagement strategies. One proposed initiative is an "Innovation Challenge" to invite market feedback on the CBDC's benefits. The central bank also plans to focus on digitally enabled early adopters, businesses, and individuals already active in the digital economy to accelerate broader uptake across the population.

7.3 The Bahamas: Pioneering the World's First Retail CBDC

While Peru's CBDC journey reflects a measured, infrastructure-focused approach to Financial inclusion, The Bahamas offers a contrasting example, one defined by bold first-mover advantage. As the first country to fully launch a Retail CBDC, The Bahamas illustrates both the opportunities and the early growing pains of national digital currency deployment in a geographically unique setting.

Understanding The Bahamas' pioneering role in CBDC deployment requires first examining the country's broader context, a small but digitally ambitious nation whose recent growth has positioned it as a regional leader in financial innovation. The Bahamas, an archipelagic nation in the Caribbean, presents a unique economic and technological landscape. Over the years, The Bahamian economy has projected growth in recent years, with GDP increasing from $14.34 billion in 2023 to an estimated $15 billion in 2024. The GDP per capita figures reflect the country's status as one of the wealthier nations in the Caribbean region, with a 2024 estimate of $36,322 from $35,896.5 in 2023. This growth is due to the improvement of tourism, technology, and finance industries despite having a smaller population of 399,440.

In terms of technological adoption, by 2023, the mobile cellular subscriptions in The Bahamas had reached 400,000, surpassing the country's population. For the financial services sector, banking penetration is relatively high, with widespread access to digital payment platforms and banking services. Credit card usage experienced significant growth, with a 203.2% increase between 2013 and 2017. Debit card usage has become increasingly popular, growing by 138% in the same period. Online banking adoption is substantial, with 62% of consumers surveyed reporting comfort with its use. The high smartphone penetration and growing comfort with digital financial services presented significant opportunities for further fintech innovation and Financial inclusion initiatives in The Bahamas.

With the progression of online banking, digital payments in The Bahamas have been evolving rapidly, with both public and private-sector players driving the transformation. The Central Bank of The Bahamas has been the primary public-sector driver of digital payments, while private companies like Island Pay and Kanoo have also played significant roles. During the late 1990s, the Central Bank acknowledged a need for payment system modernization in The Bahamas. In that effort, they introduced the Payment System Modernization Initiative (PSMI) in the country. Further, the National Payments Council was established in 2003 to oversee the development of the national payment system strategy. A significant milestone was reached in 2004 with the launch of The Bahamas Interbank Settlement System (BISS), enabling real-time electronic settlements between banks. In 2010, The Bahamas Automated Clearing House (BACH) was established to handle small-value Retail payments to reduce clearance time from five days to one day. In 2013, the government removed the stamp tax on Bahamian dollar electronic funds transfers or debits to encourage electronic payments. This trajectory was paving the way for digital payments in The Bahamas. In 2017, the government removed the stamp tax on Bahamian dollar electronic funds transfers or debits, encouraging electronic payments over a cash-based economy. After 9 years, in 2019, NZIA Limited (now Movmint) was selected to provide the technology for The Bahamas' CBDC.

Against this backdrop of rising digital infrastructure and policy reform, The Bahamas launched the world's first Retail CBDC, the Sand Dollar. The Sand Dollar pilot was launched in Exuma in late 2019 and subsequently expanded to Abaco in 2020. The primary goals of the Sand Dollar launch were: First, to foster Financial inclusion by expanding access to financial services for unbanked and underbanked communities across the Bahamian archipelago. Second, to increase efficiency by reducing service delivery costs and increasing transactional efficiency for financial services. Third, to continue the Bahamian Payments System Modernization Initiative (PSMI) that began in the early 2000s. Fourth, to improve access to financial services during natural disasters like hurricanes and reduce the risk of money laundering. Fifth, to improve transparency and payment resilience through a centralized alternative to banking platforms.

The Sand Dollar is available both in Retail and Wholesale spaces. It is available for public use, allowing individuals to make and receive digital payments. It is also used for interbank settlements and clearing house transactions. The Bahamas, with the Sand Dollar, is yet to join the cross-border CBDC projects like mBridge, but their long-term objective through CBDC is to facilitate transactions with other countries. The Sand Dollar utilizes direct distribution models, wherein the Central Bank of The Bahamas issues the Sand Dollar CBDC, maintaining control over the monetary supply and backing it with foreign reserves. The Central Bank wants to extend the front-end services to be provided by banks and other authorized financial institutions in the private sector by 2026.

To facilitate access, The Bahamas employs a tiered wallet system and an indirect distribution model through authorized financial institutions. Tier 1 includes basic access with limited holdings (Bahamian Dollars 500) and monthly transaction limits (Bahamian Dollars 1500), requiring minimal user information. Tier 2 includes higher limits (Bahamian Dollar 8000 holdings, Bahamian Dollar 10,000 monthly transactions) for users with government-issued identification. The Business Tier includes ranges from Bahamian Dollars 8000 to Bahamian Dollars 1,000,000, with limits for businesses with valid licenses and VAT certificates. The transactions are instantly validated, and there are no additional transaction fees applied to the customers. Currently, there is an indirect distribution model used for Sand Dollar, wherein the Central Bank issues Sand Dollars through authorized financial institutions (AFIs) such as commercial banks and credit unions. These intermediaries are responsible for onboarding users, verifying identities, creating digital wallets, and facilitating transactions. The Sand Dollar operates on a token-based infrastructure, with each digital token fully backed by central bank reserves and can be accessed via mobile apps or physical payment cards. The system features both sovereign wallets (direct claims on the central bank) and custodial wallets managed by AFIs, ensuring flexibility and accessibility. Interoperability is a key requirement, allowing users to transact seamlessly across different wallet providers, and businesses can integrate Sand Dollar accounts with traditional bank deposits for streamlined B2B and B2C payments. With no minimum balance requirements and a focus on Financial inclusion, the Sand Dollar aims to serve unbanked populations and enhance disaster resilience in the hurricane-prone nation.

Following its launch, the implementation of the Sand Dollar has been shaped by public–private collaboration, legislative backing, and technological innovation. Private players like Kanoo integrated CBDC into its payment app, while Island Pay, along with Mastercard in February 2021, launched the world's first CBDC-linked card through The Bahamas. A significant milestone was reached in March 2022 when the Central Bank completed the initial integration of the Sand Dollar with The Bahamas Automated Clearing House system, enabling transfers from digital wallets to local bank accounts. By 2023, the Sand Dollar Authorized Financial Institutions (AFIs) were mandated to extend bank account integration features to their platforms. Looking ahead, in 2024, the Central Bank announced plans to require commercial banks to support the Sand Dollar CBDC within the next two years, aiming to boost the adoption and usage of the digital currency.

Technologically, the Central Bank selected NZIA Limited as its solutions provider, deploying a robust, proprietary platform called Cortex to manage issuance, compliance, and transaction processing across the archipelago, with features such as real-time transaction validation, interoperability among payment service providers, and offline functionality to ensure resilience in areas with unstable communications. Legally, the rollout was underpinned by a new and updated legislative framework, including the Central Bank of The Bahamas Act 2020, the Banks and Trust Companies Regulation Act 2020, and the Central Bank (Electronic Bahamian Dollars) Regulations 2021, which collectively regulate wallet providers, set minimum standards for interoperability and Financial inclusion, and empower the Central Bank to oversee the digital currency ecosystem. To drive adoption, the Central Bank implemented a multi-pronged marketing strategy: it conducted targeted outreach to financial institutions, broad public education campaigns through media and chambers of commerce, and collaborated with payment service providers to encourage integration and merchant acceptance. The bank also worked with the government to promote Sand Dollar as a means for public payments and disbursements and addressed barriers such as digital literacy and Internet access by deploying physical kiosks and planning free Wi-Fi initiatives for remote islands. As of April 2025, these combined efforts have established the Sand Dollar as a pioneering CBDC, though ongoing work continues to expand its reach and utility across the nation.

Despite its pioneering status, the Sand Dollar has faced challenges in adoption and merchant participation, highlighting both successes and limitations in its rollout. As of early 2024, just Bahamian Dollar 2.1 million worth of Sand Dollars were in circulation—less than 0.5% of the total cash in the Bahamian economy, more than 120,000 wallets having been opened in a nation of around 400,000 people, a figure that includes a significant number of tourists who can also use the wallets. Merchant participation has lagged, with about 1800 merchants signed up, and many businesses in the informal sector remain wary of digital transactions due to Privacy concerns and a preference for cash. Accessibility has improved, particularly for residents of remote islands where physical banking services are scarce, but technical barriers such as inconsistent Internet infrastructure have hampered widespread use; the central bank is developing offline capabilities to address this. In terms of safety, the Sand Dollar is backed 1:1 by the Bahamian dollar, which itself is pegged to the U.S. dollar, ensuring virtually no currency volatility. The system incorporates multi-factor authentication and a digital ID solution to enhance user security, and Privacy is protected by limiting the central bank's access to user identities unless required for legal investigations. However, the IMF and other observers have noted the need for ongoing improvements in Cybersecurity and public education to build trust and drive greater adoption.

7.4 Zimbabwe: Digital Currency as Crisis Control

While The Bahamas represents a case of early innovation driven by Financial inclusion and technological readiness, Zimbabwe offers a starkly different narrative—one rooted in monetary crisis and urgent stabilization efforts. The introduction of its CBDC, the ZiG, reflects not just a digital shift but a high-stakes attempt to restore economic control in the face of inflation and public mistrust.

Zimbabwe's currency history has been marked by numerous changes driven by economic instability. The country has been grappling with hyperinflation, currency instability, and widespread poverty. In 2023, the country's nominal GDP was $35.23 billion, along with a per capita GDP of $2156. Zimbabwe's economy is strongly tied to agricultural output, and an El Niño-induced drought resulted in a significant economic slowdown.

Despite the economic challenges, Zimbabwe has made leaps in digital connectivity. The number of mobile cellular subscriptions increased to 15.7 million in Q4 2024, effectively covering almost the entire 16.34 million people living in the country. In terms of Internet penetration, the number of active Internet users stood at around 6.45 million at the beginning of 2024.

Financial inclusion has also improved markedly over the past decade. According to the FinScope Zimbabwe 2022 Consumer Survey, formal Financial inclusion increased from 40% in 2011 to 84% in 2022, largely due to the widespread adoption of mobile money services. EcoCash, launched in 2011 by Econet Wireless, has been a significant driver in this space, offering services such as money transfers, bill payments, and airtime purchases.

The digital payment landscape in Zimbabwe has expanded beyond mobile money, and the Reserve Bank of Zimbabwe (RBZ) has played a critical role in introducing various currencies, including the Zimbabwean Dollar and its iterations. Zimswitch, the national payment switch, processes over 75% of all card-based transactions in the country, reflecting the increasing adoption of electronic payments.

Despite these advancements, challenges remain. Approximately 40% of adults do not have a bank account, with many relying on informal financial services due to factors such as low-income, cultural norms, and financial illiteracy. Efforts are ongoing to bridge this gap through fintech solutions and financial literacy programs, aiming to integrate more citizens into the formal financial system.

Amid rising inflation and a legacy of monetary instability, The Reserve Bank of Zimbabwe (RBZ) launched the ZiG in April 2024 with the primary objectives of curbing rampant inflation, restoring public confidence in the national currency, and reducing the economy's heavy reliance on the U.S. dollar. The RBZ launched the currency with the intention of providing a more stable and trustworthy medium of exchange by backing the currency with gold and foreign currency reserves. Another goal was to further integrate the informal sector with the formal financial system. This would help increase the tax base and make Monetary policy more effective and responsive.

The ZiG is a Retail CBDC and is designed for use by the general public in everyday transactions. Its gold backing is intended to provide intrinsic value and stability, distinguishing it from traditional fiat currencies. The RBZ's approach combines elements of both digital and physical currency, with the ZiG existing alongside physical banknotes and coins.

To deliver the ZiG across the country, Zimbabwe uses a two-tier distribution model relying on both the central bank and commercial institutions, with digital integration expected through existing mobile and banking infrastructure:

1. **Central Bank**: The RBZ issues the ZiG, ensuring its backing with gold and foreign currency reserves.
2. **Commercial Banks and Financial Institutions**: Commercial banks and other financial institutions distribute the ZiG to end users, enabling transactions and conversions between the ZiG and other currencies.

While specific technological details have not been publicly disclosed, the RBZ has indicated that the ZiG leverages existing banking infrastructure to facilitate digital transactions. The integration with mobile money platforms is also anticipated to enhance accessibility, particularly in rural areas.

Despite its promising launch, the ZiG has quickly faced setbacks, with key milestones reflecting both optimism and volatility in its early months (Table 7.1).

These early developments highlight the fragility of the ZiG's rollout and the persistent macroeconomic pressures facing Zimbabwe. Despite the initial promise of a gold-backed digital currency, the rapid depreciation and inflation spikes have underscored the need for stronger institutional support and policy clarity.

In response, the government has introduced a set of legal and regulatory measures intended to formalize the currency's use and restore public confidence in its stability. These include: legal tender status: the ZiG has been designated as a Legal tender, mandating its acceptance for all transactions

Table 7.1 Timeline of key milestones in the evolution of ZiG in Zimbabwe (2024–2025)

Year	Event
April 2024	The RBZ officially launched the ZiG, replacing the Zimbabwean dollar at an initial exchange rate of 13.56 ZiG per U.S. dollar
Mid-2024	The ZiG experienced significant depreciation, with its value dropping by approximately 80% on the black market by September 2024
Early 2025	Inflationary pressures persisted, with the annual inflation rate reaching 14.6% in January 2025

within Zimbabwe; Taxation Policies: businesses are required to pay taxes in a 50/50 split between U.S. dollars and ZiG, aiming to bolster demand for the new currency; and Consumer Protection and Financial Stability: regulatory measures have been implemented to safeguard consumers and maintain financial stability, including oversight of digital transactions and anti-money laundering protocols.

Yet, adoption has been slow, and public trust remains fragile as inflation, market depreciation, and widespread use of the U.S. dollar continue to undermine the ZiG's credibility. Citizens of Zimbabwe are reluctant to adopt ZiG despite its backing by gold. Surveys and anecdotal reports indicate that many still view the U.S. dollar as a safer store of value, undermining the acceptability of ZiG as a legitimate medium of exchange. Inflation surged from 2.5% in December 2024 to 14.6% by January 2025, and the ZiG lost over 90% of its value against the U.S. dollar within months of launch, both officially and on black markets. These developments have reinforced the public perception of ZiG as unstable. Approximately 80% of Zimbabwe's economy operates informally. This sector overwhelmingly rejects ZiG due to its perceived instability, unfamiliarity, and transactional inconvenience. Informal traders continue to demand payments in U.S. dollars, and where ZiG is accepted, sellers often impose higher prices to compensate for exchange rate risks.

7.5 The Digital Euro

The digital euro is a proposed CBDC being developed by the ECB and the Eurosystem. Its goals are to enable the modernization of payments, strengthen monetary sovereignty, and reduce dependence on non-European payment providers like Visa and Mastercard. The digital euro is designed to function as a digital equivalent of cash. Additionally, it is intended to complement and not replace physical cash.

The ECB has indicated that the project is currently in its preparation phase, which began in November 2023 and is scheduled to conclude by the end of October 2025. This phase has involved the ECB finalizing the digital euro scheme rulebook, selecting technology providers, and conducting testing to ensure the currency meets user needs along with regulatory requirements. The ECB has also established what it calls an innovation platform, where it has partnered with around 70 market participants to test payment functionalities and explore a multitude of use cases, like digital euro wallets that are accessible even to those without bank accounts or digital devices. The fourth progress report was published by the ECB in April 2025 and showed significant advancements and input from numerous stakeholders.

The urgency behind the digital euro is partly driven by financial instability in Europe, exacerbated by recent geopolitical shifts and economic challenges, including rising inflation, tariff wars, and declining confidence in the ECB's policies. The ECB has faced consecutive years of losses, and the need to reinforce the Euro's role as a reserve asset has become more pressing. Additionally, the European financial sector's reliance on payment infrastructure structured around the U.S. is seen as a strategic vulnerability. This is seen as especially concerning in the context of global tensions and increased European defense spending. Across the ocean, the Trump administration's push to expand global usage of Stablecoins has increased European concerns about monetary sovereignty despite the EU's existing MiCA regulations that limit the scale of foreign Stablecoins and grant authorities intervention powers if monetary sovereignty is threatened.

ECB President Christine Lagarde has announced that the digital euro could be ready for launch by October 2025 as long as the necessary legislative framework is in place. The ECB aims to finalize all political agreements by early 2026, after which it would take an additional two to three years to fully roll out the currency.

A major challenge is reaching a consensus among all the EU member states. Despite technical and regulatory progress, there also exists a significant amount of public skepticism. A March 2025 study indicated that 58% of Europeans are "unlikely or very unlikely" to use the digital euro for everyday payments. Respondents were concerned about Privacy and the impact on traditional banking infrastructure. The ECB contends that it is working to address these issues by ensuring robust data protection standards, setting holding limits, and enabling offline payments.

While the digital euro is primarily envisioned as a Retail CBDC for everyday consumer use, there is also growing momentum for launching a Wholesale CBDC that, at first, will be aimed at institutional participants. The digital euro represents a major step in the evolution of European finance, aiming to harmonize digital payments, foster innovation, and enhance the resilience of the euro area's monetary system.

7.6 M-Pesa and CBDC Prospects in Kenya

Kenya, known for its innovative mobile money ecosystem, the M-Pesa, has been exploring the potential of a CBDC. The Central Bank of Kenya (CBK) initiated this exploration by releasing a Discussion Paper in February 2022. The paper talks about applicability, potential benefits, and risks in a digital payment landscape that's relatively well-developed.

The CBK identified potential opportunities for a CBDC, particularly in reducing transaction costs, improving interoperability, and enhancing Cross-border payments. Right now, cross-border remittances in Kenya incur high costs, averaging around 8%, well above the UN Sustainable Development Goal of less than 3% by 2030.

Given Kenya's high Financial inclusion rate (over 83% as of 2021) and the widespread use of mobile money (over 68 million accounts as of December 2021), the CBK questioned whether a CBDC could offer significant advantages over existing solutions like M-Pesa.

The CBK sought public feedback on the CBDC proposal, and the public and expert feedback generally favored a cautious approach, with many preferring a hybrid CBDC model where both the central bank and intermediaries share responsibilities for onboarding and transaction processing. Concerns were raised about potential risks, including financial system stability, technological barriers for some users, and the possibility of financial exclusion if the necessary infrastructure and digital literacy are not widespread.

The CBK concluded that, given the robustness and inclusivity of Kenya's current digital payments ecosystem, implementing a CBDC is not an immediate priority. Instead, the CBK has been advocating for strengthening and innovating within the existing payment infrastructure.

7.7 Lessons and Diverging Trajectories: Global Insights from Early CBDCs

Ghana's eCedi project exemplifies a pragmatic and inclusive approach to CBDC design. By tackling challenges like offline use early and engaging with end users and innovators, BoG has built a foundation that addresses Ghana's specific needs, such as inclusion across urban–rural divides. The project still faces hurdles, notably how to compete or integrate with the very successful mobile money sector and how to convince Ghanaians to trust and use eCedi widely. But if BoG continues on its thoughtful trajectory, Ghana could emerge as a model for other countries on how to systematically develop a CBDC that garners public trust and achieves its policy aims.

In Peru, challenges such as digital literacy and infrastructure constraints persist, but the integration of real-time payment systems and a well-structured CBDC implementation plan could revolutionize Peru's financial landscape, fostering economic growth and greater financial participation.

The Bahamian Sand Dollar has made notable strides in Financial inclusion and resilience, especially in disaster-prone areas. However, it is struggling to achieve broad, everyday usage among Bahamian consumers and merchants.

The introduction of ZIG was an ambitious effort to stabilize Zimbabwe's economic landscape, but its success has been limited. Inflationary pressures, exchange rate volatility, and a lack of widespread acceptance, particularly in the informal sector, have undermined ZIG's effectiveness. For ZIG to fulfill its potential, the RBZ should focus on restoring public trust, ensuring its independence, and integrating the currency more fully into the informal economy. Addressing these issues will be critical for ZIG's long-term success and for achieving broader economic stability in Zimbabwe.

Meanwhile, the Central Bank of Kenya, taking into account its existing robust digital payments landscape, continues to monitor global CBDC developments and remains open to reassessing the need for a Kenyan CBDC as technology and local needs evolve.

In the context of developed nations' CBDC experiments, European officials are clear: the recent U.S. support for crypto-assets and Stablecoins, combined with tariff pressures, has made it even more vital for Europe to complete the digital euro project to maintain monetary and Financial sovereignty. The push now is to move rapidly from experimentation to operationalization, with central banks across the Eurosystem working actively to bring the digital euro and related infrastructure to fruition.

Part III

Stablecoins, CBDCS, and Competing Visions of Digital Money

8

Cross-Border CBDCs: mBridge, Agora, and the Others

Main Messages

- mBridge is s cross-border Wholesale CBDC initiative led by China and BRICS nations, aimed at bypassing SWIFT and enhancing currency interchange via Smart contracts.
- Agora is a BIS-led project that integrates central banks and private firms to tokenize Cross-border payments using a unified ledger and Smart contracts.
- Other projects like Project Jura, Mariana, and Tourbillon explore Privacy, FX risk mitigation, and DeFi integration across Europe, Asia, and Africa.

In previous chapters, we have predominantly discussed the implications of introducing CBDCs within individual countries. However, the introduction of CBDCs has the potential to significantly disrupt global payment systems and, by extension, the global economic world order. While systems for currency conversions and payments across different jurisdictions have facilitated global trade for centuries, the rapid interlinking of trade and commerce in the wake of globalization has vastly increased the scale and volume of Cross-border payments. In recent decades, technology-enabled

---

The contributions of Abhi Das and Suudarshan Vaidhya to this chapter is gratefully acknowledged.

© The Author(s), under exclusive license to Springer Nature Switzerland AG 2025
M. Mobius et al., *The Digital Currency Revolution*,
https://doi.org/10.1007/978-3-032-02819-8_8

innovations have primarily shifted Cross-border payments into the realm of electronic transfers. With recent breakthroughs in Blockchain-based technologies and artificial intelligence, we are poised for a dramatic restructuring of the pipelines that allow institutional and Retail payments to keep flowing across the world.

Traditionally, transferring funds across national borders and currencies is an expensive, time-consuming, and highly bureaucratic process. Layers of regulatory complexity and the lack of interoperability between domestic systems create added hurdles toward the seamless transfer of funds. Interestingly, these hurdles were not limited to individuals or small businesses seeking to transfer funds across borders—they applied to well-resourced institutions as well (e.g., central banks, global banks, etc.). The recent advances in domestic payment systems in developed as well as developing countries throw the rather clunky nature of the current cross-border payment systems into sharper relief.

As the dust settled on a reordered global landscape following World War II, the focus shifted toward advancing economic interconnectedness and progress at a global scale. This includes the introduction of the SWIFT (Society for Worldwide Interbank Financial Telecommunication) messaging system, which has become a key player in coordinating and facilitating institutional Cross-border payments by serving as a dedicated platform to assign institutional codes and secure messaging for transactions. In the 1990s, a unique combination of geopolitical events, technology-driven innovations (e.g., the Internet and personal computing), and the liberalization of economic markets in developing countries provided impetus to the adoption of systems for Cross-border payments. In 1998, SWIFT established a new model to facilitate cross-border transactions, known as "correspondent banking." Put, correspondent banking involves a financial institution that acts as a "correspondent bank" and provides banking services to other banks, often across international borders, facilitating Cross-border payments and international trade. It is a crucial part of the global financial system, enabling domestic banks to access international markets without setting up physical branches. SWIFT's model has experienced high adoption over the past year, and it remains a key player in the global financial system. As recently as 2018, around half of the world's high-value transactions were conducted through SWIFT. That said, SWIFT is not the only player in the field.

A key feature of CBDC is its geographic nature, as it distinguishes between domestic and cross-border applications. Cutting across Retail and Wholesale types, they can be used domestically or for international purposes. One of the main reasons why CBDCs have been gaining immense traction is their cross-border application, as they provide key solutions to current issues in the globalized financial system. There are several aspects to international exchanges in the financial system, along both political and economic lines. For example, as conflicts abound with increasing regularity, economic tools are being weaponized. Phenomena such as economic sanctions and trade wars involve currency as a primary mechanism. CBDC can help navigate this volatile geopolitical landscape to insulate a country from such shocks. There are also benefits to boosting the functioning of foreign exchange markets and global transactions. Therefore, some important cross-border CBDC projects will be discussed in the following sections, providing insights into the current and emerging dynamics of the evolving subject of CBDCs.

8.1 CBDC Effects on Financial Stability and Subsequent Effects on Currency Valuation

As central banks around the world continue to explore CBDCs and observe the potential advantages and disadvantages of the new technology, it is important to consider macroeconomic implications from both domestic and international perspectives. Specifically, existing research on CBDCs suggests notable effects on a country's financial stability, as well as the global foreign exchange market. While CBDCs are not yet widespread, full CBDC launches in certain nations, pilot CBDCs in others, and economic modeling provide valuable insights into the potential ramifications of a more widespread adoption of CBDCs.

The current understanding of CBDCs suggests that the implementation of such a digital currency could pose a threat to financial stability. Primarily, CBDCs risk amplifying the financial instability linked to bank runs. As depositors rush to withdraw their deposits, the high withdrawal times and switching costs associated with switching to physical cash can sometimes mitigate instability. While CBDCs are touted for their speed of transaction and reduced costs, in the event of a bank run, these very characteristics could be those that worsen the crisis. A weakly regulated CBDC launch could also lead to "digital runs," wherein a drastic shift away from commercial banks and toward CBDC would engender severe financial instability.

Furthermore, a movement toward CBDCs could lead to bank Disintermediation. With CBDCs entering the financial market, more consumers might hold savings in CBDCs rather than in traditional bank accounts. This decrease in deposits leads to a heightened reliance on Wholesale funding for banks, and therefore, a general increase in lending rates. The relative lack of deposits to finance loans results in illiquidity. As such, consumers and businesses would be less likely to borrow from banks, reducing the role of banks in the economy as a whole.

However, CBDCs also demonstrate the potential to have a positive effect on financial stability. CBDCs are highly liquid because they serve as a form of Legal tender, offering immediate purchasing power. The resulting enhanced speed of transactions that come with such liquidity could allow for more efficient payments in both Wholesale and Retail. Such an increase in transaction efficiency could lead to greater market efficiency and financial stability.

CBDCs show particularly high potential for increasing liquidity access in underserved markets. A primary reason for the recent surge in CBDC research and development is the perceived opportunity to increase financial access for unbanked and underbanked communities. Many emerging markets feature large segments of the population without access to traditional financial services, oftentimes found in rural areas of the country. For instance, over 51% of Mexico's population is unbanked. In such cases, CBDCs can afford these segments of the population access to readily available money, which can be transferred at relatively low costs when compared with the informal money services that many such communities rely on. CBDCs can also expand access to credit systems for unbanked citizens. As such, the velocity of money in these communities could increase, further integrating them into the country's broader financial fabric and allowing for a greater flow of funds throughout the economy as a whole. Such a dynamic may significantly boost financial stability in a given country.

The aforementioned potential effects on financial stability posed by the adoption of CBDCs would have a direct impact on a given country's currency valuation. Namely, if CBDCs accentuate financial instability, a given country could experience a depreciation in its currency's value. For instance, a decrease in bank funding following the launch of a new CBDC could heighten financial instability, making potential foreign investors more wary of the risks associated with such a market. A decrease in foreign investment reduces demand for the currency, leading to its depreciation. Inevitably, this would hurt a given country's global financial standing. Conversely, an overall increase in financial stability would likely lead to an appreciation of a given country's currency. Considering the potential implications for financial stability and currency valuation resulting from the adoption of a CBDC, this offers important insight into the reasons why certain countries may be apprehensive about launching a CBDC, despite extensive investments in CBDC research in recent years.

Case studies of countries in which CBDCs have been launched or piloted may help provide a better understanding of the potential impacts of CBDCs on financial stability and currency valuation. Zimbabwe's ZiG, for instance, was launched in April 2024 to curb inflation and restore confidence in the national currency. However, initial observations have shown the launch to be unsuccessful, as a lack of public trust in the ZiG and failure to institutionalize the new currency have only raised inflation rates in the months since the ZiG's launch. At the same time, the ZiG faced severe depreciation relative to the United States dollar. While Zimbabwe has attempted to mitigate these effects by designating ZiG as Legal tender, increasing regulation, and requiring businesses to pay a portion of their taxes in ZiG, the country offers an important example of the risks associated with a CBDC launch, which can decrease financial stability and currency valuation (Fig. 8.1).

Nigeria's e-Naira presents another example of a CBDC launch with limited success. Launched in 2021, the e-naira was promoted by the Central Bank of Nigeria to offer a promise to improve nationwide Financial inclusion. Similar to the case of Zimbabwe, Nigeria also sought to strengthen its currency, particularly in comparison with the U.S. dollar. Despite a phased rollout to ensure integration into the financial system, which would limit negative effects on financial stability, a poor understanding of the new technology rendered many e-Naira wallets inactive. As such, the central bank's hopes for

Fig. 8.1 U.S. Dollar (USD) to Nigerian Naira (NGN) exchange rate, 2021–25 (*Source* Google Finance [https://g.co/finance/USD-NGN?window=5Y]; Accessed June 2025)

the e-Naira's launch to lead to widespread adoption and stabilization of the currency were not realized. Instead, inflation has risen each year since the e-Naira's launch, while the Naira has depreciated against the dollar each year since 2021 (Fig. 8.2).

India, meanwhile, piloted a Wholesale CBDC program in November of 2022, followed by the adoption of a Retail CBDC pilot in December of 2022. The Reserve Bank of India (RBI) met its daily Retail CBDC transaction goal by December of 2023 while also seeing a significant increase in Retail usage from 2023 to 2024. Since the pilot launch, inflation has cooled each year and is projected to stabilize at 4% through 2030. Additionally, the rupee generally maintained its value against the U.S. dollar. The case of India thus demonstrates promise for CBDCs in positively affecting financial stability and currency valuation. However, it is worth noting that the RBI reported only 400,000 active e-rupee users as of July 2024, a minuscule portion of India's population of 1.4 billion. It is not easy to measure the e-rupee pilot's true impact on financial stability and currency valuation.

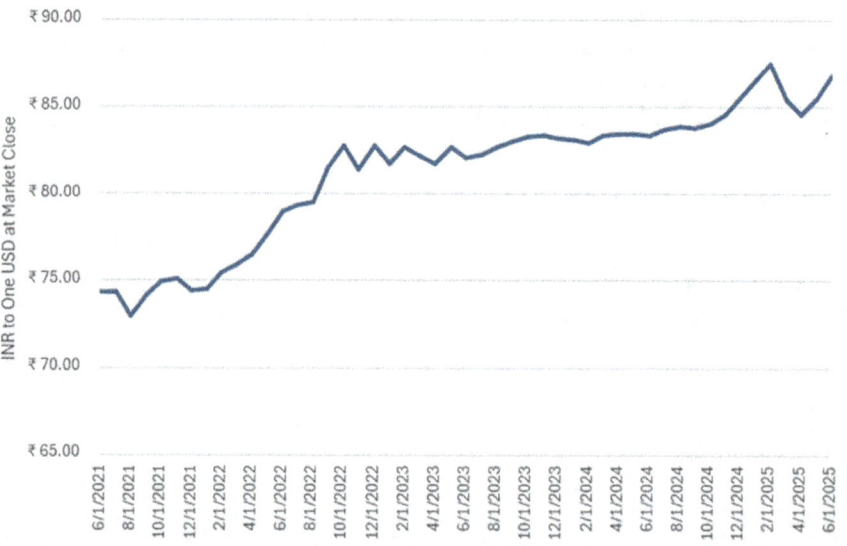

Fig. 8.2 U.S. Dollar (USD) to Indian Rupee (INR) exchange rate, 2021–25 (*Source* Google Finance [https://g.co/finance/USD-INR?window=5Y]; Accessed June 2025)

8.2 Impacts on Forex

The emergence of CBDCs has great potential to reshape the foreign exchange (FX) market and, subsequently, the global financial landscape as a whole. As more and more central banks explore the idea of implementing CBDCs, questions will undoubtedly arise about how they will influence exchange rate dynamics, Cross-border payments, and the dominance of existing reserve currencies. By enabling faster, cheaper, and more transparent transactions, CBDCs have the potential to reduce reliance on traditional FX intermediaries and alter capital flows between nations.

The current foreign exchange market is characterized as risky and inefficient, with an estimated one in three foreign exchange settlements occurring without adequate risk mitigation. Since settlement is commonly subject to delays and takes an average of at least two days to execute, banks mitigate risk using payment-versus-payment mechanisms in order to ensure that money is only exchanged once both parties fulfill their obligations. However, this requires banks to hold large amounts of capital to meet their liquidity coverage ratios, which comes with a significant opportunity cost.

With the emergence of CBDCs, there is potential for an entirely new approach to settlement, where transactions can be settled instantaneously, and both sides of the transaction either succeed or fail. This last part means that the positions of each bank will always be balanced, as one side's transaction funds the other side's, completely eliminating settlement risk and resulting in significant capital savings—possibly one of the greatest sources of cost reduction for banks. This development has the potential to create entirely new market dynamics by introducing more efficiency and potentially increasing competition in the market as the transaction costs and barriers to entry decrease.

Similarly, faster settlement would remove the delays that currently reduce the profitability of arbitrage between currency markets. Arbitrage is the act of buying something in one market and then selling it in another in order to make a profit via the price difference. This is often limited by things like settlement delays and high transaction costs mentioned previously, which means that with the adoption of CBDCs, it would be much easier for traders to take advantage of the temporary price gaps between different currencies and markets. For example, if the digital euro and the digital dollar have slightly different rates on two different exchanges, a trader could arbitrage without having to worry about the long delays and high fees eating away part of the profit. Additionally, CBDCs would enable 24/7 trading and increased transparency, making markets more accessible to smaller players and allowing for new forms of arbitrage, such as cross-border and time-zone-based strategies.

CBDCs also make possible entirely new trading opportunities by transforming how currencies are used and exchanged, such as the potential for live, around-the-clock trading. Traditional currencies often rely on banks, which have limited operating hours. However, CBDCs bypass this issue and can be exchanged directly at any time of day, allowing for continuous global trading. This would enable traders to react to news and market events instantly, rather than having to wait for markets to open. Moreover, since CBDCs are programmable, they could include built-in features such as expiration dates, spending restrictions, or interest rates, which would open doors to new types of trades. For example, one could speculate on how different CBDC policies affect currency values or design strategies around how programmable rules influence demand. Overall, CBDCs have the potential to fundamentally reshape the foreign exchange market and unlock many avenues previously considered unimaginable.

8.3 Project mBridge

Project mBridge is the most significant project for cross-border CBDCs as of date. It comprises a unique combination of a multilateral financial institution and central banks from multiple countries. The players involved are the Bank for International Settlements (BIS) and the monetary authorities of China, Hong Kong, Thailand, Saudi Arabia, and the UAE. It is aimed at a Wholesale CBDC use case, with the target of facilitating better cross-border transfers and foreign exchange interactions through direct international bank linkages. Initially, an Ethereum-based Blockchain was utilized, but later, a shift was made to the Dashing Blockchain consensus protocol developed by the People's Bank of China. The MVP stage was reached in 2024 with the next steps of private-sector consultation for applications and solutions. However, in October 2024, the BIS exited the project, with the central banks assuming the role of the main stakeholders.

In recent times, the issues with mBridge have not concerned its economic feasibility or technical aspects but rather with geopolitical considerations. The idea of mBridge being used to bypass sanctions created by Western nations was a crucial notion perceived by many to be the reason for BIS' recent withdrawal from the project. There are two dimensions associated with mBridge: one is that it serves as a vehicle for BRICS countries to establish a separate sphere of influence, and secondly, to enhance the prominence of the Chinese

8 Cross-Border CBDCs: mBridge, Agora, and the Others

yuan relative to the U.S. dollar. Now that the project is led by China, with all the countries in mBridge being members of BRICS except Thailand, there are interesting future pathways to be contemplated. The main concept is to move away from the SWIFT system, backed by the United States, due to its power in executing sanctions and freezing assets.

Project mBridge solves some key nuances of Cross-border payments. Firstly, correspondent banking networks are necessary to facilitate transactions between entities from different nations. Especially in less developed countries, the number of intermediary banks increases, leading to a multiplication of fees and time for compliance procedures. Further, the dimension of currency also adds up due to steep conversion costs for non-USD currencies.

Therefore, it is crucial to understand that there are genuine pain points that mBridge addresses, and these should not be overlooked so that political apprehensions can be allayed. In the project's infrastructure, each central bank has power over consensus and data in the permissioned DLT through Smart contracts, therefore preventing singular interests from taking hold. Some initiatives that are in process include the concept of zero-knowledge proofs, which will enhance interoperability. Moreover, the target with respect to currency systems is to reduce the costs of foreign exchange by interchange of local currencies, without any preference toward a particular one, which can enable advantages for commercial banks.

Some competition to mBridge should be taken into consideration. The utility of Stablecoins for cross-border purposes is also a strong alternative, as private companies respond better to commercial interests than the bureaucratic monetary authorities of several countries coming together. Furthermore, recent political developments with the latest election in the United States have complicated matters, with the current regime adopting a strong nationalist stance in favor of America and the U.S. dollar. Strong opposition has been displayed to any posturing regarding alternative methods to the U.S.-led system. For example, a comment by a member of the U.S. Fed in January 2025 mentioned that "trade with the United States and Europe will have to be through a common platform that we use," and the presidential remark regarding 100% tariffs if countries plan to implement strategies diverging from the U.S. dollar, is well known. However, it is expected that mBridge will persist and progress due to the very real advantages it possesses. According to Daleep Singh, the deputy NSA at the White House, said of mBridge, "It is faster, cheaper, and less frustrating if you want to move money across borders than using the legacy dollar-based architecture."

The future path of mBridge is contingent on the path its participants aim for and the responses of Western policy. According to Lu Lei, the deputy governor of the PBOC, the project should focus on social good by targeting operations such as cross-border remittances and e-commerce, which banks face complexities and lower profits, and therefore tend to be undersupplied. However, changing alliances are inevitable, as relationships with ASEAN and BRI (Belt and Road Initiative) countries are to be strengthened in mBridge due to their "close trade ties and relatively stable geopolitical conditions." There are alternatives that are gaining favor as well, with the idea of IPS (Instant Payment Systems) receiving a positive view from 47% of central banks, compared to only 13% who perceive CBDC networks as the best approach, according to the OMFIF Future of Payments 2024 survey. For example, Project Nexus was recently tested by five Southeast Asian countries for cross-border transactions. The success of Project mBridge will increasingly depend on the dynamics of multilateral governance and cooperation. Steady wins in implementation can drive the project forward, with current account exchanges of smaller ticket sizes for demand-side components, such as travel, trade, and others, having strong potential.

8.4 Project Digital Euro

The Digital Euro project is a flagship initiative of European countries, with the ECB establishing the project in July 2021. It is aimed at both Wholesale and Retail CBDC use cases from a cross-border perspective. It is currently in the preparation phase, scheduled for a two-year duration starting in November 2023. There is a dual-purpose ambition behind the plan for the digital euro: firstly, to achieve a position of "strategic autonomy" by reducing reliance on non-European financial firms, and secondly, to pursue innovation and technical advances, an area in which Europe is still largely seen as a laggard.

It has been shown that 13 countries in Europe are required to use only international card schemes and mobile payment solutions for Retail payments, which negatively affects their monetary sovereignty. The motivating needs are multiple, with geopolitical turbulence, the absence of scale for European providers, higher costs in terms of fees and data, and the current U.S. administration's resurgent push for crypto and Stablecoins. This has called for Europe to embark on its most ambitious public–private partnership yet. The progress has been substantial, with the formulation of the digital euro rulebook for a unified set of legal standards and planning of the digital euro holding limit based on Monetary policy, financial stability, and usability.

8 Cross-Border CBDCs: mBridge, Agora, and the Others

The importance of innovation has also been recognized. Last week, the ECB announced a partnership with around 70 private-sector companies in the financial domain with an innovation platform for the digital euro. There are two streams—"pioneer" and "visionary" partnerships. The former is for testing conditional payments (payments based on certain conditions) on a simulation of technical infrastructure. In contrast, the latter pertains to theoretical explorations of innovative use cases for society and the community. Further, significant dimensions of offline access, Privacy, and pan-European solutions are being explored.

It should be realized that the digital euro as a cross-border CBDC offers certain benefits that alternatives like Stablecoins may not address, political aspects notwithstanding. Stablecoins sometimes suffer from having greater sensitivity to information due to a lack of substantial regulation, leading to large deviations from their underlying currency. They would mainly be based on the sentiment between users and providers, which can result in runs akin to the historical phenomenon of treasury-backed currency issued by private banks. The deposit function of banks would also be affected due to greater competition for maintaining liquidity, resulting in higher funding costs for banks and an undersupply of credit. Hence, compared to Stablecoins, the digital euro offers better capabilities for unifying Europe's payment systems with positive effects for networked collaboration, varied use cases, and performance gains. For instance, the ECB has adopted a strategy of maintaining limits to counter deposit outflows. It has been shown that with a loose limit of 5000 euros, the overnight deposit outflow for households would not exceed 12%. Methods such as "waterfall" and "reverse waterfall" would also be employed to ensure that the limit would not hinder payment mechanisms.

Some challenges do remain for the digital euro. For example, the ECB has decided not to implement the feature of programmability at present, which has been used in other countries by designating usage for cross-border instruments. Only the feature of recurrence or automation can be used for payments without any predefined purposes. Moreover, there could be centralized points of failure, either due to technological issues or political misadventures or corruption. Europe also has its cultural legacies around Privacy and citizen autonomy to consider, as there have been policy moves to remove end-to-end encryption and impose cash limits. A crucial aspect pertains to the question of which entities will have control over frameworks that apply at a pan-European level in the cross-border context. For example, would the ECB, the member countries, or the banks themselves decide on regulations, operations, and decisions? This is because the proportion of effects and costs would vary across these stakeholders, which necessitates an equitable distribution of power.

The digital euro represents a key milestone in assessing the future of cross-border CBDC. This is because, fundamentally, although Europe is integrated in terms of a common currency (the euro), there is no integrated digital payments or CBDC solution so far for the continent. There have been some initial successes for specific nations, such as the Bizum wallet in Spain and iDEAL in the Netherlands, but the expansion of these initiatives has not been significant. Therefore, the creation of a CBDC system that spans the borders of 20 member nations having interlinked economies could prove to be a game changer. Some concerns will need to be addressed, as a seven-hour blackout at the ECB a few months prior led to questions from multiple groups in the European Parliament regarding the requisite preparedness and operational capabilities. Done right, the digital euro can be a strong global contender in cross-border CBDC and a boon for Europe to regain a robust geo-economic footing in the world.

8.5 Project Agora

Project Agora was launched by the BIS in April 2024, in partnership with France (representing Europe), the United States, Switzerland, Japan, Korea, Mexico, and the UK. The objective is to develop a Wholesale application that tokenizes Cross-border payments through an integrated and programmable infrastructure connecting various central banks and commercial financial institutions. It also began the involvement of private-sector firms, brought together under the Institute of International Finance (IIF), in May 2024. A key strength of the project is its synergy between the private and public sectors, with the participation of prominent companies such as JP Morgan and Mastercard. This will allow for the development of innovative use cases by private players on top of ensuring the smooth working of the global financial system with public stakeholders.

The project aims to enhance the global monetary landscape by tokenizing central bank money and bank deposits, featuring dual capabilities of programmability and Smart contracts. The two-tier system of the central bank and commercial banks will be maintained, but the common financial platform will be through a public–private collaboration. This will enable new ideas for settlements and exchanges through the combination of Tokenization and Blockchain technology. It aims to address core inefficiencies that plague

Cross-border payments, including differing technological and legal standards, as well as the complexity of financial control procedures.

A key concept underlying the project is Tokenization. It refers to the process of creating a digital representation of a physical, intangible, or financial asset, usually on Blockchain. This allows better performance and operations to be done on the asset, which is not possible without Tokenization, as it combines the functions of data recording and transfer logic. The integration of the current system, which is heavily fragmented across legacy technology systems and market processes, along with a tokenized nature of assets, offers the potential for faster operations, greater transparency, and better financial infrastructure. According to the World Economic Forum, Tokenization can lead to annual cost savings of around $15 billion in operations of global infrastructure and liberation of financial institutions' capital worth more than $100 billion per year. By tokenizing bank deposits and central bank money, Project Agora aims to simplify frictions in Wholesale cross-border flows through efficient and secure transfers on the common Blockchain platform with embedded functionalities. It also solves many incentive problems that arise in contracting, for example, moral hazard and adverse selection, as Tokenization clearly determines the purposes of monetary flows in the system.

The second concept that is linked to the one above is the **unified ledger** concept. Most projects have occurred in a siloed manner without the cornerstone of trust, i.e., central bank money. The unified ledger is a new method of infrastructure for a financial market in which all three—tokenized assets, deposits, and central bank money—are present. The premise rests on the fact that emerging Web 3.0 capabilities, such as Tokenization, Smart contracts, and programmability, may not have a long life without an anchor of trust and leadership at the helm of a two-tier system, which the central bank represents. Due to different databases, requirements for separate messaging and reconciliation, and settlement risks in cross-border transactions, there is much scope for enhancement. The combination of a unified ledger and Tokenization provides a crucial advantage—the "settlement finality" that arises from the presence of central bank money alongside other claims. Furthermore, the bundling of transactions through composability, executed via automation in real-time, enhances functionality. There can be a second level in the manner of multiple unified ledgers, with each ledger serving a specific application like bonds, trade, and so on, and interoperability between ledgers can be ensured through application programming interfaces (APIs). From a cross-border perspective, it is key to enable governance and unification across countries with different regulations and private payment service providers (PSPs).

Some characteristics of the project are paramount in addressing present and future concerns pertaining to Cross-border payments. The design of an open architecture allows for flexibility, accounting for factors like multiple time zones and country-specific scenarios. Another aspect is the separation of Wholesale CBDC and tokenized deposits in the unified ledger, with their relationship managed by Smart contracts. This approach enables complementarity by maintaining the singleness of money, credit, and liquidity. However, these technical advantages have led to contested notions of the project's definition. For example, due to the US' opposed position against CBDC, Christopher Waller, the governor of the Fed, commented in February 2025 on Project Agora, of which the New York Innovation Center is a participant: "That project is really not about creating a Wholesale CBDC. It is like taking bank reserves that we have now, and how can you trade these on a platform to cut out intermediate steps and make the correspondent banking system more efficient? We are not trying to replace anything." This introduces a fundamental clash in the conceptualization of whether cross-border Wholesale CBDC is merely a technological improvement or a reimagining of the monetary paradigm altogether.

Project Agora is the most complex and largest cross-border CBDC project undertaken by the BIS to date, due to its large number of participants and the diversity of represented geographies. It is significant for its forward-looking orientation on revamping existing compliance processes and redesigning financial infrastructure. By building on key technology features with the monetary authorities of advanced economies and diverse companies as stakeholders, there is immense potential for solving the most pressing issues in global finance. It remains to be seen whether this will be delivered upon in the face of changing headwinds in foreign policy and international trade.

8.6 Other Projects

Several other cross-border CBDC projects are currently underway in various parts of the world. There is a dual contrast in their nature of advancement, with many projects in the research or pilot stage, but at the same time, a sizable number of projects are inactive as well. It is interesting to note that developed countries have formulated many projects. They are targeted at both Wholesale and Retail CBDC, contrary to the common notion that Retail cross-border use cases may not be as relevant for advanced economies. Some examples include Project Jura, which involves France and Switzerland, Project Polaris in the Nordics, and the Venus Initiative, among others. A large number of projects are in the research stage in Africa, whereas Eurasian countries have progressed in large numbers to the pilot stage. It is important to understand that many projects delve into specific dimensions of cross-border CBDC. For example, Project Mariana, by France, Switzerland, Singapore, and the BIS, involved using Blockchain and decentralized finance technology with Automated Market Makers (AMMs), showing that foreign exchange market risks could be mitigated. Another instance is Project Tourbillon, which addressed features of Privacy and cyber resilience, demonstrating that payer anonymity could combat crime while also ensuring user security. Some projects utilize private-sector firepower, with Project Helvetia studying the feasibility of Wholesale CBDC on the digital platform of SIX Group, a financial center infrastructure company.

Therefore, there are rapid developments on multiple fronts of cross-border CBDC. The advancements and potential future directions of these various projects should be carefully contemplated, as they provide impetus for the global evolution of how cross-border CBDCs shall be formulated, analyzed, and implemented.

8.7 Will the Cross-Border CBDCs Work?

This chapter has explored the concept of CBDC and the most important dimension of its application—the cross-border aspect. It is worth noting that many such projects were completed in 2023 or 2024. By delving deep into a variety of projects across different motivations and targets, several interesting solutions on how cross-border CBDC can transform the ways of working of the global financial system for both consumers and financial institutions have been looked at. This is particularly pertinent at a time when fragmentation is becoming increasingly prominent in the world, yet high levels of financial integration have made the refinement of cross-border interactions imperative. The amount of variation in the focus of the projects discussed is relevant, for it gives insights into how considerations of a multifaceted nature—ranging from geopolitical need to technological advancement—can drive enhancements in an area that is a direct consequence of heavy financialization and globalization. The magnitude of specificity in certain projects is unique, and this can be seen as a reflection of contextual requirements stemming from each group's developmental and structural characteristics. As cross-border CBDCs progress with more ambitious plans to unify various countries' financial interactions comprehensively, it remains to be seen whether the evolving contours of global conflict will affect this progress. However, one thing is clear—the performance benefits from advancing new amalgamations of technology and finance will take the world to unexplored horizons.

9

Stablecoins: An Alternative to CBDCs

Main Messages

- Stablecoins have emerged as a transformative force in global finance, offering price stability, cross-border efficiency, and a viable alternative to volatile cryptocurrencies and legacy payment systems.
- Their rapid adoption has prompted both innovation and concern, with regulators exploring CBDCs to preserve monetary sovereignty and address associated risks.
- The broader crypto ecosystem is evolving rapidly, with key players like Tether and Circle, while the SEC adapts its regulatory approach to asset Tokenization and decentralized finance.

The digitization of money has emerged as a defining theme in the evolution of the global financial systems over the last two decades. Anchored by a new group of alternative financial services companies, their technological advances are redefining how value is stored, transferred, and recorded. Stablecoins, a novel form of digital currency, have emerged as one of the most consequential innovations in this shift in global payments. Designed

---

The contribution of Abubakar Idris, MBA student and EMI fellow at Cornell University is gratefully acknowledged as well as Carlos Bernós Amorós.

to minimize volatility by pegging their value to real-world assets, Stablecoins combine the programmability of crypto-assets with the familiarity and stability of fiat money.

Over the last five years, Stablecoin adoption has accelerated dramatically, evolving from a trading-specific tool into a foundational mechanism for digital value transfer. Today, Stablecoins facilitate trillions of dollars in both human-initiated and automated transactions annually, increasingly rivaling traditional banking and payments infrastructure in scale, speed, and accessibility. However, as Stablecoins gain global appeal, central bank authorities worldwide are examining their risks to the financial system and the long-term implications, particularly their impact on sovereign control over monetary systems in an increasingly borderless digital world. In response, many central banks are developing Central Bank Digital Currencies (CBDCs) to preserve monetary sovereignty and modernize public payment systems. However, to be effective, CBDCs must appreciate the multiple value propositions of Stablecoins. In this article, we will explore the emergence of Stablecoins and their role as a powerful force in the global financial system.

9.1 What Are Stablecoins?

A stablecoin is a digital token built on a blockchain that is designed to maintain a stable value by being pegged to a real-world asset, such as the U.S. dollar, gold, or other commodities and currencies. There are different types of Stablecoins, with the most common being fully reserved, collateralized, and algorithmic models.

Fully reserved Stablecoins are digital assets pegged to fiat currencies like the U.S. dollar or commodities such as gold, and are backed 1:1 by equivalent reserves. The most traded Stablecoin in the crypto industry today is Tether (USDT), which is pegged to the U.S. dollar. In theory, one USDT equals one U.S. dollar. However, since Stablecoins are actively traded on exchanges, a loss of trust in the issuer could lead users to sell their holdings below $1 to avoid further losses—a phenomenon known as depegging.

Another prominent fully reserved Stablecoin is USD Coin (USDC), issued by Circle, a U.S.-based company known for its regulatory compliance and transparency, including regular audits of its reserves. In March 2023, Silicon Valley Bank (SVB) collapsed, and since Circle had deposits with SVB, USDC temporarily lost its peg. Although Circle later confirmed its reserves were safe and restored the peg, the incident highlighted the importance of trust and transparency between a Stablecoin and its issuer.

Notably, episodes of depegging have occurred with other stablecoins as well—regardless of the type of collateral or asset backing. This reflects a broader risk tied not just to market conditions, but to the issuer's credibility, operational risk, and reserve management. Maintaining the peg ultimately depends on users' confidence in the issuer's ability to honor redemptions at par value, particularly during periods of market stress.

Crypto-collateralized Stablecoins follow a different model. Instead of holding fiat assets, these Stablecoins are backed by other cryptocurrencies, with the collateral locked in Smart contracts on the Blockchain. A well-known example is DAI, issued by the MakerDAO protocol. To mint DAI, users must overcollateralize their positions by depositing crypto-assets like Ether (ETH) into a smart contract. This mechanism helps maintain DAI's peg to the U.S. dollar, even if the underlying collateral is volatile. Unlike fully reserved Stablecoins, these models rely on decentralized protocols rather than a centralized issuer, which introduces a different risk profile but enhances transparency and censorship resistance.

Finally, algorithmic Stablecoins attempt to maintain their peg without being backed by fiat or crypto reserves. Instead, they use algorithms and incentive mechanisms to expand or contract supply in response to market demand—much like a central bank manages monetary supply. The most infamous example is TerraUSD (UST), developed on the Terra Blockchain. UST relied on its sister token, LUNA, to maintain its peg. However, in May 2022, a sharp decline in the price of Bitcoin triggered a wave of redemptions, destabilizing the peg. UST collapsed from $1 to nearly zero within days, wiping out over $40 billion in market value and shaking trust in algorithmic Stablecoins.

In summary, Stablecoins have evolved into critical infrastructure for the digital economy, enabling stable value transfer in volatile markets. Each model—fully reserved, crypto-collateralized, and algorithmic—comes with its own trade-offs in terms of stability, transparency, decentralization, and risk. Understanding these differences is essential for users, developers, and regulators as the role of Stablecoins continues to grow in global finance.

The first Stablecoin, BitUSD, was launched in 2014 on the BitShares Blockchain. Since then, many companies—including major financial firms like PayPal—have entered the Stablecoin space with their own tokens. However, over the last decade, two fiat-collateralized Stablecoins have emerged as dominant in terms of market capitalization and usage: Tether (USDT), issued by iFinex, a Hong Kong-based company incorporated in the

British Virgin Islands, and USD Coin (USDC), issued by Circle, a U.S.-based company that launched the Stablecoin in partnership with Coinbase under the Centre consortium.

Stablecoins were initially developed to support Cryptocurrency adoption by enabling global payments with minimal volatility—a major limitation of early digital assets like Bitcoin and Ether. Over time, their use cases have expanded to include remittances, trading, decentralized finance (DeFi), and on-chain settlements.

By 2024, Stablecoin usage had grown significantly. According to Visa, human-initiated Stablecoin transactions—often referred to as adjusted transaction volume—reached $5.67 trillion, up from $560 billion in 2020. When including all activity, such as automated transactions via Smart contracts and bots, the total value transferred by Stablecoins reached nearly $28 trillion in 2024—exceeding the combined annual transaction volume of Visa ($15.9 trillion) and Mastercard ($9.8 trillion).

As transaction volumes surged, the total market capitalization of Stablecoins also grew. In 2020, the Stablecoin market was valued at around $14 billion; by May 2025, it had grown to approximately $250 billion, according to data from CoinMarketCap and the Bank for International Settlements (BIS). This valuation is roughly equivalent to the combined market capitalizations of Citigroup, U.S. Bancorp, and Truist Financial Corporation—three of the top ten U.S. banks by market value. A recent report from Citi projects that the total market capitalization of Stablecoins could exceed $1.6 trillion within the next five years.

9.2 Use Cases of Stablecoin and Key Growth Drivers

Stablecoins have become one of the most important forms of digital currencies and are increasingly gaining users worldwide, with over 250 million active, unique crypto wallets sending and receiving fund transfers. As adoption surges in the global financial system, market participants need to understand why these tokens are becoming popular.

Globally, there are a few key use cases of Stablecoin. Inherently, the reliance on real-world assets such as U.S. government treasury bills and gold has bolstered confidence in Stablecoins and quelled concerns about the health of their underlying assets. However, there are other reasons propelling the growth of these tokens, including that they serve as an accessible hedge against devaluation in emerging markets and facilitate faster cross-border transactions, among others, which we will discuss below.

Serves as a Buffer in Economies with Monetary Instability and inflation: As discussed in our case studies in previous chapters, one crucial use case for Stablecoins over the last decade is to mitigate the impact of monetary instability in countries of the global south. Developing and emerging economies, such as Argentina, Nigeria, and Turkey, tend to experience frequent macroeconomic shocks that trigger higher inflation and erode the value of their local currencies due to devaluation.

Nevertheless, as the Internet becomes ubiquitous in these locations and Cryptocurrency trading platforms expand globally, it has increased access to financial services for millions of the world's financially excluded demographics. Now, in the absence of stable macroeconomic conditions or trusted banking infrastructure, a growing number of people in emerging markets are increasingly adopting USD-pegged Stablecoins to make payment transactions and hedge against further decline in their local currency's value.

Utilization for Remittances and Cross-border payments: Stablecoins reduce frictions associated with traditional remittance systems. For example, the average (global) cost of sending $200 across borders hovers around 6.35% of the transfer value, a figure that can be much higher in certain emerging markets, according to Coinbase. However, with Stablecoins, these transactions are faster and cheaper, with fees between 0.5 and 3%, compared to alternatives such as Western Union or even Bitcoin. Migrant workers, freelancers, and small exporters increasingly rely on USD-based Stablecoins to efficiently send money to family members in their home countries.

Beyond remittances, Stablecoins also facilitate faster payments for a wide range of cross-border transactions, including business-to-business transfers. With fiat currency, Cross-border payments are handled by the Society for Worldwide Interbank Financial Telecommunication, called SWIFT, a global messaging system that helps over 11,000 international banks and financial institutions communicate with one another to authorize fund transfers within minutes.

However, correspondence banking relationships are significantly limited outside developed economies, and transactions tend to focus on liquid currencies. This means that fund transfers from a U.S. business to suppliers in West African countries, such as Ghana, can be painfully slow and expensive. Stablecoins solve this problem for businesses in emerging markets.

Increased Interoperability Across the Crypto Ecosystem: The familiar user experience of Stablecoins has made it an accessible entry point for Cryptocurrency participants who are unfamiliar with the complicated digital currency universe. Stablecoins serve as a crucial on-ramp to help people convert their fiat currencies into digital assets, after which they can trade over 11,000 cryptocurrencies. When users want to take money out of the crypto ecosystem and convert it in fiat currency, also called an off-ramp, Stablecoins provide a faster liquidity solution, especially during times of volatility. As of May 2025, around 90% of daily Cryptocurrency trading volume is driven by Stablecoin activity, including automated or algorithmic transactions.

Growing Regulatory Clarity and Integration by Traditional Financial Services Companies: As the adoption of Stablecoin, which mirrors fiat money more closely than Bitcoin, increases, governments are paying attention and have issued a slew of working papers to influence policymaking. Financial services regulators in more than two dozen key markets, such as Japan and Switzerland, have implemented Stablecoin regulations over the last few years. In 2023, the European Union adopted the Markets in Crypto-Assets Regulation (MiCA) framework to provide further legal support for cryptocurrencies across member states.

This clarity has bolstered the confidence of traditional companies, such as banks and card payment companies, to develop or signal their willingness to introduce new crypto products. In 2023, PayPal launched its own dollar-backed Stablecoin. In April 2024, Visa partnered with Bridge, a Stripe-owned Cryptocurrency company, to offer Stablecoin-linked Visa cards. As we will discuss in Chapter 12, the United States government has also developed a bipartisan bill called the Guiding and Establishing National Innovation for U.S. Stablecoins Act, or the GENIUS Act, a first-of-its-kind legislation to regulate Stablecoins. As of May 2025, the bill has quickly advanced through the Senate, awaiting a vote in the House of Representatives.

9.3 Challenges for Stablecoins in a CBDC World

Stablecoins' growing adoption is not without several risks. Indeed, the Cryptocurrency sub industry continues to face a myriad of challenges. These include concerns over fraud, debugging, and geopolitics, which could negatively impact its growth. We will discuss these issues below.

Reserve Transparency and Asset Quality: Stablecoin operators are private businesses with a combined market value of over $250 billion as of May 2025. However, as their value grows, there are concerns over a lack of transparency in their practices, including whether these tokens are fully backed by high-quality, liquid reserves. Some issuing companies hold commercial paper, corporate bonds, or other riskier assets, making customer redemption uncertain during a worst-case scenario, such as a financial crisis.

Importantly, despite growing regulatory support, Stablecoins do not have the same level of deposit insurance coverage as banks. As a result, customers could lose all their funds during a crisis, and a run on redemptions could lead to insolvency or a loss of the peg, especially for under-regulated issuers.

Risk of Depegging: Stablecoins are constantly at risk of losing the peg to their reference assets. Market volatility, operational failures, or flawed algorithms can exacerbate the situation and cause a Stablecoin to break its peg to the underlying currency. The collapse of TerraUSD[1] in 2022 remains instructive for the rest of the industry. Meanwhile, peg instability undermines trust and can cause contagion to spread across crypto markets or even affect traditional finance through connected firms.

Regulatory Uncertainty and Fragmentation: Stablecoin regulation remains uneven across jurisdictions, with countries taking divergent approaches to licensing, reserve requirements, and legal classification. While the European Union's MiCA framework provides some clarity, countries such as the United Kingdom still lack comprehensive national legislation, leaving issuers uncertain about whether their products will be treated as payment instruments, securities, or commodities. This lack of regulatory harmonization creates legal risk for issuers and users, impedes cross-border interoperability, and deters institutional adoption.

The resulting fragmentation enables regulatory arbitrage, as issuers gravitate toward jurisdictions with looser oversight. This undermines global efforts to ensure consumer protection and financial stability. Without coordinated international standards, particularly for reserve transparency and redemption rights, Stablecoins may continue to operate in legal gray zones, exposing the financial system to potential misconduct or collapse under stress.

Systemic Risk and Financial Contagion: As Stablecoins become embedded in both crypto and traditional financial systems, their failure poses a growing systemic risk. In decentralized finance (DeFi), Stablecoins serve as core collateral and liquidity instruments; a depegging event can trigger smart contract liquidations cascading through the ecosystem. More broadly, if a large Stablecoin faces a redemption run, issuers may be compelled to liquidate their reserve assets rapidly, disrupting short-term funding markets and potentially spilling over into the traditional economy.

---

[1] TerraUSD (UST) was an algorithmic stablecoin designed to maintain a 1:1 peg to the U.S. dollar, using the LUNA token as a mechanism for price stabilization, part of the broader Terra blockchain ecosystem. Because of a number of allegedly fraudulent transactions by the founders, the UST stablecoin and its sister token, LUNA, collapsed in May 2022, resulting in significant losses for investors.

Regulators are increasingly viewing large Stablecoins as potential systemically important financial institutions. The absence of clear capital requirements, backstops, or coordinated resolution mechanisms means that even credible issuers could destabilize financial markets if confidence collapses. Effective oversight must evolve from sector-specific crypto rules to broader macroprudential frameworks that address this emerging class of monetary instruments.

Concentration and Counterparty Risk: The Stablecoin market is highly concentrated, with Tether and Circle dominating issuance. This centralization introduces counterparty risk: if either issuer mismanages reserves, faces regulatory action, or experiences operational failures, user funds and systemic trust could be jeopardized. Despite their similarities to traditional money instruments, most Stablecoins lack the depositor protections and institutional backstops typically found in the formal banking system. However, the banking system can also go bankrupt as not all the liabilities could be covered.

Further, these issuers rely on a limited number of banks and custodians, amplifying vulnerabilities. The 2023 USDC-Silicon Valley Bank (SVB) incident, when Circle's USDC broke its dollar peg after the firm revealed it had a $3.3 billion exposure to the failing SVB, demonstrated how problems in reserve custody can affect peg stability even when the underlying assets are sound. As adoption grows, regulators may need to impose diversification mandates and enhanced disclosures to mitigate concentrated points of failure.

Exploitation in Illicit Finance: Stablecoins are increasingly used in illicit transactions due to their speed, global reach, and ease of transfer without intermediaries. Criminal networks have leveraged Stablecoins for money laundering, sanctions evasion, and ransomware payments, especially when using non-custodial wallets or decentralized platforms. This undermines AML enforcement and creates significant geopolitical and reputational risk for issuers.

Although some issuers have implemented blacklisting tools or integrated wallet surveillance, enforcement remains uneven and technically difficult across jurisdictions. Without stronger on-chain identity standards and cross-border cooperation, Stablecoins may continue to be a preferred tool for illicit finance, prompting a regulatory backlash that could hinder legitimate use cases.

Over-Reliance on the U.S. Dollar and Geopolitics: Most Stablecoins are pegged to the U.S. dollar, reinforcing the dollar's dominance in global digital finance. While this provides stability and liquidity, it also subjects Stablecoin infrastructure to the geopolitical influence of the United States. Issuers may be compelled to enforce U.S. sanctions or restrict access to users in politically sensitive regions, turning Stablecoins into instruments of financial diplomacy or exclusion.

This reliance also poses risks for monetary sovereignty, especially in emerging markets where Stablecoins may displace local currencies. Governments may resist adoption to preserve control over Monetary policy, while rival powers may accelerate the development of non-dollar CBDCs or local-currency Stablecoins. As Stablecoins scale, their geopolitical implications will become increasingly salient in the design of global digital currency regimes.

9.4 Stablecoins in a CBDC World

The existence and growing adoption of Stablecoins for international payments is posing a dilemma for monetary authorities across the world as they try to grasp this converging shift in the global financial system. As Internet penetration and smartphone adoption become widespread, central bank authorities are looking to modernize and secure their domestic payment systems while preserving the role of the sovereign currency in an increasingly digitized economy. To accomplish this goal, they are turning to CBDCs, which are essentially digital equivalents of their local currencies, as a counterweight to Stablecoins.

Stablecoins, particularly those pegged to the U.S. dollar, have demonstrated the capacity to operate across borders, offering real-time settlement and lower fees compared to traditional correspondent banking systems. This functional efficiency, combined with growing trust in Stablecoin issuers, has led to their increasing use not only in speculative markets but also in practical economic activity such as remittances, cross-border e-commerce, and payroll disbursements in low-trust monetary environments. Consequently, their proliferation is now viewed by many central banks as a challenge to the primacy of sovereign currencies, particularly in smaller economies with weak monetary frameworks or high inflation.

CBDCs are, therefore, positioned not merely as technical upgrades but as strategic instruments to reassert state control over money. By digitizing central bank liabilities and embedding them in modern payment infrastructure, authorities aim to provide a publicly backed digital alternative that maintains user confidence while offering programmability, security, and potential inclusion benefits. However, the policy design of CBDCs often involves trade-offs between Privacy, financial surveillance, and the risk of disintermediating commercial banks—features that Stablecoins, operating under lighter or fragmented regulation, may avoid altogether.

This has created a dual-track trajectory in monetary innovation: one path led by public institutions, emphasizing stability and trust, and another by private issuers, emphasizing speed and flexibility. In many jurisdictions, Stablecoins have reached market maturity faster than CBDCs, particularly in cross-border use cases where central banks face regulatory, technical, and geopolitical barriers. Rather than eliminating Stablecoins, CBDCs may coexist alongside them, with governments focusing on regulation, interoperability, and the use of Stablecoins for certain classes of transactions where private innovation outpaces public infrastructure.

Ultimately, as discussed in Chapter 5, the effectiveness of CBDCs as a counterbalance will depend not only on technical design but also on their ability to replicate the network advantages and user experience that have made Stablecoins attractive. If CBDCs fail to meet user needs in terms of accessibility, Privacy, or transaction cost, Stablecoins may continue to function as de facto global payment instruments. This tension reflects a broader shift in monetary governance, where the credibility and utility of money are increasingly determined by its function and interoperability, rather than by its Legal tender status alone.

Stablecoins have redefined the trajectory of digital finance by offering a pragmatic alternative to both volatile cryptocurrencies and legacy banking systems. Their appeal lies not only in technical efficiency but in their real-world utility—providing faster payments, hedging against inflation, and enabling financial access across borders. As a result, they have shifted the locus of monetary innovation from central banks to the private sector, challenging traditional notions of what constitutes money and who gets to issue it.

However, this rise is not without consequence. Stablecoins now sit at the heart of a complex policy debate about the future of sovereign currency, systemic stability, and global financial governance. Their coexistence with CBDCs is not a matter of if but how, and the outcome will hinge on whether central banks can match the flexibility and functionality of their private-sector counterparts. As Stablecoins continue to evolve, the challenge for regulators and policymakers will be to build frameworks that both harness their potential and contain their risks before the digital currency future is defined without them.

9.5 Tokenization of Assets

The SEC's position on tokenization has evolved considerably over the past decade, shaped by technological advances, market experimentation, and a series of high-profile enforcement actions. Understanding this evolution provides essential context for the agency's current regulatory approach.

In the initial years of blockchain adoption, particularly during the 2017 Initial Coin Offering (ICO) boom, the SEC faced a rapidly growing market for digital tokens that often blurred the line between securities and non-securities. Many ICOs promised returns to investors but failed to register with the SEC or provide adequate disclosures, leading the agency to initiate its first wave of enforcement actions. The SEC's focus was on projects that marketed tokens as investment opportunities without complying with federal securities laws, often resulting in investor harm or outright fraud.

During this period, the SEC relied on the Howey Test—a legal standard from a 1946 Supreme Court case—to determine whether a digital asset constituted an "investment contract" and thus a security. If a token met the Howey criteria (an investment of money in a common enterprise with an expectation of profits derived from the efforts of others), it fell under the SEC's jurisdiction. However, the application of this test to digital assets was not always straightforward, leading to significant uncertainty for issuers and market participants.

Throughout the late 2010s and early 2020s, the U.S. regulatory landscape for Tokenization was characterized by fragmentation and ambiguity. The SEC, Commodity Futures Trading Commission (CFTC), and Financial Crimes Enforcement Network (FinCEN) each assert jurisdiction over different aspects of the digital asset ecosystem, creating a complex compliance environment. For security tokens—digital representations of traditional securities—the SEC's oversight was clear; however, for other tokenized assets, jurisdictional boundaries were less defined.

This patchwork approach created several challenges:

- **Classification Uncertainty:** Determining whether a token was a security, commodity, or something else was often a complex, case-by-case process, resulting in inconsistent regulatory interpretations and enforcement actions.
- **Compliance Burden:** Companies faced overlapping regulations and significant compliance costs, which stifled innovation and deterred new entrants from pursuing Tokenization projects.

- **Limited Market Growth:** The lack of regulatory clarity discouraged institutional participation and limited the development of secondary markets for tokenized assets.

SEC Guidance and Notable Enforcement

In response to industry demand for clarity, the SEC issued several statements and no-action letters, but these often left room for interpretation. The agency's enforcement actions against major projects—such as Ripple, Telegram, and Kik—reinforced its view that many token offerings were, in substance, unregistered securities offerings. These actions sent a strong message to the market but also highlighted the need for more tailored regulatory guidance.

By 2024, the SEC began to participate more actively in public roundtables and industry dialogues, acknowledging both the innovative potential of Tokenization and the regulatory gaps that needed to be addressed. The agency's approach remained grounded in investor protection, emphasizing disclosure, registration, and anti-fraud measures as central pillars of its oversight.

A significant shift occurred in 2024 with the passage of landmark legislation, including the Lummis-Gillibrand Act and the Digital Commodity Exchange Act. These laws clarified the division of regulatory authority between the SEC and CFTC, with the SEC retaining oversight of security tokens and the CFTC assuming primary responsibility for most other digital assets. This legislative clarity, combined with ongoing SEC engagement with industry stakeholders, has helped to foster innovation while maintaining robust investor protections.

In 2025, the U.S. Securities and Exchange Commission (SEC) took decisive steps to bring greater clarity to the rapidly evolving landscape of asset Tokenization. As digital transformation reshapes financial markets, the SEC has sought to strike a balance between encouraging technological innovation and upholding its core mandate of investor protection.

Asset Tokenization—the digital representation of traditional assets such as securities, real estate, or commodities on distributed ledger technology (DLT)—has gained substantial traction in recent years. Advocates tout its potential to enhance market efficiency, transparency, and access. However, this shift also presents regulatory challenges, particularly in defining how traditional laws apply to digital assets. In 2025, the SEC responded with comprehensive guidance and a more open approach to stakeholder engagement, reflecting both the promise and the complexity of tokenized finance.

A major milestone was reached in April 2025, when the SEC's Division of Corporation Finance released updated guidance to clarify how the agency determines whether a digital token constitutes a security under U.S. law. Central to this determination is the application of the Howey test, a long-standing legal standard used to assess whether an instrument qualifies as an "investment contract." Under this test, if individuals purchase tokens with a reasonable expectation of profit derived from the efforts of a central team or promoter, those tokens are likely to be considered securities.

To bring greater precision to this assessment, the SEC introduced a three-pronged framework:

1. **Initial Sale Context**—Was the token marketed primarily as an investment opportunity?
2. **Ongoing Use**—Does the token provide genuine functional utility within a decentralized network?
3. **Issuer Influence**—How much control does the founding team continue to exercise over the asset or protocol?

According to the SEC's interpretation, tokens that are marketed with profit potential, feature revenue-sharing mechanisms, or remain under the influence of a centralized entity are likely to fall within the definition of security. On the other hand, tokens designed for functional use—such as Stablecoins backed by transparent reserves or utility tokens operating on decentralized platforms—may escape that classification, provided they are not positioned as investment vehicles.

While the SEC remains vigilant about investor protection, its evolving posture in 2025 demonstrates a growing recognition of the need to foster innovation. In a May 2025 speech, Commissioner Hester Peirce emphasized the importance of "well-balanced regulation," which allows for experimentation without sacrificing oversight. To this end, the SEC is exploring conditional exemptions for firms involved in tokenized securities, enabling them to issue, trade, and settle assets on DLT-based systems without full compliance with traditional registration requirements.

This approach is inspired by regulatory sandboxes seen in other jurisdictions, where innovative projects operate within a controlled environment under regulatory supervision. The SEC's Crypto Task Force is leading the charge on these initiatives, aiming to address a key hurdle in Tokenization: the so-called chicken-and-egg problem. Few tokenized securities exist because there are limited compliant trading venues, and venues are hesitant to develop without a sufficient asset supply. By offering limited exemptions, the SEC hopes to stimulate both sides of the market simultaneously and observe developments that inform future rulemaking.

Throughout 2025, the SEC made a concerted effort to include industry voices in the regulatory process. Multiple public roundtables were held to gather insights from technologists, legal experts, institutional players, and decentralized communities. One notable event, the May 12 roundtable on Tokenization, served as a forum to explore the real-world implications of the SEC's evolving guidance. Participants discussed key issues such as the applicability of securities laws to various token models, the regulatory treatment of decentralized autonomous organizations (DAOs) and DeFi platforms, and the operational challenges surrounding custody, settlement, and disclosure. These discussions signaled a shift in tone from prior years, moving away from an adversarial stance toward digital assets and instead fostering a more collaborative, informed regulatory approach.

Despite the progress made, challenges remain. The line between a security and a utility token is often blurred, and many digital assets exhibit characteristics of both. Projects that claim decentralization may still be subject to SEC oversight if a central team controls key decisions. While legal opinions and no-action letters from the SEC can offer guidance, each token issuance still requires individualized legal analysis. Issuers and platforms must, therefore, approach compliance with care, consulting legal counsel and maintaining transparent operations. The SEC's guidance aims to provide greater predictability, but it also expects a higher standard of diligence from market participants.

The SEC's actions in 2025 represent a pivotal moment in the evolution of digital finance in the United States. By clarifying the application of securities laws to tokenized assets, exploring conditional exemptions, and engaging directly with stakeholders, the Commission is laying the groundwork for a regulatory framework that supports responsible innovation. As asset Tokenization continues to redefine capital markets, the SEC's evolving approach will play a crucial role in shaping how the industry matures—balancing the need for investor protection with the imperative to embrace technological progress.

9.6 Key Players in the Crypto Space

The Cryptocurrency landscape is undergoing a monumental transformation, driven by innovative Blockchain-enabled companies alongside established players in the digital asset space. Additionally, many traditional legacy corporations are getting into this space at a rapid pace and are continuously developing, as seen through the actions of J.P. Morgan and Meta Platforms, Inc. Meanwhile, leading digital asset exchanges continue to solidify their positions, reflecting a broader industry shift toward integrated, compliant, and globally accessible financial solutions that are reshaping how we interact with money and digital assets.

Tether Limited Inc

Tether is a Blockchain-enabled fintech company based in Hong Kong, founded in 2014 to modernize the use of fiat currencies in a digital manner across the Blockchain. Tether is related to Bitfinex (or iFinex, the parent company) and started as a virtual asset. The company's core mission is to disrupt the traditional financial system by enabling users to transact in government-backed currencies, such as USD or EUR, without the volatility and complexity typically associated with cryptocurrencies. It is the first Blockchain-enabled platform to achieve this. With 165 employees and a profitable and successful operating model, Tether has grown into a global force, supported by a recent $600 million investment from Cantor Fitzgerald, which valued the company at $12 billion.

Tether operates on a global scale, with its technology serving cross-border payment and a broad international investment strategy. The company has invested across diverse sectors and regions, including agriculture in Latin America (Adecoagro), media in North America (Rumble), fintech in Europe and Asia (Zengo, Fizen.io), and sports in Italy (Juventus). These investments support Tether's larger goal of expanding Cryptocurrency adoption and improving financial infrastructure through decentralized, Blockchain-backed platforms.

While year-to-year revenue growth and net income figures have not been disclosed, Tether reported normalized EBITDA of $13 million in 2024 and $7.4 million in 2025. Additionally, the company raised undisclosed debt in 2024, taking on some financial leverage. Tether is now a key player in the space.

Unlike traditional financial institutions, there is no indication that Tether relies on customer deposits or loan portfolios, limiting its exposure to typical credit risks. However, as a Blockchain company dealing in fiat currency and crypto infrastructure, Tether is inherently affected by regulatory developments. Under the current U.S. administration, the crypto industry has received some regulatory clarity, as well as reduced SEC enforcement. On a global level, the company's leadership and compliance team suggest active navigation of global financial policy shifts.

With a profitable business model, a $12 billion valuation, and aggressive global expansion through strategic investments, Tether is well-positioned to shape the future of digital finance. Its unique value proposition of bridging traditional currencies with Blockchain infrastructure continues to differentiate it in a competitive fintech landscape.

Circle Internet Group, Inc

Circle Internet Group, Inc. (CRCL) is a Blockchain-based fintech firm with headquarters in New York. Founded in 2013, their goal is to bring transparency and usability to digital finance through Stablecoins and programmable money. Unlike some crypto companies that are primarily focused on trading or DeFi, Circle has distinguished itself by prioritizing regulatory compliance and developing institutional-grade infrastructure to bridge the gap between traditional finance and Web3. The company's flagship product, USDC, is a fully backed, U.S. dollar-denominated Stablecoin that has become one of the most widely adopted in the market, supported across multiple Blockchain ecosystems.

Over the last five years, Circle has experienced extraordinary growth, with revenue increasing by more than 17,700% from December 2019 to March 2025, currently standing at $1.89 billion. In 2024, the company reported a net income of $171.8 million, showcasing its sustainable profitability. Its market capitalization now stands at $30.4 billion, with a 24% increase in stock price over the last year. Circle has continued to invest in expanding its product offerings, launching services such as Circle Mint, which allows institutions to mint and redeem USDC seamlessly, the Cross-Chain Transfer Protocol (CCTP) for Blockchain interoperability, and a smart contract platform for developers building scalable Web3 applications.

Circle completed two major transactions: the acquisition of CYBAVO Pte Ltd in 2022 to strengthen security infrastructure and a private placement by Everbright Investment Limited Company in 2025. With around 900 employees, Circle has affirmed its position as a foundational layer of the Internet financial system.

Circle's close alignment with regulators and its focus on easy usability have given it a unique advantage in navigating the regulatory landscape. Its services have helped financial institutions and developers integrate Blockchain into real applications like payments, treasury management, and commerce. As Blockchain adoption continues to grow globally, Circle is well-positioned to lead the next wave of digital finance through tokenized dollars, cross-border transactions, and real-world Blockchain utility.

Coinbase Global, Inc

Coinbase Global, Inc. (NASDAQ: COIN) is a publicly traded Cryptocurrency company headquartered in New York that operates both in the United States and abroad. It was founded in 2012 to offer secure and regulated access to the emerging world of digital assets and stands out in the crypto space as one of the few U.S.-based, compliant exchanges listed on NASDAQ, offering transparency and great services in a market often characterized by volatility and limited oversight.

Over the years, Coinbase has expanded its product suite to cater to Retail users, institutions, and developers. Key offerings include Coinbase One, a subscription-based service with over 600,000 members, and Coinbase Prime, a platform tailored to institutions that offers services such as custody, trading, and staking, both of which reflect Coinbase's broader strategy to deepen user engagement and grow recurring revenues. The company's overall customer base has continued to grow in tandem with broader Cryptocurrency adoption, particularly as it builds momentum among institutions and internationally.

Financially, the company has seen a phenomenal turnaround, with total revenue reaching $6.56 billion as of December 2024, representing a 1,129.83% increase since 2019. Following a $2.6 billion loss in 2022, Coinbase rebounded to a $2.58 billion net income. The company also acquired Deribit FZE in 2025 for $2.862 billion, expanding its footprint in global crypto derivatives markets, particularly through its presence in Dubai. Coinbase currently has a market capitalization of $61.8 billion and employs 3,772 people globally.

Coinbase's stock, currently trading at $242.71 as of June 13, 2025, is performing well due to several key drivers, including increased adoption of institutional products, positive political sentiment toward Cryptocurrency, and the recent dismissal of an SEC lawsuit. Regulatory clarity has also played a pivotal role in Coinbase's recent success. With the SEC lawsuit dropped in early 2025 and progress toward EU licensing underway, the company is poised to benefit from both domestic and international regulatory momentum. Coinbase's ability to operate within regulatory frameworks while pushing forward innovation makes it a unique player in the evolving financial landscape.

Binance

Binance is a Blockchain-based digital asset exchange platform founded in 2017, headquartered in George Town, Malta, created to increase the freedom of money for users by facilitating affordable Cryptocurrency trading. In a market filled with exchanges offering limited scope and high fees, Binance worked to differentiate itself by building a comprehensive, multi-service crypto ecosystem, including trading, finance, education, research, and a strong focus on decentralization and social good initiatives.

Binance has grown to become one of the most influential and key players in the Cryptocurrency industry, operating on a global scale and employing 9,204 people. Its strength stems from the company's ability to leverage scale and infrastructure, enabling high liquidity, low trading fees, and fast transaction speeds. Binance also stands out for its diversified service offerings, which extend beyond trading to include investment and incubation, educational outreach, and digital asset infrastructure. In March 2025, Binance secured a $2 billion venture capital investment aimed at strengthening its efforts in AI, Blockchain, and financial innovation, indicating a strong commitment by the company to technological leadership and market evolution.

Binance has been actively investing in and acquiring businesses to expand its reach and capabilities. Recent acquisitions, such as Streami and Tokocrypto, have reinforced its offerings in crypto finance and infrastructure. Strategic investments have also supported growth in sectors such as entertainment software (MEET48), financial software (Bitstaker, PrismaStake), and decentralized services, with a focus on early-stage fintech and Blockchain integration.

Despite a 55% decline in revenue in 2023, which brought total annual revenue to $9 billion, Binance remains resilient and forward-looking, driven by global expansion and platform enhancements. It holds a strong venture capital exit profile, with a 90% likelihood of success and an 89% probability of IPO, according to recent data. Operating across regions and jurisdictions, Binance benefits from Blockchain-friendly environments but also potentially faces challenges in more tightly regulated markets. However, Binance's decentralized and international structure helps position it well to navigate these changes.

In the future, Binance is expected to continue expanding its global presence while promoting and advancing innovation in decentralized finance, AI, and financial technology. With its range of products, strategic investments, and proactive funding strategy, the company is set to remain a leading force in the evolving digital asset market (Table 9.1).

Table 9.1 Crypto ecosystem: platforms, exchanges, and newcomers

Main players

Stablecoin issuers

Company	Founder(s)	Type	Market cap (USD)	Revenue/income	Strengths/focus areas
Tether Limited Inc. (founded 2014) HQ: Hong Kong https://tether.to/en/	Not disclosed; Paolo Ardoino (CEO)	Platform/stablecoin issuer	$12B (2025)	$13M EBITDA (2024), $7.4M EBITDA (2025), Debt raised	Fiat-backed Stablecoins, Cross-border payments, global crypto investments
Circle (founded 2013) HQ: New York https://www.circle.com/	Jeremy Allaire	Platform/Stablecoin issuer	$45.43B (2025)	$1.89B revenue (2025), $171.8M net income (2025)	USDC issuance, regulated Stablecoin infrastructure, strong institutional partnerships

Exchanges

| Binance (founded 2017) HQ: Malta https://www.binance.com/en | Yi He and Changpeng Zhao | Platform/exchange | Private (Not disclosed) | $9B revenue (2023, post-55% decline) | High liquidity, fast settlement, early-stage Blockchain/AI investments |
| Coinbase Global, Inc. (founded 2012) HQ: New York https://www.coinbase.com/ | Brian Armstrong and Frederick Ehrsam | Platform/exchange & institutional services | $61.8B (2025) | $6.56B revenue (2024), $2.58B net income (2024) | Exchange, Coinbase prime (institutions), Coinbase one (subscription) |

Other players

(continued)

Table 9.1 (continued)

Main players

Stablecoin issuers

Company	Founder(s)	Type	Market cap (USD)	Revenue/income	Strengths/focus areas
Meta Platforms, Inc. (founded 2004) HQ: California https://www.meta.com/	Mark Zuckerberg	Platform / Big Tech	$1.75T (2025)	$170.36B revenue (2025), $66.63B net income (2025)	Exploring Stablecoin payments, interest in cross-border creator payments Announced and withdrew the launch of Libra (then Diem) in 2019
JPM Chase & Co (founded 1799) HQ: New York https://www.jpmorgan.com/global	J.P. Morgan	Financial Institution/ Institutional Blockchain	$761.36B (2025)	$168.71B revenue (2025), $59.7B net income (2025)	JPM Coin (settlements), Onyx (Blockchain platform), asset Tokenization, institutional focus

Source Capital IQ and PitchBook; Accessed June 2025

10

The Debate over CBDCs

Main Messages

- CBDCs offer major benefits such as faster payments, reduced physical currency costs, and expanded Financial inclusion, especially in emerging markets.
- They also present strategic and regulatory advantages, strengthening monetary sovereignty and enabling better oversight of illicit financial activity through traceable transactions.
- CBDCs pose significant risks, including Privacy concerns, banking Disintermediation, Cybersecurity threats, and public resistance.

Central Bank Digital Currencies have spurred a wide spectrum of opinions. Economists, policymakers, and the general public within the same country often disagree with each other on the pros and cons and the extent to which CBDCs should be adopted.

10.1 Advantages of CBDCs

As discussed in previous chapters, the creation of CBDCs has opened the door to a new era of monetary and technical innovation. There are many advantages to CBDC adoption, which is being further driven by the rise in fintech, global economic competition, and the shortcomings of traditional currency systems. These issues have paved the way for the adoption of modern and digital monetary solutions. CBDCs are a crucial step in enhancing payment infrastructure and improving financial access while modernizing traditional and outdated currencies.

CBDCs promise to revolutionize the payment landscape by facilitating real-time, low-cost, and secure transactions. These benefits cover both domestic and cross-border transfers, simultaneously addressing inefficiencies that have long plagued the global financial system. For instance, the Financial Times has noted that CBDCs "have the potential to reduce transaction costs, decrease government interest burdens, and bolster GDP by about 3%." Denmark National Bank reinforces this by stating that "Wholesale CBDC can potentially form the basis for faster and more effective payments between financial institutions, including Cross-border payments across currencies."

This promise and perspective are also found in Asia. The Bank of Korea views CBDCs as a way to "enhance the efficiency of the payment system and support financial innovation." The Monetary Authority of Singapore believes they "can enhance the efficiency of Cross-border payments and support Financial inclusion." Thailand's central bank is exploring how "a Retail CBDC [can] enhance the efficiency and security of the payment system," with similar sentiments expressed by the central banks of Malaysia, Taiwan, and the Philippines.

10.2 Fiscal Sustainability and the Elimination of Physical Currency Costs

CBDCs also present substantial fiscal advantages by dramatically reducing the costs associated with the lifecycle of physical currency. Governments currently spend a significant amount of effort and money on minting coins and printing banknotes. The process involves sourcing raw materials, maintaining specialized production facilities, and implementing sophisticated anti-counterfeiting technologies. Once produced, currencies must also be transported with the utmost security to banks, ATMs, and Retailers. It must then be stored securely, counted regularly, and replaced as it becomes worn or damaged. Each stage of this cycle incurs not only monetary cost but also time, labor, and environmental impact.

A clear example of these inefficiencies is the US Treasury's decision to cease production of the penny in 2026. This is due to an economic inefficiency, as producing one penny has now started to cost more than its actual face value, resulting in a net loss for the federal government with every coin minted. The penny is not the only case. Other low-denomination coins and certain paper notes also approach or exceed cost ineffectiveness when materials, labor, and distribution are taken into account. Similar debates have emerged in countries such as Canada, which discontinued its penny in 2013, and the United Kingdom, where calls to phase out the 1 and 2 pence coins have intensified.

CBDCs offer a compelling alternative. By digitizing sovereign currency, governments can bypass the entire infrastructure required to produce, secure, and circulate physical money. This shift not only leads to immediate cost savings but also frees up public resources that can be redirected toward building and maintaining modern digital financial infrastructure. These investments may include the development of nationwide digital payment infrastructure, Cybersecurity enhancements to protect against digital fraud, and interoperable systems that facilitate efficient monetary transfers between individuals, businesses, and institutions.

From a long-term strategic perspective, reducing dependence on physical currency also aligns with broader environmental goals. The materials used to mint coins, such as metals, inks, and cotton-linen blends, all carry ecological costs. The production and transport of cash contribute to carbon emissions, and worn-out notes must be incinerated or processed, further impacting the environment. By transitioning to a digital currency model, governments can take a meaningful step toward more sustainable financial ecosystems.

10.3 Expanding Financial Inclusion

As mentioned earlier in the book, perhaps one of the most widely cited and compelling justifications for the implementation of Central Bank Digital Currencies (CBDCs), especially in emerging markets, is their potential to enhance Financial inclusion significantly. In many developing economies, large segments of the population remain outside the formal financial system, lacking access to basic banking services such as savings accounts, credit facilities, or secure payment mechanisms. This exclusion is often driven by a combination of structural barriers, including geographic isolation, a lack of trust in financial institutions, insufficient documentation, and high transaction costs. Traditional banks have been unable or unwilling to overcome many of these challenges due to risk management and financial reasons.

However, these same regions, which face a lack of Financial inclusion, frequently exhibit high rates of mobile phone penetration, even in remote and low-income communities. This paradox of being digitally connected yet financially excluded presents a unique opportunity for CBDCs to act as a transformative bridge. Unlike commercial bank accounts, CBDC wallets could be accessed through simple mobile applications without the need for a traditional bank intermediary. In Africa, M-Pesa has developed as a leading a payment facilitator that can work with SMS messages without the need for Internet or smartphone connectivity. This model lowers entry barriers by eliminating the need for in-person account openings, minimum balance requirements, or credit histories, which often prevent individuals from entering the formal financial system. If countries can implement CBDC infrastructure similar to M-Pesa, which can work across smart and traditional phones via SMS capabilities, Financial inclusion will drastically change for the better.

The potential for CBDCs to bring financial access to unbanked populations is widely acknowledged. This access is not limited to money storage or peer-to-peer payments, but it also opens the door to broader digital participation. From microloans to buy now pay later (BNPL) services and insurance products to e-commerce and government services, the new era of digital money can facilitate an upward trajectory toward greater financial empowerment.

Policymakers are increasingly embracing this vision. In Latin America, for example, Mexico's central bank has explicitly cited Financial inclusion as a cornerstone of its CBDC development strategy. The proposed "digital peso" is seen as a tool for modernizing the national payment infrastructure and expanding service access to millions currently underserved by the banking sector. In Asia, Indonesia and the Philippines have emphasized the traceability of CBDC transactions as a mechanism to bring economic activity out of the shadows. Greater transparency not only supports tax collection and anti-money laundering efforts but also helps individuals build a digital footprint who previously operated solely in cash-based environments. This digital history can be leveraged to unlock access to formal credit, social protection programs, and Digital identity systems.

Moreover, CBDCs can offer a more equitable and inclusive framework for the disbursement of government benefits. Traditional cash-based welfare programs often suffer from leakages, delays, and corruption. A CBDC-based system can enable governments to directly deposit funds into digital wallets with minimal cost and maximum speed, ensuring that subsidies, pensions, or emergency relief payments reach the intended recipients with greater accuracy and efficiency. This is particularly critical during crises such as pandemics or natural disasters, where rapid financial response can have life-saving consequences.

Beyond enabling basic transactions and digital payments, CBDCs also hold the potential for broader financial participation for the newly financially included individuals. This includes access to savings accounts that bear interest, CDs and fixed deposits, and investment products that have historically been out of reach for the unbanked. Once individuals possess a CBDC wallet linked to a verified Digital identity, governments and fintech providers can build platforms that connect users to government bond marketplaces, Retail investment portals, or fractional ownership schemes in equity markets.

For example, a central bank could allow CBDC wallet users to purchase small-denomination sovereign bonds directly through a mobile app, offering a safe, low-risk savings option with minimal onboarding requirements. In time, this infrastructure could expand to include regulated access to equity markets through simplified micro-investment platforms. By embedding these services into CBDC ecosystems, emerging economies could dramatically broaden household participation in capital markets, helping individuals build wealth, hedge against inflation, and participate more fully in national economic growth. The democratization of investment, made possible by the foundation of inclusive digital currency, would have significant benefits for the economy as a whole.

The implications for CBDC benefits and Financial inclusion extend beyond the individual. Small and micro enterprises, which frequently operate outside the formal economy due to banking access constraints, can also benefit from CBDCs. Imagine buying a hot dog from a street vendor in Central Park. By enabling fast, low-cost digital transactions and reducing reliance on physical cash, CBDCs can help these businesses legitimize their operations by building verifiable income history, flourishing with greater profit margins, and unlocking access to credit to facilitate expansion. By helping small business owners transition from the informal to the formal economy, CBDCs open the door to broader financial tools such as credit, savings products, and insurance, all of which support the growth and long-term success of their operations.

In essence, CBDCs offer more than a technical upgrade to payment systems—they represent a pathway toward inclusive economic development. When implemented with thoughtful design and robust support infrastructure, they can empower the financially excluded, reduce inequality, and lay the foundation for a more integrated and accessible financial future.

10.4 Technological Sovereignty and the Preservation of Monetary Authority

CBDCs are increasingly viewed not only as domestic financial innovations but also as strategic geopolitical tools. One of their most compelling use cases lies in facilitating faster, cheaper, and more secure Cross-border payments, a process that remains notoriously slow, expensive, and opaque under the existing correspondent banking model. By utilizing CBDCs issued by central banks, countries can build a new global payment infrastructure that reduces reliance on intermediaries, streamlines settlement processes, and increases transparency across borders. This infrastructure has the potential to revolutionize remittances, trade finance, and capital flows, especially for emerging markets that often face high fees and currency conversion barriers when interacting with global financial systems.

From a strategic standpoint, CBDCs are also viewed as crucial to maintaining monetary sovereignty in the digital era. As private digital currencies, cryptocurrencies, and privately run tech companies expand across borders, they threaten to erode national control over currency and payments. In response, central banks are accelerating CBDC development to maintain oversight, protect domestic Monetary policy, and uphold the integrity of their financial systems.

Lael Brainard of the US Federal Reserve articulated this motivation clearly when she stated that "a U.S. CBDC may be one potential way to ensure that people around the world who use the dollar can continue to rely on the strength and safety of U.S. currency to transact and conduct business in the digital financial system." In other words, a digital dollar would serve as a modern extension of the US dollar's global role, reinforcing its status as the world's primary reserve currency while ensuring it remains relevant in a future where money moves instantly and digitally across borders. But, as discussed in Chapter 11, the current opposition to a CBDC in the United States renders the possibility of such a digital dollar being rolled out unlikely in the coming years.

This concern is mirrored in Europe, where the European Central Bank and its national counterparts have framed the digital euro as a tool to safeguard monetary autonomy in the face of growing foreign and private competition. Spain has explicitly underlined the CBDC's strategic value as a counterweight to the expansion of cryptocurrencies and as a means to strengthen European identity and control over monetary affairs. Germany's Deutsche Bundesbank views a digital euro as a catalyst for harmonized innovation, stating that it could "foster competition and innovation in payments across Europe" by enabling seamless pan-European financial integration. France's Denis Beau echoed this sovereignty-focused vision, describing the digital euro as a "digital banknote," a modern instrument designed to carry forward the core values of physical cash, including accessibility, stability, and public trust, into the digital economy.

Thus, CBDCs are not merely about improving efficiency; they are a means of asserting influence in a rapidly digitizing global financial order. For the United States, failure to offer a digital version of the dollar could gradually cede ground to competing digital currencies, particularly those from rival geopolitical actors. For Europe, a digital euro is essential to avoiding dependence on foreign payment infrastructures and reinforcing economic cohesion within the region. CBDCs are emerging as instruments of both economic modernization and strategic defense. They can help preserve the dominance of trusted fiat currencies, such as the dollar, while offering countries the tools to shape the future rules of digital finance rather than being shaped by them.

10.5 Policy Precision and the Fight Against Illicit Activity

CBDCs grant central banks significantly greater oversight and enforcement capabilities in the fight against illicit financial activity. Unlike cash, which is anonymous and difficult to trace once it changes hands, CBDC transactions can be designed to offer varying degrees of traceability, depending on policy goals. This transparency creates a powerful deterrent against a range of illicit activities, including money laundering, tax evasion, and terrorism financing.

As discussed in Chapter 5, one of the most disruptive impacts of CBDCs in this context is their ability to generate detailed, immutable, and real-time transaction records. These digital trails can be monitored using advanced analytics and AI to flag suspicious patterns, identify shell operations, or detect cross-border money flows that fall outside of regulatory norms. Authorities can then intervene more rapidly and with far greater precision than under current systems, which depend heavily on delayed reporting from financial institutions or limited visibility into cash-based activity.

Additionally, the programmability of CBDCs offers unprecedented regulatory tools. Specific wallet types could be restricted from transacting with known high-risk entities or jurisdictions. Limits could be placed on transaction sizes, frequency, or use cases for unverified accounts, all of which would make it more difficult for bad actors to move large volumes of illicit funds. These capabilities align with the goals of existing financial intelligence frameworks (like FATF guidelines) but take enforcement one step further by programming compliance mechanisms into the currency itself.

Central banks around the world have acknowledged this enforcement potential. France's Nathalie Aufauvre, General Secretary of the Banque de France, noted that CBDCs "can ensure the safe settlement of transactions… and thereby contribute to the secure development of these innovations," highlighting the dual role of digital currencies in enabling innovation while reinforcing financial integrity. Similarly, the Bank of Thailand has emphasized that CBDC design must balance innovation with robust regulatory oversight, suggesting that traceable, policy-aligned currencies can reduce systemic risk while responding to the public's need for security.

In regions where the shadow economy constitutes a significant portion of GDP, such as parts of Southeast Asia, Latin America, and Africa, CBDCs offer governments a practical mechanism to rein in illicit trade and broaden the tax base. By drawing transactions into a regulated and auditable system, CBDCs could significantly disrupt underground economies that have long operated beyond the reach of enforcement agencies.

10.6 Drawbacks and Concerns Surrounding CBDCs

While the benefits of CBDCs are compelling, their implementation introduces equally serious risks that must be acknowledged and addressed. The greatest of these threats are those in relation to financial Privacy, disruption of the traditional banking model, cyberattacks, and the challenge of public adoption in technologically saturated or politically sensitive environments.

The aspect of expanded visibility is a double-edged sword as it also raises critical debates around Privacy, surveillance, and the role of the state in everyday financial life. These concerns must be addressed transparently if CBDCs are to achieve both legitimacy and effectiveness in combating illicit finance. While CBDCs offer powerful tools for combating illicit financial activity, they also introduce serious concerns about surveillance, data Privacy, and governmental overreach. For a CBDC system to function effectively as a deterrent to crime, it must be designed with traceability. However, this very feature can conflict with the fundamental expectation of financial Privacy if every transaction is potentially visible to a central authority; even when not criminal, citizens may feel that their economic freedoms are being compromised.

Concerns related to Privacy and surveillance for CBDCs are not unfounded. Cointelegraph described concerns over Privacy with the digital pound as "not entirely overblown," while Taiwan's central bank noted public fears over "data Privacy and the potential for government surveillance." In the Philippines, a leading fintech commentator warned that "CBDCs do nothing for Financial inclusion. Instead, they actually reduce financial freedom because monitoring always implies censorship."

This concern is amplified in regimes with more centralized power structures. In Turkey, analysts warned that "if [the country] continues to subordinate the central bank to the government, the digital lira will not solve its problems. It could even aggravate them." In Malaysia, the Human Rights Foundation raised the prospect that "a CBDC could be used to target opposing voices and cut them off from society through direct financial controls." In countries where there is already a lot of government oversight, the idea of implementing a CBDC would add another layer of surveillance on citizens.

In the absence of robust legal safeguards and independent oversight, CBDCs could be weaponized to monitor, restrict, or penalize lawful behavior under the guise of regulatory enforcement. For example, governments could use CBDC data to track political donations, religious contributions, or purchases deemed "undesirable," leading to chilling effects on expression, association, and dissent. In authoritarian regimes, this level of financial transparency could be exploited to exert control, punish opposition, or enforce discriminatory policies.

Users must trust that their financial data will remain secure and that governments will act with restraint. Without strong Privacy protections, clear limitations on data usage, and transparent governance frameworks, public adoption of CBDCs could falter. In democratic societies, especially where trust in institutions is lacking, the perception of state overreach can spark public backlash and drive users toward alternative, less-regulated digital assets, such as cryptocurrencies, which may undermine the very financial integrity that CBDCs aim to protect.

Ultimately, the challenge is to strike a balance between security and freedom. If central banks and policymakers fail to convincingly articulate and guarantee this balance, CBDCs could risk becoming tools of control rather than instruments of trust.

10.7 Disintermediation of the Banking Sector

CBDCs also raise serious concerns about the future role of commercial banks and legacy payment providers. One of the most frequently cited risks is the potential for CBDCs to disintermediate the traditional banking system by pulling deposits away from private financial institutions. If individuals choose to store a significant portion of their funds in central bank digital wallets, commercial banks could face a rapid erosion of their deposit base. These deposits form the backbone of a bank's liquidity and are essential for supporting its lending operations. Large-scale migration of funds to CBDCs could limit banks' capacity to extend credit, dampening economic activity and disrupting the traditional model of financial intermediation.

This scenario is especially concerning during times of financial stress, when depositors may view government-issued CBDCs and bonds as safer alternatives to bank deposits, effectively triggering digital bank runs. In a conventional system, such runs are slowed by logistics, such as the need to withdraw cash or wait for transfers to settle physically. CBDCs could eliminate these frictions, enabling instantaneous mass withdrawals from commercial banks with a few taps on a phone, potentially leading to greater uncertainty.

The Banque de France has warned that a Wholesale CBDC "available to a large number of market participants could affect the role of financial intermediaries and the transmission of Monetary policy," highlighting fears that CBDCs could upend the entire structure of money markets and bank funding. Similarly, South Korea's central bank has voiced strong concerns about how CBDCs might weaken the traditional banking model and potentially introduce new sources of financial instability. If central banks begin offering interest-bearing CBDCs or highly convenient alternatives to bank accounts, the competition could fundamentally reshape how banks attract and retain customers.

Beyond deposit displacement, credit card networks and payment processors also face potential disruption. CBDCs could allow users to conduct peer-to-peer or Retail payments directly through central bank-supported apps or wallets. This would allow for bypassing intermediaries such as Visa, Mastercard, or commercial payment gateways, which would drastically reduce the fees that card networks can charge their customers and merchants. Many merchants already resent the cost and complexity of accepting card payments and push for cash-based transactions by offering discounted prices or other benefits to their customers. In a CBDC-enabled world, cash equivalents can be moved instantly with low fees and fast settlement so that credit cards may lose their appeal.

While some argue that banks and card providers could adapt by building services around CBDC infrastructure, the core threat remains: CBDCs challenge the primacy of banks and private payment systems by offering a government-backed alternative that is often cheaper, safer, and more direct. CBDCs could unintentionally hollow out the financial institutions they are meant to complement.

10.8 Systemic Cybersecurity Risks

The digitization of national currencies through CBDCs introduces a new class of Cybersecurity risks that traditional cash and even many bank-based systems are largely insulated from. While CBDCs promise enhanced efficiency and traceability, they also make sovereign currencies directly dependent on complex digital infrastructure. This opens a new opportunity for cybercriminals, state-sponsored hackers, and other malicious actors. These risks extend beyond individual wallets or user endpoints, threatening the integrity and stability of entire national financial systems.

A fully digital currency system must maintain constant uptime, transactional integrity, and data security, all while serving millions of users simultaneously. Any vulnerability in the underlying architecture, whether at the user interface, smart contract layer, or central infrastructure, could lead to devastating consequences. For example, a breach of the central ledger or digital wallet provider could result in the theft, freezing, or unauthorized manipulation of funds. Worse still, a coordinated cyberattack on a national CBDC platform could lead to widespread loss of confidence in the currency itself, triggering economic panic and eroding central bank credibility.

The Monetary Authority of Singapore (MAS) has explicitly raised these concerns, warning that "the introduction of a Retail CBDC could pose significant risks to financial stability." In a highly interconnected financial system, the cascading effects of a compromised CBDC platform could extend to commercial banks, payment processors, and international markets. The scale and real-time nature of CBDC transactions offer no margin for error. A single point of failure could have immediate, far-reaching consequences for trust in the system.

Denmark's central bank has echoed this skepticism, stating that due to the potential costs, technological uncertainty, and security challenges, "it is not clear how Retail CBDCs will create significant added value relative to the existing solutions in Denmark." This view reflects a broader hesitation among technologically advanced countries, where digital payments already function reliably, and the marginal gain from introducing a CBDC may not justify the heightened Cybersecurity exposure.

Unlike traditional banknote issuance, which is decentralized and resilient in physical form, CBDCs centralize currency issuance and management into a high-value digital target. As such, they will require significant investment in Cybersecurity protocols, as well as new forms of risk modeling, rapid response systems, and international coordination. Questions remain about how central banks will address threats from Quantum computing, supply chain vulnerabilities, and insider threats.

To succeed, CBDC frameworks must go beyond the technical safeguards of today's banking systems. They will require secure digital identities, encrypted communications, multi-layer authentication, and possibly even offline payment capabilities to ensure resilience during cyber incidents or network outages. Without this, a cyberattack could not only bring down a national payments system but also challenge the sovereignty and trust that central banks are built to uphold.

In short, while CBDCs may modernize financial infrastructure, they also transform national currencies into Cybersecurity assets, with all the risks and responsibilities that this entails.

10.9 Barriers to Adoption and Market Readiness

In jurisdictions where digital payments are already mature, efficient, and widely trusted, the introduction of a CBDC often faces not only technical scrutiny but also growing public skepticism. In such environments, where cashless transactions are already handled seamlessly by commercial banks and private fintech platforms, CBDCs risk being perceived as redundant bureaucratic solutions in search of a problem. This perception is especially acute when the costs of implementation appear to outweigh the marginal gains in payment efficiency or Financial inclusion.

Denmark again stands out as a leading example. The country already enjoys near-universal access to digital payments, and confidence in existing infrastructure is high. For Danish citizens, a CBDC could feel more like a state-imposed redundancy than a meaningful innovation. Similarly, France's Denis Beau has drawn attention to the fundamental shortcomings of many existing digital currencies, focusing on the lack of clear convertibility into central bank money and the absence of a credible issuing authority, while implicitly casting doubt on whether CBDCs themselves can overcome these flaws.

Spain offers a more nuanced case. While its central bank, the Banco de España, expressed support for the digital euro project, it also delivered a pointed message about physical currency, stating that "the physical cash format does not allow [us] to exploit all the advantages offered by the growing digitalization of the economy and society." While this can be read as an endorsement of CBDCs, it also highlights the delicate communication balance policymakers must navigate. Pushing CBDCs too aggressively can alienate populations that still value the tangible, anonymous, and universally accepted nature of cash. For many citizens, cash is not just a payment method; it is a symbol of Privacy, autonomy, and financial freedom.

This tension underscores a broader challenge: public understanding and trust in CBDCs remain limited across many parts of the world. In Japan, for example, the Bank of Japan shelved its Retail CBDC pilot after discovering that only 3.1% of the surveyed consumers were familiar with the concept. According to DailyCoin, the cancelation was attributed to a "lack of interest from the public," signaling that even in technologically sophisticated societies, central banks cannot assume automatic trust and confidence in digital currency initiatives. The skepticism is rooted not only in unfamiliarity but also in a broader unease about state involvement in personal finance.

In Thailand, while enthusiasm for CBDCs is strong among policymakers and regulators, media coverage has spotlighted growing concerns over surveillance and loss of financial freedom. Outlets like the Financial Times have cautioned against "dystopian futures" where digital money becomes a tool for excessive governmental or corporate control. These concerns reflect deep-seated public anxieties about Privacy, autonomy, and the potential for power abuse. Without transparent design choices and communicated boundaries around data usage, CBDCs risk being seen less as public goods and more as instruments of centralized oversight.

Public trust is not a given; it must be earned. In nations where the existing digital payment infrastructure is already functional, central banks face a dual challenge. They must prove that CBDCs add value beyond current systems while simultaneously assuring citizens that these new tools will not compromise their financial freedoms. Without a compelling and clearly articulated vision, CBDCs may struggle to overcome resistance, even in the same societies that appear prepared to adopt them.

CBDCs are not merely digital analogs of existing currency; they represent a fundamental shift in how societies conceptualize and interact with money. Their potential to transform financial systems is vast and nuanced.

They promise more efficient payments, broader inclusion, improved policy execution, and enhanced monetary sovereignty. However, they also challenge deeply held principles regarding Privacy, decentralization, and the role of financial institutions.

Policymakers now face a complex set of technical, ethical, and political challenges as they look forward. The success of CBDCs will ultimately rely on the ability of central banks and governments to strike a delicate balance: fostering innovation while protecting individual rights, enhancing efficiency without compromising financial stability, and promoting adoption without undermining public trust. The road ahead presents numerous hurdles, including Cybersecurity risks, institutional resistance, and societal skepticism. However, if these challenges are addressed through thoughtful design and transparent governance, the full-scale adoption of CBDCs could yield transformative and substantial benefits for the global financial system as a whole.

11

2025, a New Opportunity

Main Messages

- While over 130 countries are exploring CBDCs, rollouts remain limited; the EU and India are advancing cautiously, while China pushes ahead with broad but uneven adoption.
- In a landmark 2025 pivot, the United States banned CBDC development, created a Bitcoin reserve, and signed the GENIUS Act into law to regulate Stablecoins and foster private innovation.
- With forward-thinking regulation and public–private partnerships, Dubai has built a global model for tokenized real estate and digital asset ecosystems.

In 2025, interest in CBDCs remains at an all-time high, with the number of countries having explored CBDCs jumping from 35 in 2020 to more than 130 countries, representing 98% of the global economy. Every G20 country has engaged with the CBDC as a concept, with 13 countries introducing a pilot. However, as interest in CBDCs continues to gather momentum, actual rollouts and advanced pilots are still on the horizon for most countries.

As per a recent survey of central banks conducted by the Official Monetary and Financial Institutions Forum (OMFIF), while 84% expected to eventually develop and launch a CBDC, less than 15% anticipated launching a CBDC in the next 1–2 years. While some of this hesitation stems from a lack of consensus regarding the nature and path to launch among central banks and governments, difficulties related to digital infrastructure, privacy, and security, as well as organic adoption, remain significant roadblocks.

That said, 2025 has seen significant advances in the development and adoption of CBDCs in some countries. In this chapter, we will focus on exciting developments related to the Digital Euro (expected to launch in 2025). We will also review updates from the pilots and rollout of CBDCs in India and China. Finally, we will discuss the United States' policy approach away from CBDCs and explore its implications for the U.S. dollar and the global economy.

11.1 The Digital Euro: An Exercise in Building Consensus in 2025

Although most of the European Union is unified under a single currency (the euro), the existing digital infrastructure has not enabled seamless payments and transfer of funds across the Eurozone. As discussed earlier, 13 out of 20 countries are reliant on international card schemes for card payments despite sharing the same currency. This creates a discrepancy between cash and digital forms of payment—while the same physical note can be carried, exchanged, and used across all these 20 countries, the same is not true of current digital payment means in at least 13 countries.

The rapid shift in geopolitical risks and tech-based disruptions has prompted the EU to accelerate the rollout of the Digital Euro. A recent announcement in February 2025 to expand the Eurosystem to program to settle transactions on DLT with money issued by the central bank. The European Central Bank (ECB) outlines a "two track" approach: first, developing a safe and efficient platform to settle transactions in central bank money through an interoperability link with TARGET (financial infrastructure services developed by the Eurosystem). Second, the ECB plans to explore more long-term solutions to settle DLT-based transactions in central bank funds in an integrated manner.

Speaking before the European Parliament in April 2025, Piero Cipollone from the European Central Bank (ECB) reiterated the importance of the Digital Euro in securing Europe's strategic and economic autonomy amidst rising global uncertainty. Underlying this communication is the concern that currently, European retail payments are heavily reliant on non-European providers. More than 60% of Europe's payment market is served by non-European providers, which increases risks related to security, monetary sovereignty, and financial stability. The Digital Euro aims to address these risks, along with the broader use case of "bringing cash into the digital age." Potential features being discussed would include capped digital wallets offering QR code and linked payments, as well as offline capabilities.

As of mid-2025, the EU is racing to meet an October 2025 deadline to conclude the two-year preparatory phase for the Digital Euro and publish a "Rulebook" outlining the technical and regulatory guidelines for the Digital Euro. Based on a comprehensive report to be released at the time, an official announcement regarding the proposed launch and the legislative requirements for it will be made. Given the EU's advantages in terms of strong privacy and regulatory frameworks, technological capabilities, and existing digital infrastructure, the Digital Euro could be a significant strategic advantage if executed successfully. It could improve the ease of business and the economic consolidation of the bulk of the Eurozone, helping the EU gain a stronger foothold in the global economic order. In the rapidly shifting geopolitical and financial landscape of 2025, the Digital Euro will require a steady base of support from a diverse range of stakeholders for a seamless and successful rollout.

11.2 China and India: Staying on Course

As this book goes to press, China remains a leading adopter and promoter of CBDCs globally. China has one of the most advanced pilots at full-scale implementation and continues to declare e-Yuan reserves as part of its central ledger officially. Still functioning primarily as a retail CBDC, the e-Yuan has now seen robust adoption across almost 30 cities, with 261 million e-CNY wallets reportedly in use. In the coming months, China will need to overcome several key hurdles to achieve widespread, organic adoption of the e-Yuan, including delivering on use cases for financial inclusion and domestic adoption, addressing the growing centralization of the e-Yuan, and establishing itself as one of the preferred currencies for cross-border and Wholesale transactions. To its credit, China has taken significant strides toward achieving each of these outcomes.

However, adoption is primarily concentrated in urban and coastal areas. For China to truly unlock widespread financial inclusion and increased geopolitical influence through CBDCs, it will have to drive targeted rural and international cross-border adoption. As discussed earlier in the book, just under a third of the country's population resides in rural areas. The current pattern of adoption in urban centers thus limits the fulfillment of use cases around financial inclusion for rural and/or unbanked communities. This is not to say China has not made significant and robust efforts to drive domestic adoption of Retail CBDCs—it was one of the three official forms of payment accepted during the Winter Olympics in Beijing in 2022 and is now accepted for payments on the public transit system. Although the e-Yuan is designed to be interest-free and pegged at 1:1 with the Yuan, deeply entrenched consumer preferences for private wallets such as Alipay and WeChat remain a hurdle for the e-Yuan's widespread adoption.

Another significant hurdle remains the use of alternate currencies/assets such as bitcoin. The Chinese central bank continues to maintain an unfavorable outlook toward Bitcoin and its peers while seeking to be an alternative to it. However, with the e-Yuan's requirement for users to share personal identifiers and phone numbers, Bitcoin and its peers remain attractive outlets for users seeking to conduct transactions with a higher degree of Privacy and anonymity.

Similarly, while measures to drive cross-border adoption through mBridge and bilateral agreements with individual states support the growing influence of the e-Yuan, China has yet to see the organic adoption of the e-Yuan on a significant scale.

As China seeks to add e-Yuan to its arsenal of financial tools to challenge the dominance of the U.S. dollar, its aggressive top-down approach to drive adoption will have to be bolstered with organic stickiness of the use cases for e-Yuan to truly unlock the critical mass required to provide a credible alternate currency and payment system.

India: An Incremental Story

While vying for a similar set of outcomes, India has taken a more grass-roots with its rollout of the e-rupee. As seen earlier in the book, the approach has been more measured and cautious, with smaller pilots and incremental additions of features since 2023. As discussed earlier, the introduction of offline functionalities and integration within UPI and other existing players such as PayTM and Google Pay lays the groundwork for financially inclusive, organic growth. Another notable policy decision has been to leverage the pre-existing India stack to develop the e-rupee—displaying the CBDC's placement in a larger policy setup for digital services developed by the state (other examples of digital services built using this stack include AADHAR and the Unified Payments Interface).

The RBI's slower ramp-up of the e-rupee pilots has begun to see organic adoption, with a tenfold increase in the circulation of the e-rupee. As of mid-2025, the pilot covers 17 banks and is actively used by 6 million users. Interestingly, this has coincided with a reduction in the use of physical cash in India—as per the RBI, India's currency-GDP ratio continued its trend of moderation in 2025, indicating reduced reliance on physical cash. Our anecdotal experience complements these statistics—try paying your roadside chai-wallah, your Uber driver, or your vegetable vendor in cash, and you'll be met with a quizzical look—they don't have loose change for your cash, and they would rather you scanned the QR code and paid using any of the range of digital wallets on offer.

Looking forward, India's exploration of CBDCs has multiple promising spheres of impact. The successful scaling of offline features and offering capabilities in multiple languages can bring a significant portion of India's unbanked population in rural and remote regions into the formal banking system. This will have to be complemented with extensive socialization of these tools, with measures such as awareness campaigns, buy-in from local leaders, and sustained government programming to ensure effective use of these capabilities. Initial progress shows encouraging signs, with activity within the digital payments and banking spaces suggesting a pathway to sustainable, organic growth in the use of CBDCs. For example, in March 2025, PayPal backed Indian start up, Mintoak, acquired Digilege, which specializes in CBDC and bill payments services. Mintoak's existing partnerships with major Indian banks (e.g., HDFC, the State Bank of India (SBI)) will enable banks to offer more comprehensive CBDC-related payment solutions to their clients.

India can also leverage a scaled-up version of its digital currency to drive increased cross-border payments, with use cases extending from remittances sent by the global Indian diaspora back home to bilateral/multilateral Wholesale-equivalent payments without using the dollar as an intermediary. But for all these use cases to come to fruition, India will have to execute the transformation of the e-rupee from a promising pilot to a full-scale launch in the coming months of 2025.

11.3 United States: Drawing a Line in the Sand

In the United States, the early months of 2025 saw a very significant shift in policy related to cryptocurrency and digital asset regulation through a series of sweeping presidential executive orders. In recent years, the United States has taken cognizance of digital assets such as cryptocurrencies through ad hoc actions or deliberative policy memos. However, there was no definitive national policy regarding CBDCs or cryptocurrencies. An example of ad hoc actions included proceedings initiated by the SEC against multiple blockchain-based cryptocurrencies to determine if they were securities under the Howey test, often derailing planned Initial Coin Offerings (ICOs) or sending their value into a downward spiral.

Recent actions in 2025, although unprecedented in scope, have defined the first national policy on cryptocurrencies and stablecoins for the United States and also signaled a new era in how the federal government views blockchain technology, digital currencies, and the broader fintech ecosystem.

An Intensifying Debate: CBDCs in the United States Congress and Senate

Over the past decade, the United States has engaged in an intensifying debate within its legislative branches over the potential implementation of a CBDC. From early-stage exploration to formal legislative proposals to a definitive pause in early 2025, the discussions within Congress and the Senate reflect a range of ideological, technology-based, and economic considerations.

During the early 2020s, multiple papers and discussions ensued within the legislative branches of the U.S. government. In the early 2020s, congressional engagement with the CBDC concept can be categorized as exploratory. In January 2022, the Federal Reserve released an exploratory report seeking public comments from public stakeholders on the potential issuance of a CBDC for the United States. The paper positions CBDCs as another potential innovation in line with the historic innovations adopted or pioneered by the Federal Reserve and the United States—such as the national checking system, the automated clearing house (ACH) system from the 1970s, and the most recent FedNow service introduced for real-time interbank transfers in 2019. The paper was explicit in its exploratory nature, and clearly stated its lack of position for or against the implementation of a CBDC. Rather, it sought to set parameters and considerations for discussion.

In May 2022, the House Financial Services Committee invited testimony from the Vice Chair of the Federal Reserve Commission, Lael Brainard, who had served as a leading voice on CBDC research. Lawmakers highlighted the need for alignment from the legislative and executive branches for the potential for CBDCs to be considered by the Federal Reserve. Discussions also included the importance of the benefits outweighing the risks for a CBDC in the United States, and reviewing whether use cases for the CBDCs were already being served by solutions in the private sector.

Over the past two years, global developments, such as China's expanding digital currency pilot—gave new urgency to discussions around a CBDC in the U.S., and began to be reflected in policymaking. Congressional members introduced formal proposals either in support of or in opposition to a digital dollar. This legislative activity revealed deepening partisan divides.

Opponents of the U.S. CBDC highlighted concerns related to Privacy, surveillance, and an overreach by the Federal Reserve. They highlighted the dangers of a Retail CBDC issued directly to consumers enabling the federal government to monitor private financial transactions, suppress political dissent, or cannibalize private banking services. These fears were amplified by a broader skepticism toward centralized authority.

Champions of CBDCs presented a more fragmented perspective. Some viewed a CBDC as a potentially transformative tool that could enhance Financial inclusion, streamline government benefits, and modernize payment infrastructure. Others, however, echoed Privacy concerns and emphasized the need to balance innovation with civil liberties and market freedom.

During this time, several proposed bills highlighted the fault lines of the CBDC debate. One of the more prominent bills included the CBDC Anti-Surveillance State Act (2023–24), which sought to bar the Federal Reserve from issuing a Retail CBDC or opening digital accounts directly for consumers. Emphasizing Privacy protections, the bill passed the House in 2024 and was referred to the Senate Banking Committee, and has been reintroduced multiple times. In a similar but more absolutist vein, the No CBDC Act (2025–26), seeks to prohibit the Federal Reserve from developing any form of CBDC, whether direct-to-consumer or intermediated.

Over the past years, both chambers of Congress, through the House Financial Services Committee and the Senate Banking Committee have hosted multiple hearings, engaging Federal Reserve officials on technical design, Privacy architecture, and economic implications.

The Federal Reserve's Neutral Stance

Throughout this period, the Federal Reserve maintained a position of institutional neutrality. Further, the Federal Reserve reiterated that it will not proceed without clear legislative authorization. Executive sentiment has varied by administration. The Biden administration encouraged research and interagency collaboration with a focus on responsible innovation, while the Trump administration has taken an oppositional stance based on concerns related to privacy and market freedoms, among others. The following sections explore the evolution of the current position of the United States with a broader lens of regulating digital assets and the opposition to the CBDC.

The Strategic Bitcoin Reserve and U.S. Digital Asset Stockpile

In January 2025, President Trump signed an Executive Order (Strengthening American Leadership in Digital Financial Technology). This order revoked the Executive Order 14,067 (Ensuring Responsible Development of Digital Assets), signed by President Joe Biden in 2022, that had called for a coordinated approach to the responsible development of digital assets, including the exploration of a central bank digital currency (CBDC). It also rescinded the Treasury's "Framework for International Engagement on Digital Assets" issued in July 2022. These actions reset the federal government's approach to Blockchain and Cryptocurrency, effectively discarding the prior administration's emphasis on oversight, consumer protection, and global regulatory harmonization in favor of a more market-friendly, innovation-driven stance.

Alongside this, the Executive Order in January 2025 introduced additional changes. First, it defined "digital assets" to mean "any digital representation of value that is recorded on a distributed ledger, including cryptocurrencies, digital coins, and stablecoins" and also rescinded the Treasury's "Framework for International Engagement on Digital Assets." Second, it instituted a President's Working Group on Digital Assets Markets, tasked with developing a federal regulatory policy for digital assets. Finally, and perhaps most significantly, the order barred all agencies from continuing or initiating any actions related to the issuance or exploration of Central Bank Digital Currencies in the United States, or abroad. This drew a clear line in the sand for the United States and its stance on CBDCs.

Chaired by a Special Advisor to the President on artificial intelligence and Cryptocurrency, the Working Group for Digital Asset Markets included high-level officials from the Treasury, Securities and Exchange Commission (SEC), Commodity Futures Trading Commission (CFTC), Department of Commerce, Department of Justice (DOJ), and other relevant agencies.

The Executive Order in January 2025 was followed by another order in March 6, 2025, when President Trump signed an executive order establishing a "Strategic Bitcoin Reserve" and a "U.S. Digital Asset Stockpile." Simply put, strategic reserves or stockpiles are resources stored by governments as a safety net during times of financial or other national crisis. According to the White House, the Strategic Bitcoin Reserve is intended to hold Bitcoin (BTC) currently held by the United States. The order highlighted the strategic management of Bitcoin seized or forfeited through criminal and civil enforcement actions. These holdings will not be sold; instead, they will be retained as a strategic store of value. This approach mirrors the concept of gold reserves, positioning Bitcoin as a sovereign-grade financial asset.

The accompanying Digital Asset Stockpile extends this policy to other digital assets, including Ethereum (ETH), XRP, Solana (SOL), and Cardano (ADA). These tokens will also be held by the federal government when obtained via forfeiture. Management responsibilities fall to the Treasury Department, which must ensure the safekeeping and responsible administration of these assets. Additionally, federal agencies are required to report their digital asset holdings to the Treasury and the newly established President's Working Group on Digital Asset Markets.

A United States CBDC? An Outright Ban

As discussed earlier, one of the most controversial elements of the new orders is the outright ban on the development and issuance of a U.S. central bank digital currency. The executive orders explicitly prohibit all federal agencies from undertaking any work toward a CBDC. Existing plans or projects in progress are to be immediately terminated. The rationale cited includes strong concerns over Privacy, individual liberty, and Financial sovereignty. The administration expressed the belief that CBDCs pose a potential threat to the decentralized nature of financial markets and could lead to government overreach into citizens' financial lives. This decision places the United States at odds with numerous other nations that are actively exploring or piloting CBDC programs.

Support for Dollar-Backed Stablecoins

Unlike CBDCs, the Trump administration has embraced the concept of Stablecoins—specifically those backed by the U.S. dollar. According to the White House fact sheet, legitimate USD-backed Stablecoins are seen as tools for expanding global dollar usage and reinforcing U.S. monetary sovereignty.

The administration's position is that Stablecoins can enhance the competitiveness of the dollar in international financial markets, especially as countries like China promote their digital currencies. Encouraging the use and development of private-sector Stablecoins also aligns with the administration's broader strategy of limiting government interference in digital markets.

Regulatory Reform: Clarity and Innovation for the Digital Asset Ecosystem

Another key objective of the executive orders is to bring regulatory clarity to the digital asset ecosystem. Many industry participants have long criticized the U.S. regulatory environment as fragmented and inconsistent, with overlapping jurisdictions between the SEC, CFTC, and other agencies. The administration has directed agencies to eliminate unnecessary duplication and to ensure that all regulations are technology-neutral.

This commitment to clarity includes the expectation that agencies will issue actionable guidance to market participants. By doing so, the administration hopes to create an environment in which businesses can innovate without fear of sudden enforcement actions or ambiguous compliance standards.

Reactions to the executive orders have been swift and polarized. Cryptocurrency advocates and many Blockchain entrepreneurs welcomed the moves, viewing them as long-overdue support from the federal government. The creation of a Bitcoin reserve, in particular, was hailed as a milestone, placing the United States among the first nations to treat digital assets as a strategic national interest.

On the other hand, critics—including some lawmakers, financial institutions, and Privacy advocates—have expressed concern. The ban on CBDCs, while applauded by those who fear government surveillance, has drawn criticism from those who see CBDCs as essential to modernizing financial infrastructure. Additionally, some fear that aggressive deregulation could increase the risk of fraud, money laundering, and financial instability.

11.4 A GENIUS Move?

As discussed above, the new U.S. crypto policy sets it apart from most other developed nations. While the European Union, China, and several Latin American countries continue to pilot or implement CBDCs, the United States has charted a different path—rejecting centralized digital currencies in favor of decentralized innovation and private-sector solutions.

This divergence could influence global financial dynamics. If successful, U.S. support for Stablecoins and crypto-friendly regulation could spur further adoption of dollar-backed assets globally, countering the rise of alternative digital currencies, such as China's e-Yuan.

On July 18, 2025, President Trump signed into law the GENIUS Act, a pivotal piece of legislation that aims to establish a comprehensive federal framework for regulating payment Stablecoins. The Act, officially titled the "Guiding and Establishing National Innovation for U.S. Stablecoins Act," passed with bipartisan support in the House of Congress and the Senate, signaling a shift in federal strategy to bring clarity, security, and oversight to the rapidly evolving digital asset market.

The passage of the GENIUS Act marks the first time the U.S. federal government has created tailored legislation for a subset of digital assets. By defining legal standards for issuance, reserves, and redemption, this Act can become a model for future digital asset regulation domestically and internationally.

Supporters of the Act included a wide range of financial institutions, crypto-native companies, and policy think tanks. They argue that the GENIUS Act provides essential clarity that could unlock the broader use of Stablecoins for payments and settlements.

Critics of the Act, however, point to potential regulatory blind spots, including limited federal oversight of some state-level issuers. Additionally, concerns have been raised about conflicts of interest, particularly given the growing involvement of former public officials in crypto ventures.

Payment Stablecoin Definitions: What Is Included?

The legislation defines a payment Stablecoin as a "digital asset that is designed to be used as a means of payment or settlement that the issuer is obligated to convert, redeem, or repurchase for fixed monetary value and that the issuer represents will maintain, or creates the reasonable expectation that it will maintain, a stable value."

The Act excludes national currencies, deposits, or securities under federal securities law from the definition of "digital assets" within the scope of this Act. Importantly, the Act clearly delineates payment Stablecoins issued by permitted payment Stablecoin issuers to be outside the scope of the Securities and Exchange Commission (SEC), by precluding it from the definition of a "security."

Defining Permitted Issuers and Regulatory Thresholds

A core component of the GENIUS Act is its establishment of a class of regulated entities known as "permitted payment Stablecoin issuers." Under the law, only these entities are legally authorized to issue payment Stablecoins within the United States. Foreign entities from jurisdictions deemed compatible with the GENIUS Act will be allowed to hold Stablecoins in the United States after registering with the OCC.

Issuers are subject to regulatory oversight from the OCC, and will require registration or certification from requisite authorities in order to issue and offer Stablecoins. Notably, public companies that are not primarily engaged in financial activities must pass a separate review showing no systemic risk to the U.S. banking system to become permitted payment Stablecoin issuers.

Typically, issuers can issue/manage Stablecoins, manage reserves (e.g., maintain one-to-one reserves in highly liquid assets), and offer limited services related to digital assets. The Act also bars payment of interest or yield by issuers to holders to payment Stablecoin holders, and heavily regulates use of payment Stablecoins for interbank settlements. The measure barring interest payments is presumably intended to prevent these digital assets from functioning as unregulated savings accounts or investment vehicles.

However, an approximate one year transition period has been set for these regulations to come into force. Until such time, Stablecoins can be issued and offered by anyone.

Supervisory and Enforcement Mechanisms

Supervision under the GENIUS Act is bifurcated based on the nature and scale of the issuer. The Office of the Comptroller of Currency (OCC) regulates federal issuers, and federal banking agencies regulate subsidiaries of insured banks. States can regulate issuers with under $10B in Stablecoins if their standards are "substantially similar" to federal rules, subject to federal certification.

The law also imposes compliance requirements with existing anti-money laundering (AML) and counter-terrorism financing (CTF) laws.

Preservation of Traditional Banking Roles

The GENIUS Act ensures that the legislation does not alter the eligibility of banks for Federal Reserve master accounts. It also preserves the current practice of banks holding Stablecoin reserves, thus providing continuity for existing institutional custodial relationships. This clarification was seen as necessary by banking industry groups to prevent regulatory uncertainty.

Legislative Process and Political Context

As discussed above, the GENIUS Act is now law, having passed the Senate by a vote of 66–32 after months of bipartisan negotiations, followed by House approval with a 308–122 vote. Key amendments were added to enhance consumer protections, mitigate systemic risk, and clearly define eligibility criteria for permitted stablecoin issuers. Supporters of the law include a wide range of financial institutions, crypto-native companies, and policy think tanks. They argue that the GENIUS Act provides essential clarity that could unlock the broader use of stablecoins for payments and settlements.

Critics of the Act, however, point to potential regulatory blind spots, including limited federal oversight of some state-level issuers. Additionally, concerns have been raised about conflicts of interest, particularly given the growing involvement of former public officials in crypto ventures. One of the most prominent examples is President Donald Trump's launch of his own stablecoin USD1 which follows the very framework required and established by the GENIUS Act. This has fueled accusations with critics arguing that the Act's passage under his administration could create a favorable regulatory environment for ventures he stands to personally benefit and profit from. Supporters emphasize the importance of preserving a level playing field while safeguarding consumers and the broader financial system.

The passage of the GENIUS Act marks the first time the U.S. federal government has created tailored legislation for a subset of digital assets. By defining legal standards for issuance, reserves, and redemption, the law could become a model for future digital asset regulation domestically and internationally in the future.

11.5 A Red Carpet for Crypto and a Closed Door for CBDCs in 2025

At first glance, the inherent contradiction between banning CBDCs and encouraging cryptocurrencies and Blockchain-based digital assets seems counterintuitive. Why would the state encourage the private pursuit of a digital asset class but refrain from creating one themselves?

In the case of the United States, three primary arguments undergird this set of policy decisions: crypto's massive, influence-wielding user base, fear of government control and surveillance, and a market failure perspective.

The Crypto Community—A New Constituency?

The U.S. decision is rooted in the recognition that millions of Americans participate in some form of engagement with cryptocurrencies, forming an influential, politically active constituency. Estimates suggest tens of millions of Americans own Bitcoin or Ethereum, and millions more use Stablecoins and DeFi platforms. According to the Congressional Research Service, Retail Cryptocurrency ownership in the United States exceeds tens of millions—comparable in scale to major utility services.

This massive base has shaped policymaking. Regulators prioritized crypto-friendly legal clarity rather than pursuing a CBDC, shifting resources toward private digital asset regulation. For example, in May 2024, the House passed the "CBDC Anti-Surveillance State Act" (216–192), effectively blocking a Fed-issued CBDC out of concern that it would surveil crypto users and infringe on their preferences. As discussed earlier in this chapter, the White House executive order in January 2025 explicitly banned U.S. agencies from establishing or promoting CBDCs while supporting an environment conducive to digital asset innovation.

Government Control and Surveillance—A Challenge to Individual Liberties?

A second pillar of resistance is based on deep-rooted concerns about Privacy and the consolidation of state control. U.S. citizens and lawmakers alike have highlighted the potential of CBDCs to drive unprecedented government surveillance and control. This concern is not limited to policymakers and citizens of the United States; one of the most significant drawbacks of implementing CBDCs remains their ability to enable unprecedented financial surveillance in ecosystems without requisite checks and balances. This includes the potential for government agencies to have direct access to every transaction—raising fears of funds being frozen, lifestyles being targeted, or Privacy being routinely infringed.

Learning from other nations' experiences plays a role. Extensive debate has emphasized that a CBDC could allow the government to "flip a switch" and monitor or block private transactions at will, potentially clashing with individual liberties. To this extent, the United States' reticence to embrace CBDCs reflects an academic and public concern about tracking every dollar a person spends or receives. The conviction to prevent a "surveillance state" overreach is not unmerited. However, a balanced view that weighs the potential benefits and the opportunity cost of other major economies engaging in bilateral/cross-border transitions using their CBDCs is valuable.

A "Solution Without A Problem"?—The Market Failure Perspective

The third fundamental argument lies in economic analysis. CBDCs, despite technological promise, could introduce material market distortions—unlike cryptocurrencies, which operate alongside banks and financial intermediaries.

One concern is the potential Disintermediation of existing banking structures. Nearly all research indicates that if citizens could hold funds directly at the Fed, money would migrate from commercial banks, harming their ability to lend and manage liquidity. Examples of the Bahamian Sand Dollar and the e-Naira underscore that CBDCs can threaten traditional banking stability unless they are highly constrained. CBDCs centralize power in a single trusted issuer. This can make them not just a new payment method but a powerful instrument of state control, affecting not only market dynamics but also Cybersecurity, Privacy, and competitive innovation.

From the perspective of market failure, the private sector in the United States already delivers fast, low-cost digital payments; public digital implementations (e.g., FedNow) compete well with Visa and Mastercard. Unlike such optional infrastructures, a mandatory CBDC would have no market discipline, potentially lowering systemic resilience. This concern is not unfounded either—as discussed earlier, the existence of similar private digital payment services has diluted the use case for the adoption of CBDCs in countries like China. This perspective has also been echoed over the past few years by major policymakers in the United States—with a senior leader from the Federal Reserve famously calling CBDCs a "solution without a problem" in an address to the American Enterprise Institute in Washington, D.C., in 2021.

11.6 More Than a Token Gesture—Dubai's Visionary Ecosystem for Tokenization

To round out an understanding of developments in 2025, this section highlights Dubai's policy-backed actions to become a leading center of financial innovation.

Dubai has rapidly positioned itself as a global frontrunner in Blockchain-based Tokenization, leveraging a blend of forward-thinking regulation, strategic infrastructure investment, and robust institutional collaboration. Dubai's approach is marked by a sophisticated regulatory framework that provides clarity for real-world asset (RWA) Tokenization while offering investor protections that foster trust in this emerging financial paradigm. This foundation has allowed Dubai to evolve into a vibrant hub for fractional ownership and Blockchain innovation.

Dubai's Tokenization ecosystem is anchored by a multi-tiered regulatory framework that seeks to strike a balance between innovation and prudence. At the forefront is the Virtual Asset Regulatory Authority (VARA), which, in its May 2025 Rulebook update, introduced a new class of digital instruments known as Asset-Referenced Virtual Assets (ARVAs). These tokens enable regulated entities—such as exchanges and broker-dealers—to offer tokenized representations of real-world assets, including real estate and commodities. VARA's mandate includes strict anti-money laundering (AML) measures, comprehensive client screening, and mandatory Cybersecurity audits for all virtual asset service providers (VASPs). Working in concert with the Dubai Land Department (DLD), VARA also facilitates the integration of Blockchain-verified property title deeds with traditional land registries.

Complementing VARA's oversight is the Dubai International Financial Centre (DIFC), which operates under the Digital Assets Law No. 2 of 2024. The DIFC framework expressly prohibits Privacy coins and algorithmic tokens to maintain transparency and regulatory compliance. In March 2025, it launched a dedicated Tokenization sandbox—an experimental zone where participants can test the Tokenization of equities, bonds, and sukuk under relaxed regulatory conditions. Even for public Blockchain deployments, the DIFC requires permissioned access for any consumer-facing tokenized assets, ensuring a level of control and security even within decentralized environments.

At the federal level, collaboration between the Securities and Commodities Authority (SCA) and the Central Bank of the UAE ensures consistent oversight across the nation. The SCA enforces AML compliance in crypto markets, while the Central Bank regulates fiat-to-crypto onramps and offramps. Government-aligned think tanks, such as the Dubai Future Foundation, further support the ecosystem by backing initiatives like the Real Estate Sandbox, which aims to integrate Blockchain-based property transactions with legacy systems.

Transformative Projects and Industry Players

Dubai's commitment to real estate Tokenization is evident in several key ventures. Prypco Mint, in partnership with the DLD and Blockchain infrastructure provider Ctrl Alt, has pioneered the Tokenization of property title deeds on the XRP Ledger. This enables fractional ownership of real estate with entry points as low as AED 2,000 (approximately $540). The platform has ambitious goals: By 2033, it aims to tokenize 7%—around $16 billion—of Dubai's real estate market.

Other Blockchain firms, such as MANTRA, are also contributing to this movement by working with developers to fractionalize premium properties. Meanwhile, Ctrl Alt continues to provide the backend Tokenization infrastructure that ensures real-time synchronization between Blockchain systems and government land registries. Chainalysis, a leading analytics firm, supports the ecosystem by offering compliance tools that monitor illicit activity and ensure regulatory adherence.

On the institutional side, Zodia Markets—a crypto trading platform backed by Standard Chartered—offers institutional-grade services under the oversight of Abu Dhabi's ADGM. Crypto.com, another major player, has partnered with the Dubai Department of Finance to facilitate crypto payments for government fees, aligning with the city's broader push toward a cashless economy.

Catalysts Driving Growth

Dubai's aggressive digital transformation strategy is a major catalyst behind the rise of Tokenization. The Dubai Cashless Strategy, for example, aims to achieve 90% digital transaction adoption by 2026. As part of this initiative, residents can already pay for utilities, visas, and licenses using Cryptocurrency.

On the technological front, Dubai's Blockchain infrastructure is among the most advanced globally. The DLD has deployed direct API integrations between its registry and platforms like Prypco Mint, enabling seamless real-time updates for tokenized assets. Furthermore, Dubai mandates that all public Blockchain projects, including those on the XRP Ledger, adhere to internationally recognized ISO security standards to ensure system interoperability and data integrity.

Investor accessibility is also a key factor. Fractional ownership models dramatically lower the entry threshold for Retail investors, making luxury apartments and commercial towers accessible to a broader audience. At the same time, the city's tax-free zones and streamlined licensing processes continue to attract Blockchain firms from across the globe.

Remaining Risks and Challenges

Despite its progress, Dubai's Tokenization ecosystem is not without challenges. Regulatory gaps persist in areas such as cross-border asset transfers and inheritance laws related to tokenized holdings. Market volatility remains a concern as well, especially when RWA tokens are tied to unstable cryptocurrencies or collateralized by volatile assets. Technical risks, including smart contract bugs and potential Blockchain outages, also pose threats to the reliability of Tokenization platforms.

11.6.1 A Blueprint for the Future

Dubai's success in building a thriving Tokenization ecosystem stems from its unique mix of regulatory clarity, technological sophistication, and strategic public–private collaboration. With a strong initial focus on real estate and institutional finance, the city has created a replicable model for scalable RWA Tokenization. However, sustaining this momentum will require further innovation—particularly in achieving cross-border interoperability and expanding the types of assets that can be tokenized.

Projects like the DLD's $16 billion real estate digitization plan and VARA's ARVA framework illustrate the city's long-term commitment to Blockchain. As global markets continue to explore the potential of tokenized economies, Dubai stands as a bold and proactive leader—one that is setting the standard for the digital financial systems of tomorrow.

11.7 Case Study: EMAAR

Strategic investments, visionary governance, and the active participation of major private-sector players have shaped Dubai's meteoric rise as a global leader in Blockchain innovation. Among the pioneers in this transformation is EMAAR Properties—the developer responsible for some of the city's most iconic landmarks, including the Burj Khalifa and Dubai Mall. EMAAR has leveraged Blockchain technology to reimagine the dynamics of real estate ownership and investment.

This section explores EMAAR's Tokenization journey—from early experiments with loyalty tokens to the ambitious digitization of real estate assets—within the broader context of Dubai's national objective to tokenize 7% (approximately $16 billion) of its real estate market by 2033.

From Loyalty to Liquidity: The EMR Token (2019)

EMAAR's foray into Blockchain began in 2019 with the launch of EMR, a Blockchain-based loyalty token designed to reward customer engagement across its diverse portfolio of properties, hotels, Retail outlets, and leisure experiences. Rather than tokenizing real estate directly, EMR represented a strategic first step into the digital asset economy—an initiative focused on user incentivization and digital engagement.

EMR was developed on Quorum, JPMorgan's enterprise-grade variant of Ethereum, offering a permissioned Blockchain with smart contract capabilities. The token was not just a points-based loyalty mechanism; it was tradable and redeemable, offering users the ability to exchange tokens for services and goods across EMAAR's ecosystem. This functionality gave EMR tangible monetary value, an innovation that positioned EMAAR at the intersection of customer experience and digital finance.

The token was accessible via a mobile application (available on both iOS and Android), reflecting EMAAR's intent to appeal to digitally native consumers with a "blockchain rewards" application. While this initial phase did not tokenize real estate itself, it set the groundwork for a more ambitious vision: leveraging Blockchain to redefine ownership models in high-value property markets.

Phase Two: Real Estate Asset Tokenization (2020–2025)

In 2020, EMAAR transitioned from utility tokens to the more complex endeavor of real estate asset Tokenization. The goal was to democratize access to premium real estate by fractionalizing ownership of high-value assets such as the Burj Khalifa. This move would allow both institutional and Retail investors to gain exposure to historically inaccessible properties.

EMAAR partnered with IBM's Hyperledger Fabric, highlighting the emerging trend related to enterprise Blockchain: technical infrastructure must be tailored to both regulatory compliance and operational complexity. EMAAR's partnership with Swisscom Blockchain, a recognized player in digital infrastructure, ensured the architecture was enterprise-ready and future-proof.

The Tokenization effort was ambitious in scale. EMAAR aimed to tokenize a significant portion of its portfolio, which had seen the sale of over 30,500 residential units during the preceding decade. This move was not merely a digitization exercise but a structural transformation intended to bring liquidity, divisibility, and transparency to real estate markets.

Regulatory Alignment: Working with VARA and the Dubai Land Department

EMAAR's Tokenization initiative coincided with—and benefited from—the launch of Dubai's Real Estate Tokenization Project in March 2025. Spearheaded by the Dubai Land Department (DLD) in coordination with the Virtual Assets Regulatory Authority (VARA), this project established the legal and technological infrastructure needed to support tokenized real estate in the emirate.

Under the new framework, tokenized real estate assets had to comply with VARA's Asset-Referenced Virtual Assets (ARVA) regulations. These rules mandated anti-money laundering (AML) checks, Cybersecurity audits, and strict governance mechanisms. Tokens could also be synchronized with the DLD's Blockchain-based land registry, ensuring that ownership rights could be verified, transferred, and enforced with legal backing.

The collaboration with regulators gave EMAAR's initiative a crucial layer of legitimacy and investor confidence, distinguishing it from many informal or unregulated Tokenization attempts. For example, DLD's initiatives for tokenizations allowed investors to start investing in real estate tokens for as little as 500 dirhams (approximately 135 USD) provided that they follow standard compliance norms (e.g., Know Your Customer verification). This taps into a massive network of small and medium scale investors that can provide momentum to Dubai's vision.

While EMAAR is one example, Dubai's ecosystem extends its tokenization infrastructure and opportunities to a range of applicable players.

Challenges Along the Way

Despite its progress, EMAAR's Tokenization journey has not been without challenges. The technical pivot from Hedera Hashgraph to Hyperledger Fabric highlighted the complexity of choosing the right distributed ledger technology for asset Tokenization at scale. The initial promise of speed and scalability had to be weighed against compliance, governance, and enterprise integration needs.

Additionally, while fractionalization increased access for Retail investors, traditional institutional buyers remained cautious. For many, the leap from brick-and-mortar real estate to digital tokens still raised concerns about legal enforceability, valuation standards, and market volatility. Bridging this perception gap will be essential for broader adoption.

Nevertheless, EMAAR's leadership in this space—alongside other notable players, such as Prypco and MANTRA—has added significant momentum to Dubai's ambitious Tokenization roadmap.

Strategic Impact and the Road Ahead

EMAAR's evolution from a loyalty token innovator to a full-fledged leader in real estate Tokenization is emblematic of Dubai's broader push toward Blockchain-integrated capital markets. By embedding Digital ledger technologies into its core business strategy, EMAAR is not merely digitizing assets—it is reengineering how value is created, transferred, and owned in the twenty-first-century property market.

The alignment with government initiatives ensures that EMAAR is not operating in a regulatory vacuum. Instead, it is contributing to the $16 billion tokenized real estate goal laid out in Dubai's digitization strategy. This synergy between public infrastructure and private enterprise is critical to creating an interoperable, trustworthy, and scalable Tokenization ecosystem.

Looking ahead, the challenge will be twofold: scaling up tokenized offerings across more real estate categories and addressing legacy investor skepticism through education, legal clarity, and transparent performance metrics. However, the foundation has been laid. EMAAR's journey provides a replicable blueprint for real estate developers worldwide seeking to leverage Blockchain for structural transformation.

11.8 Looking Ahead: What Does 2025 Promise?

2025 marks a pivotal year in the evolution of CBDCs. With the United States' decision not to pursue a CBDC, other major economies will likely draw their own lines in the sand based on their opportunities and roadblocks. While only a handful of countries (e.g., Bahamas, Jamaica, Nigeria) have fully launched CBDCs, 2025 is expected to bring more concrete decisions and potential launches, particularly as central banks finalize pilot programs and address outstanding policy issues. Collaborative projects such as Project mBridge are pioneering cross-border CBDC interoperability.

The success of CBDCs will depend on striking a balance between innovation, stability, and trust—ensuring that digital currencies enhance, rather than disrupt, the global financial ecosystem. As we will discuss in the upcoming chapter, the coming years will likely see accelerated adoption, deeper integration with traditional finance, and a reshaping of how money moves across borders and societies.

12

Moving Forward

Main Messages

- Trust, education, and interoperability are critical for CBDC adoption, requiring strong public communication, secure systems, and seamless cross-border integration.
- Regulatory fragmentation, infrastructure gaps, and privacy concerns must be addressed to build public acceptance and ensure global scalability.
- CBDCs offer growth in financial inclusion, cross-border trade, programmable money, and sustainable finance through public–private innovation and global collaboration.

As Central Bank Digital Currencies (CBDCs) continue to evolve from concepts to real-world implementations, the focus now shifts toward the future. Technological advancement is imperative for CBDCs, but global adoption would also be crucial for their success and implementation. The roadmap for the widespread adoption of CBDCs is a challenging one, but there are plenty of opportunities and areas of exciting growth that will shape their future.

12.1 The Road to Adoption: Key Drivers

To successfully move forward with CBDC adoption, several key drivers must align. The first and most fundamental aspect is trust. Central banks and governments need to work diligently to build public confidence in CBDCs, ensuring that the benefits of digital currencies, including security, efficiency, and accessibility, outweigh any perceived risks. This will require transparency, robust security measures, and clear communication from central banks about how these currencies will function in practice. There will also need to be a form of backing for these digital currencies. This could involve offering insurance similar to that provided by the Federal Deposit Insurance Corporation (FDIC) in the United States, which insures bank account deposits up to $250,000. By extending this insurance to digital wallets or through other alternative methods, government-backed digital wallets may gain some more credibility over privately offered digital wallets, which do not provide such a service.

Education and awareness are also crucial. CBDCs will not just be adopted because they are offered. Different countries may choose to implement a CBDC for different purposes. In the European Union, a CBDC might be introduced to preserve monetary sovereignty. In China, it may serve multiple purposes, offering financial inclusion and programmable welfare funds domestically, while strengthening China's ability to conduct bilateral trade and enable Cross-border payments.. In India or the Philippines, however, CBDCs may be introduced to address issues in Financial inclusion in a largely unbanked society. Other reasons for implementation include stronger oversight, combating illicit activity, or utilizing transaction data to inform monetary policy, among other objectives. Once a country has a reason for implementing a CBDC, it is then crucial for digital currencies to grow among both consumers and businesses to be effectively implemented throughout the economy. This will only be accomplished through education on how to use digital currencies and how to stay informed and vigilant of any potential scams. If people are confused and fall victim to scams involving CBDCs, faith and trust in the system can collapse rapidly. Once a country develops a bad or negative reputation, it will be very difficult to turn things around. Central banks must provide resources, support, and incentives for the adoption of CBDCs, and businesses must be encouraged to integrate them into their systems.

A third key driver is interoperability. As countries move toward developing their CBDCs, ensuring these digital currencies can work seamlessly with other countries' currencies will be critical for global adoption. Interoperability will enable frictionless cross-border transactions and reduce barriers for businesses and individuals operating across borders. This is also very important for the USD to accomplish, as it is the world's de facto global currency. In order to maintain this dominance, interoperability is key, as well as seamless cross-border capabilities.

12.2 Challenges to Overcome

While the future of CBDCs holds promise, significant challenges remain on the path to their widespread adoption. One of the most pressing issues is regulatory alignment. Governments and central banks must collaborate on international standards and regulations for CBDCs. Without a unified global approach, the adoption of CBDCs could be slow and fragmented. Countries will need to collaborate to establish a unified legal framework that facilitates secure and efficient cross-border transactions. Democracies may disagree over how much the government should be involved in a CBDC offering, what level of insurance or incentives is appropriate, and who will bear the costs of development and maintenance.

A challenge that is often overlooked but equally important is technological infrastructure. While many nations are developing their CBDCs, the actual infrastructure to support them, from secure digital wallets to blockchain-based platforms, is still in the process of being built. Central banks will need to make substantial investments in technology, ensuring that the systems are scalable, secure, and capable of handling the volume of transactions that will accompany the adoption of CBDCs.

Public acceptance is another challenge. While the financial and technological aspects of CBDCs may be robust, convincing the general public to adopt digital currencies requires addressing concerns over privacy, security, and the potential for digital currency misuse. To foster public trust, central banks must prioritize not only security measures but also the privacy of user data. Another way to incentivize people to switch to a CBDC offering is by ensuring that they are a cheaper method of transacting.

12.3 Opportunities for Growth

While challenges exist, the opportunities for growth in CBDC adoption are vast. One of the most exciting areas is financial inclusion. By providing digital access to a country's currency, CBDCs can empower millions of people around the world who are excluded from traditional banking systems. This could be particularly transformative in developing countries where banking infrastructure is scarce, allowing citizens to transact securely and access financial services via smartphones.

The integration of CBDCs into consumer and business ecosystems presents another major growth opportunity. Once CBDCs become mainstream, businesses will need to adapt their payment systems to accept digital currencies, creating new avenues for innovation in payments, lending, and financial products. This will stimulate new startups, fintech companies, and platforms built around the CBDC ecosystem, driving economic activity and growth.

CBDCs will also open doors to a new era of cross-border trade. By providing instant, low-cost, and transparent international payments, CBDCs can greatly reduce the friction involved in global commerce. As central banks develop infrastructure for cross-border digital currency transactions, international trade will become more efficient, enabling companies to expand into new markets and individuals to make seamless Cross-border payments. The ease of cross-border payments will also drive a reordering of global financial networks and payment corridors, offering countries more flexibility to trade bilaterally with each other.

Another exciting opportunity is the potential for collaboration between the public and private sectors. Governments and central banks could work with fintech companies and digital infrastructure providers to design and implement CBDC solutions that are both secure and accessible. This collaboration can foster innovation while ensuring that CBDCs remain aligned with public policy goals.

12.4 Exciting Areas of Growth: What Is Next for CBDCs?

Looking ahead, several areas are primed for growth in the CBDC space:

- **Programmable Money**: One of the most exciting possibilities for CBDCs is the ability to program them for specific uses. Governments and central banks could design CBDCs that are programmable, allowing for Smart contracts, targeted stimulus payments, and other advanced financial instruments. This could lead to the rise of new, efficient ways for central banks to conduct monetary policy, as well as new business models that leverage programmable digital currencies.
    - However, programmable money also comes with risk and adds another level of government involvement in people's funds. This could be met with pushback as money that is limited to certain shops or with an expiration date could create inefficiencies within the economy.
- **Digital identity Integration**: The future of CBDCs may also involve the seamless integration of digital identities with Central Bank Digital Currencies (CBDCs). By combining CBDCs with secure Digital identity systems, governments could streamline access to public services, reduce fraud, and enable easier access to financial products for consumers. This could also simplify Know Your Customer (KYC) and Anti-Money Laundering (AML) processes, further enhancing the security and efficiency of digital currency transactions.
    - This also creates a problem where people have less Privacy in their transactions. This is a significant concern and one of the primary arguments people raise when advocating against the adoption of CBDCs.
- **Central Bank Collaboration**: As more countries develop their own CBDCs, the potential for international collaboration is growing. Central banks could collaborate to create shared digital currency networks that facilitate global trade and investment. These networks could reduce the need for intermediaries, streamline foreign exchange transactions, and reduce costs for both businesses and consumers.
    - This has already been observed in coalitions such as BRICS (Brazil, Russia, India, China, South Africa), which are implementing their own currency to avoid transacting in USD and paying fees for doing so. As coalitions like BRICS begin to take hold and issue their own forms of currency, CBDC implementation could be massive in frictionless,

cross-border, secure payments of their own currency among partner countries.

- **Tokenization of Assets:** CBDCs could pave the way for the broader tokenization of assets, from real estate to commodities to shares in companies. With CBDCs as a base currency, tokenized assets could be traded on decentralized exchanges or within secure digital platforms. This could revolutionize the way people invest, enabling fractional ownership and increased access to markets that were previously inaccessible to the general public.
  - This is already happening in many countries, such as the United Arab Emirates, which has been researching the use of blockchain and tokenization to track property ownership. By implementing tokenization alongside the blockchain, the transfer of ownership could be seamless and done without major government approvals.
- **Sustainability:** A growing area of interest is the use of CBDCs to drive sustainable finance. Central banks could implement mechanisms within CBDCs that incentivize sustainable practices, such as rewarding environmentally conscious transactions or directing investments toward green projects. This could turn CBDCs into powerful tools for promoting sustainable growth and aligning financial systems with global sustainability goals.

12.5 The End of the Beginning: Charting the Future of Money with CBDCs

The journey toward integrating Central Bank Digital Currencies (CBDCs) into everyday life will be a marathon, not a sprint—but the potential rewards are substantial. For CBDCs to advance successfully, a concerted effort is needed from governments, central banks, the banking sector, fintech firms, and the general public. Most importantly, trust, transparency, and clear communication among these stakeholders will be essential to their success. While the path to mainstream adoption presents significant challenges, the opportunities to drive economic growth, Financial inclusion, and innovation are too important to ignore.

It is particularly noteworthy that CBDC pilots and launches are, so far, taking place in emerging markets—in countries often grappling with persistent currency volatility, capital outflows, and macroeconomic instability. In these economies, a common structural challenge lies in the mismatch between the denomination of income and that of debt: while households and businesses primarily earn in local currency, governments and large corporations frequently rely on U.S. dollar funding to access global capital markets. This dynamic exposes countries to severe financial strain whenever their local currencies depreciate, eroding purchasing power and investor confidence.

In response, several emerging markets have explored alternative monetary frameworks in pursuit of greater stability. Some, like Ecuador, Panama, El Salvador, or Zimbabwe, have opted for full or partial dollarization to anchor trust in their financial systems. Others have turned to digital alternatives such as Bitcoin—as in El Salvador's highly publicized experiment—or are now actively trialing Central Bank Digital Currencies as a state-backed solution to long-standing currency vulnerabilities.

CBDCs, in particular, offer these nations a potentially transformative tool: one that could enhance monetary sovereignty, reduce dependence on foreign currencies, and improve the efficiency and security of domestic payment systems. While the outcomes of these initiatives remain uncertain and success is far from guaranteed, what is clear is the growing determination among emerging market policymakers to explore new pathways toward currency stability and financial resilience in the digital age.

Looking ahead, we can anticipate an increasingly interconnected world powered by secure, efficient, and programmable CBDCs. These digital currencies are likely to be integrated into broader digital finance ecosystems, enabling real-time cross-border payments, automated regulatory compliance, and personalized financial services through smart contracts and AI-powered platforms. Their programmability could unlock transformative capabilities—from conditional welfare disbursements to more targeted and responsive Monetary policy tools tailored to specific sectors or regions.

Interoperability among national CBDCs will be vital in reshaping the global financial landscape. Initiatives such as the mBridge project and cross-border trials spearheaded by the Bank for International Settlements (BIS) Innovation Hub suggest the emergence of a multipolar digital currency system. This evolution could reduce dependence on traditional intermediaries while enhancing the resilience and efficiency of global payments infrastructure.

However, the future of CBDCs will be shaped by ongoing debates around privacy, security, governance, and the role of the state in digital finance. Striking the right balance—between regulatory transparency and user privacy—will be critical for building public trust and ensuring widespread adoption. The decisions made by early adopters will serve as influential models, offering both inspiration and cautionary lessons for others.

CBDCs also offer promising avenues for advancing sustainable finance. With enhanced traceability, digital currencies can support compliance monitoring, promote green investments, and encourage responsible consumption through data-driven incentives. In emerging and developing economies, CBDCs could significantly expand access to financial services, empower micro-entrepreneurs, and lower remittance costs—fostering more inclusive and equitable growth.

The evolution of CBDCs will not only redefine the future of money but also lay the foundation for a more efficient, inclusive, and resilient financial system. As technological innovation converges with regulatory reform and international cooperation, CBDCs are poised to become a cornerstone of twenty-first-century economic infrastructure. The journey is just beginning, but the future holds immense promise—and the decisions made today will shape how that future unfolds.

Appendix

Acronyms

AEPS
Aadhaar Enabled Payment System. A bank-led model in India that allows customers to make financial transactions using their Aadhaar number and biometric authentication. (NPCI)

AFI
Authorized Financial Institution. A financial institution approved by a regulatory body to offer certain banking or investment services. (Oxford Reference)

AML
Anti-Money Laundering. A set of regulations and practices aimed at preventing criminals from disguising illegally obtained funds as legitimate income. (Oxford Reference)

BACH
Bahamas Automated Clearing House. A national electronic network that facilitates bulk payments and interbank transfers in The Bahamas. (Central Bank of The Bahamas)

BCRP
Central Reserve Bank of Peru. The central bank of Peru, responsible for monetary policy and currency issuance. (BCRP)

BHIM
Bharat Interface for Money. A mobile app developed by NPCI based on UPI to promote cashless payments in India. (NPCI)

BISS
Bahamas Interbank Settlement System. A real-time settlement system managed by the Central Bank of The Bahamas for interbank transactions. (Central Bank of The Bahamas)

CBDC
Central Bank Digital Currency. A digital form of fiat money issued and backed by a central bank, intended as legal tender. (BIS)

CTF
Counter-Terrorism Financing. Measures and practices aimed at preventing the flow of funds to terrorist organizations. (Oxford Reference)

DLD
Dubai Land Department. The government agency responsible for overseeing land registration, real estate regulation, and transactions in Dubai. (Government of Dubai)

DLT
Distributed Ledger Technology. A digital infrastructure that records and synchronizes data across multiple locations in a decentralized manner. (Oxford Reference)

ECB
European Central Bank. The central bank responsible for managing the euro and monetary policy for the eurozone. (ECB)

e-CNY
China's Digital Yuan. The digital version of China's currency issued by the People's Bank of China, part of its CBDC initiative. (PBoC)

IBFT
Istanbul Byzantine Fault Tolerance. A consensus mechanism used in blockchain systems that ensures fast finality through validator agreement. (Ethereum Developer Docs)

IMF
International Monetary Fund. An international organization that fosters global monetary cooperation and provides financial support to member countries. (IMF)

IMPS
Immediate Payment Service. An Indian electronic funds transfer system that allows instant bank-to-bank payments 24/7. (NPCI)

KYC
Know Your Customer. A regulatory process requiring financial institutions to verify customer identities and assess potential risk. (Oxford Reference)

mBridge
Multiple CBDC Bridge Project. A cross-border payments initiative using DLT to enable instant, low-cost transactions between participating central banks. (BIS Innovation Hub)

NACH
National Automated Clearing House. An Indian centralized payment system for bulk, high-volume, recurring transactions like salaries and subsidies. (NPCI)

NCMC
National Common Mobility Card. India's interoperable contactless smart card for payments across transit, tolls, and retail. (Ministry of Housing and Urban Affairs, India)

NEFT
National Electronic Funds Transfer. A nationwide payment system in India enabling one-to-one fund transfers between banks. (RBI)

NETC
National Electronic Toll Collection. An Indian system for cashless toll payments using RFID tags (FASTag), allowing interoperability across toll plazas. (NPCI)

NPCI
National Payments Corporation of India. The umbrella organization for retail payment systems in India, including UPI, IMPS, and NACH. (NPCI)

NPCI-I
NPCI International. The subsidiary of NPCI focused on expanding Indian digital payment solutions like UPI and RuPay globally. (NPCI)

OCC
Office of the Comptroller of the Currency. A U.S. federal agency regulating and supervising national banks and federal savings associations. (U.S. Department of the Treasury)

PBFT
Practical Byzantine Fault Tolerance. A consensus algorithm that enables agreement among distributed systems even when some nodes act maliciously. (MIT/Blockchain Literature)

PoA
Proof of Authority. A blockchain consensus mechanism where pre-approved validators confirm transactions, enabling fast, energy-efficient operations. (Ethereum Developer Docs)

PPI

Prepaid Payment Instrument. A financial tool (e.g., wallet or card) that allows users to store value and make purchases without a linked bank account. (RBI)

PSMI

Payment System Modernization Initiative. A strategy to upgrade and digitize legacy payment infrastructures, promoting efficiency and real-time capabilities. (Policy Reports)

RBI

Reserve Bank of India. India's central bank, responsible for monetary policy, regulation of the banking sector, and issuance of currency. (RBI)

RTGS

Real-Time Gross Settlement. A payment system that enables the real-time, individual settlement of high-value transactions without netting. (BIS)

SWIFT

Society for Worldwide Interbank Financial Telecommunication. A global messaging network used by financial institutions to securely transmit payment and securities data. (SWIFT)

UPI

Unified Payments Interface. A real-time Indian payment system that allows users to transfer funds instantly across banks using mobile devices. (NPCI)

USSD

Unstructured Supplementary Service Data. A GSM-based communication protocol enabling mobile banking and payments without Internet access. (Telecom Regulatory Authority of India)

VARA

Virtual Assets Regulatory Authority. The regulatory body overseeing virtual asset services and providers in Dubai. (Government of Dubai)

ZiG

Zimbabwe Gold-Backed Digital Token. A digital currency introduced by Zimbabwe's central bank, backed by gold reserves. (Reserve Bank of Zimbabwe)

Glossary

AML

Anti-Money Laundering. A set of procedures, laws, and regulations designed to stop the practice of generating income through illegal actions. (Oxford Reference)

Appendix

API
Application Programming Interface. A set of routines and protocols used for building software and allowing different programs to communicate. (Oxford English Dictionary)

Accessibility
The quality of being able to be reached or entered; in a digital finance context, it refers to the ease with which users can access and use financial systems. (Oxford English Dictionary)

Account
A record or arrangement where financial transactions are tracked for individuals or entities, typically by a financial institution. (Oxford English Dictionary)

Account-Based
A system in which access to funds or services is determined by verification of identity linked to an account, rather than possession of tokens. (Bank for International Settlements)

Agent
A person or entity authorized to act on behalf of another in a business transaction. In finance, often refers to a payment agent or representative institution. (Oxford Reference)

Agreement
A negotiated and legally binding arrangement between parties, often detailing obligations, payments, or terms of service. (Oxford English Dictionary)

Algorithm
A set of defined, step-by-step instructions used for calculations or problem-solving, especially by a computer. (Oxford English Dictionary)

Anonymity
The condition of being anonymous; in digital finance, the state in which user identities are not tied to transactions. (Oxford English Dictionary)

Application Programming Interface
See "API."

Auditability
The ability of a system to be audited—i.e., examined for accuracy, integrity, and compliance with standards. (Oxford Reference)

Authentication
The process of verifying the identity of a person or system, particularly before granting access to services or data. (Oxford English Dictionary)

Authorization
The process of granting someone permission to do or have something, often following authentication in digital systems. (Oxford English Dictionary)

Automated
Operated automatically using pre-programmed instructions or technology, without human intervention. (Oxford English Dictionary)

Automation
The use of technology to perform tasks with reduced human assistance, increasing efficiency and reducing error. (Oxford English Dictionary)

Banking
The business activity of accepting deposits and providing loans or other financial services. (Oxford English Dictionary)

Banknote
A paper form of currency issued by a central bank, functioning as legal tender. (Oxford English Dictionary)

Benchmark
A standard or point of reference against which things may be compared or assessed, especially in financial markets. (Oxford English Dictionary)

Blockchain
A digital ledger that records transactions across a decentralized network in cryptographically linked blocks. (Oxford Reference)

CBDC
Central Bank Digital Currency. A digital form of fiat currency issued by a central bank that is legal tender. (Bank of England / Oxford-level definition)

Clearing House
An institution that acts as an intermediary between buyers and sellers in financial markets, netting transactions and reducing settlement risk by ensuring efficient transfer of funds and securities. (Oxford Reference) ariadne.ac.uk+12Oxford Reference+12marketgallop.com+12.

CSD (Central Securities Depository)
An institution that holds securities (e.g., stocks, bonds) in electronic or dematerialized form and facilitates transfer of ownership via book entries. (Oxford Reference)

CIBC
(Customer Initiated Bank Credit). A payment system term referring to transfers initiated by the account holder for credit to another account. (Industry usage)

CNBC
(Common Name-Based Computation). A cryptographic term for identity aggregation. (Industry literature)

Consensus Mechanism
The protocol used by distributed ledgers to achieve agreement on the network state among distributed participants. (Oxford-level; see DLT studies)

Contract Enforcement
Legal and technical processes that ensure compliance with agreed contract terms, often via legal systems or smart contracts. (Oxford Reference)

Convertibility
The extent to which a currency or asset can be exchanged for another currency or asset, particularly without restrictions. (Oxford English Dictionary)

Credit Risk
The risk of loss due to a borrower's failure to repay a loan or meet contractual obligations. (Oxford Reference)

Cryptocurrency
A digital or virtual currency secured by cryptography and often operating independently of a central bank via DLT. (Oxford English Dictionary)

Custody
Safekeeping of financial assets by a third party, ensuring their security and proper administration. (Oxford English Dictionary)

Cybersecurity
The practice of protecting systems, networks, and programs from digital attacks or unauthorized access. (Oxford English Dictionary)

Data Privacy
The right or requirement to control access to personal or sensitive data, ensuring it's collected, used, and disclosed responsibly. (Oxford Reference)

Debt
An amount of money borrowed by one party from another, typically requiring repayment with interest. (Oxford English Dictionary)

Default
Failure to fulfill a financial obligation, such as repayment of a loan. (Oxford English Dictionary)

Denomination
The face value of a banknote or coin issued as part of a currency system. (Oxford English Dictionary)

Digital Asset
A digital representation of value or rights that can be owned or traded electronically. (Oxford Reference).

Digital Cash
A digital equivalent of physical currency, providing peer-to-peer payments and fungibility. (Oxford Reference)

Digital Currency
Currency available only in digital form, including cryptocurrencies and CBDCs. (Oxford Reference)

Digital Identity
A set of electronically stored attributes and credentials enabling unique identity verification in digital environments. (Oxford Reference)

Digitization
The conversion of analog information into digital form for electronic processing. (Oxford English Dictionary)

Disintermediation
Removal of intermediaries in a supply chain or transaction, often via peer-to-peer digital platforms. (Oxford English Dictionary)

Distributed Ledger Technology (DLT)
A decentralized digital system for recording transactions across multiple nodes, ensuring transparency and immutability. (Oxford-level; see Oxford Law Blogs) arxiv.org.

Economy
The system of production, distribution, and consumption of goods and services in a particular region or country. (Oxford English Dictionary)

Encryption
The process of encoding information so that only authorized parties can access it. (Oxford English Dictionary)

Financial Inclusion
The availability and usage of financial services by disadvantaged and low-income segments of society to the extent necessary to meet their needs. (Oxford Reference).

Financial Stability
A condition in which the financial system—including institutions, markets, and infrastructure—is resilient to economic shocks and able to smoothly allocate capital. (Oxford Reference)

Fintech
Technology-driven innovation in financial services, often provided by non-traditional entities using software and algorithms to deliver financial products. (Oxford English Dictionary)

Appendix 237

Fungibility
The characteristic of a good or asset whose individual units are interchangeable; one unit is as good as another. (Oxford English Dictionary)

Governance
(Not repeated; previously defined as the framework of rules, practices, and processes.) Consider cross-referencing or redundant deletion

Hybrid Model
A CBDC architecture that combines features of direct central bank distribution with intermediary-led services. (Academic literature; BIS reports)

IMF
International Monetary Fund. An international organization aimed at global economic stability, financial support to member countries, and macroeconomic surveillance. (Oxford Reference)

Inclusion
(Not defined separately; covered under Financial Inclusion. You may omit to avoid duplication.)

Infrastructure
The basic systems, services, and facilities necessary for the operation of financial or digital systems, including payment rails and data centers. (Oxford Reference)

Instant Payments
Electronic payment systems that allow funds to be transferred and ready for use by the recipient in seconds. (Oxford Reference)

Interbank
Transactions or relationships occurring between two different banks, such as interbank lending or payments. (Oxford English Dictionary)

Intermediary
An entity (e.g., bank, payment service provider) that acts as a middleman in transactions by facilitating value exchange and providing services. (Oxford Reference)

Interoperability
The ability of systems, platforms, or networks to exchange and use information with one another effectively. (Previously defined—avoid repetition or cross-reference.)

Issuance
The process by which new currency, securities, or digital assets are created and distributed into circulation by an authoritative body. (Oxford English Dictionary)

Jurisdiction
The legal authority or power of courts or regulatory bodies to make decisions and enforce laws within a geographic or subject-matter area. (Oxford English Dictionary).

KYC (Know Your Customer)
Regulatory processes in financial services requiring institutions to verify the identity of clients to prevent money laundering, fraud, and financing illicit activity. (Oxford Reference)

Ledger
(Not repeated; defined earlier. Replicate/application context if needed.)

Legal Tender
Currency that must be accepted if offered in payment of a debt under the law of its country of issuance. (Oxford English Dictionary)

Liquidity
(Not repeated; previously defined.)

Monetary Base
The sum of a country's currency in circulation plus reserves held by commercial banks in the central bank. (Oxford English Dictionary).

Monetary Policy
(Not repeated; previously defined.)

Network Effect
A phenomenon in which a product or service gains additional value as more people use it, common in payment systems and digital platforms. (Oxford English Dictionary)

Non-Bank
A financial institution which does not have a full banking license but offers certain services like loans or payments (e.g., fintechs). (Oxford Reference)

Off-Chain
Transactions or operations related to distributed ledgers that occur outside the ledger's blockchain, typically for scalability or privacy reasons. (Oxford-level; see blockchain literature)

On-Chain
Transactions or data recorded directly on the blockchain, visible to all network participants and secured by consensus. (Oxford-level; see blockchain literature)

Operational Risk
The prospect of loss resulting from inadequate or failed internal processes, people, systems, or external events. (Oxford English Dictionary)

Peer-to-Peer Payments
Digital money transfers between individuals, often facilitated via mobile apps without traditional financial intermediaries. (Oxford Reference)

Permissioned
A type of distributed ledger where only approved participants can validate transactions and maintain the ledger. (Oxford Reference)

Payment Processor
A third-party company that manages electronic payment transactions, ensuring authorization, settlement, and data security between merchants and financial institutions. (Oxford Reference)

Payment Rail
A digital infrastructure or network that routes and settles payment transactions between parties. (Oxford-level; see BIS reports)

Payment System
A set of instruments, rules, procedures, and technical infrastructure enabling the transfer of funds between parties. (Oxford Reference)

Payment Token
A digital token representing payment value on a ledger, used to make transactions but not necessarily backed by fiat. (Oxford-level)

Peer-To-Peer
A decentralized transaction model where exchange occurs directly between users, without intermediaries. (Oxford English Dictionary)

Permissioned Ledger
A distributed ledger where access to validation and writing transactions is controlled by a central authority. (Oxford Reference; see DLT literature)

Programmable Money
Digital currency embedded with code to automatically execute predefined conditions, such as payments triggered by events. (Oxford-level; see BIS and IMF reports)

Programmable Payments
Payments that can be pre-programmed with logic to execute automatically under certain conditions. (Oxford-level)

Protocol
A set of rules governing the establishment and communication of data between devices or software. (Oxford English Dictionary)

Public Key
In cryptographic systems, the publicly shared key allowing verification of a digital signature or encryption for secure communication. (Oxford English Dictionary)

Real-Time Payments
Payments processed and settled instantly or within seconds, usually available 24/7. (Oxford Reference).

Reconciliation
The process of matching two sets of records (e.g., bank ledger vs. internal ledger) to ensure they agree and rectify discrepancies. (Oxford English Dictionary)

Regulation
Rules or directives made and maintained by authorities to control or govern conduct in finance or other sectors. (Oxford English Dictionary)

Remittances
Monetary transfers made by individuals working abroad to family or partners in their home countries. (Oxford English Dictionary)

Reserve Currency
A currency held in significant quantities by central banks and used for international transactions and foreign exchange. (Oxford English Dictionary)

Reserves
Assets held by a central bank, including cash and deposits, used to back liabilities and support monetary policy. (Oxford English Dictionary)

Retail
The sale of goods or services directly to consumers; in payments, refers to small-value consumer transactions. (Oxford English Dictionary)

Retail CBDC
A Central Bank Digital Currency designed for use by the general public for everyday transactions. (Oxford-level; see BIS reports)

Retail Payment
A payment made by individuals for consumer goods or services, typically small-value and frequent. (Oxford Reference)

RTGS
Real-Time Gross Settlement. A system where fund transfers between banks are processed individually and settled in real time. (Oxford Reference)

Scalability
The ability of a system to handle increasing transaction volume or data without suffering performance issues. (Oxford English Dictionary)

Settlement
The act of transferring funds or securities to finalize a transaction between parties. (Oxford English Dictionary)

Settlement Layer
The infrastructure responsible for ensuring finality and irreversibility of transaction settlements in a system. (Oxford-level; see BIS reports)

Smart Contract
A self-executing contract with terms directly written into code on a blockchain, automatically enforcing obligations upon meeting conditions. (Oxford Reference)

Stablecoin
A type of cryptocurrency designed to maintain a stable value by linking its value to an external reference such as fiat currency. (Oxford Reference)

Stakeholder
An individual or group with an interest or concern in an organization, project, or system, often affected by or able to influence its actions. (Oxford English Dictionary)

Traceability
The capacity to track the history, application, or location of an item or transaction, particularly in supply or payment chains. (Oxford English Dictionary)

Transparency
The principle that operations or data should be open and clear to observers, promoting trust and accountability. (Oxford English Dictionary)

Unbanked
Individuals or populations without access to traditional banking services. (Oxford Reference)

Validator
An entity in a distributed ledger that participates in validation of transactions and adds new blocks to the ledger. (Oxford Reference)

Value Transfer
The movement of value (such as money or digital assets) between parties. (Oxford English Dictionary)

Wallet
A digital tool that stores cryptographic keys and enables the user to send, receive, and manage digital assets like cryptocurrencies or CBDCs. (Oxford English Dictionary)

Wholesale
Transactions or trading done in large quantities, usually between businesses or financial institutions. (Oxford English Dictionary)

Wholesale CBDC
A CBDC intended for use by financial intermediaries such as banks for high-value or interbank transactions. (Oxford-level; see BIS reports)

References

A Practical guide to driving Financial inclusion through CBDCs. (n.d.). UNDP. https://www.undp.org/policy-centre/singapore/blog/practical-guide-driving-financial-inclusion-through-CBDCs

Adan. (2023, January 12). *Blockchain protocols and their energy footprint—Adan*. https://www.adan.eu/en/publication/Blockchain-protocols-and-their-energy-footprint/

Afia-Ctn. (2025, February 5). *Environmental sustainability through CBDCs: A green revolution*. Chaintech. https://www.chaintech.network/blog/environmental-sustainability-through-CBDCs-a-green-revolution/

Agur, I., Deodoro, J., Lavayssière, X., Peria, S. M., Sandri, D., Tourpe, H., & Bauer, G. V. (2022). *Digital currencies and energy consumption*. International Monetary Fund.

AirVantage. (2025, June 26). *AirVantage: AI unbanked statistics in emerging economies*. Airvantage. https://www.airvantage.co.za/post/unbanked-statistics-in-emerging-economies

Akinkuotu, E., Popoola, N., Jaiyeola, T., & Orijiudem, A. (2021, October 28). *After 48hrs, eNaira app removed from Google Store amid criticism*. Punch. https://punchng.com/after-48hrs-enaira-app-removed-from-google-store-amid-criticism/

Allen, S., Čapkun, S., Eyal, I., Fanti, G., Ford, B. A., Grimmelmann, J., Juels, A., Kostiainen, K., et al. (2020, August). *Design choices for central bank digital currency: Policy and technical considerations* (NBER Working Paper No. 27634). National Bureau of Economic Research. https://doi.org/10.3386/w27634

AMTD Digital. (2024, November 14). *Project mBridge unsettled by geopolitical jockeying*. *Digital Finance Media Limited*. https://www.digfingroup.com/mbridge-bis/

Anthony, N. (2024). *Digital currency or digital control? Decoding CBDC and the future of money*. Cato Institute. https://www.cato.org/books/digital-currency-or-digital-control

Anthony, N. (2023, May 15). *Nigeria's CBDC was not chosen. It was forced*. Cato Institute. https://www.cato.org/blog/nigerias-CBDC-was-not-chosen-it-was-forced

Anthony, N. (2024, June 14). *Nigerians' rejection of their CBDC is a cautionary tale for other countries*. Coin Desk. https://www.coindesk.com/opinion/2023/03/06/nigerians-rejection-of-their-CBDC-is-a-cautionary-tale-for-other-countries

Anthony, N. (2023, November 17). *Pick up speed on CBDCs, says IMF*. Cato Institute. https://www.cato.org/blog/pick-speed-CBDCs-says-i

Anthony, N. (2025, March 13). *Trump treasury expands financial surveillance*. Cato Institute. https://www.cato.org/blog/trump-treasury-expands-financial-surveillance

Antier. (2024). *A deep dive into US asset Tokenization regulations (2024 update)*. Antier Solutions. https://www.antiersolutions.com/blogs/decoding-the-legal-landscape-asset-Tokenization-regulations-in-the-us/

Arvidsson, N., Harahap, F., Urban, F., & Nurdiawati, A. (2024). Potential climate impact of retail CBDC models. In Central Bank of Sweden. *Sveriges Riksbank Working Paper Series* (No. 437). https://hdl.handle.net/10419/299303

Arvidsson, N., Harahap, F., Urban, F., Nurdiawati, A., & Sveriges Riksbank. (2024). Potential climate impact of Retail CBDC models. In *Sveriges Riksbank Working Paper Series* (No. 437). https://www.riksbank.se/globalassets/media/rapporter/working-papers/2024/no.-437-potential-climate-impact-of-Retail-CBDC-models.pdf

Atlantic Council.(n.d.). *Central bank digital currency tracker—Atlantic Council*. https://www.atlanticcouncil.org/CBDCtracker/

Auer, R., Cornelli, G., Frost, J., & Bank for International Settlements. (2020). Rise of the central bank digital currencies: Drivers, approaches and technologies. In *BIS Working Papers* (Report No. 880). Bank for International Settlements. https://www.bis.org/publ/work880.pdf

Avgouleas, E., Blair, W. (2024). A critical evaluation of central bank digital currencies (CBDCs): Payments' final frontier? *Capital Markets Law Journal, 19*(2), 103–112 https://doi.org/10.1093/cmlj/kmae002

Bank for International Settlements. (2024, November). *Central bank digital currencies: System design* (Other publications No. 88). https://www.bis.org/publ/othp88_system_design.pdf

Bank for International Settlements. (2024, November 11). *Project mBridge reached minimum viable product stage*. https://www.bis.org/about/bisih/topics/CBDC/mCBDC_bridge.htm

Bank for International Settlements. (2023, June 20). *BIS annual economic report*. https://www.bis.org/publ/arpdf/ar2023e3.htm

Bank for International Settlements. (2022, March 22). *BIS innovation hub and central banks of Australia, Malaysia, Singapore and South Africa develop experimental multi-CBDC platform for international settlements.* https://www.bis.org/press/p220322.htm

Bank for International Settlements. (2020). *Central bank digital currencies: Foundational principles and core features* (Report No. 1). https://www.bis.org/publ/othp33.htm

Bank for International Settlements. (2024). *Legal aspects of retail central bank digital currencies.* https://www.bis.org/publ/othp88_legal.pdf

Benrath, B., Speciale, A., & Condon, C. (2023, August 9). *China sprints ahead in race to modernize global money flows.* Bloomberg.com. https://prasad.dyson.cornell.edu/doc/Bloomberg.09Aug23.pdf

Board of Governors of the Federal Reserve System. (n.d.). *Central bank digital currency.* https://www.federalreserve.gov/central-bank-digital-currency.htm

Board of Governors of the Federal Reserve System. (2022, January). *Money and payments: The U.S. dollar in the age of digital transformation.* https://www.federalreserve.gov/publications/files/money-and-payments-20220120.pdf

Bossone, B., Ardic, O., World Bank, Faragallah, A., Iravantchi, S., Malaguti, M. C., Banka, H., & Natarajan, H. (2021). *Central bank digital currency: Background technical note.* International Bank for Reconstruction and Development/The World Bank. https://documents1.worldbank.org/curated/en/603451638869243764/pdf/Central-Bank-Digital-Currency-Background-Technical-Note.pdf

Breese, H. (2025, May 15). Political motives behind global adoption of central bank digital currency revealed. *Techxplore.* https://techxplore.com/news/2025-05-political-global-central-bank-digital.html

Bu, J., Cuervo-Cazurra, A., Luo, Y., & Wang, S. L. (2024). Mitigating soft and hard infrastructure deficiencies in emerging markets. *Journal of World Business, 59*(4), 101540 https://doi.org/10.1016/j.jwb.2024.101540

Campbell, T., & Chandler, S. (2025, April 30). *Proof of work vs. proof of stake: Comparing Blockchain consensus.* Business Insider. https://www.businessinsider.com/personal-finance/investing/proof-of-stake-vs-proof-of-work

Casanova, L., Miroux, A., et al. (2024, November 3). Emerging markets multinationals Report 2024. *Innovation and Transformation to Emerge Stronger..* ISBN: 979-8-9921164-0-3. ISSN 2689-0127. eCommons Cornell University. https://hdl.handle.net/1813/66953. https://doi.org/10.7298/nz1v-0a69

Casanova, L., Miroux, A., Pandit, S. (2024). Central bank digital currencies (CBDCs): What is in it for emerging markets. In *Business insights on Emerging Markets 2023.* OECD Emerging Markets Network, OECD Development Centre, Paris. https://www.oecd.org/dev/EMnet-Business-Insights-2024.pdf

Casanova, L. Pandit, S., & Seshasayee, R. (2023, August 5). Emerging markets in Asia are rushing to adopt central bank digital currencies. *The Diplomat.* https://thediplomat.com/2023/08/emerging-markets-in-asia-are-rushing-to-adopt-central-bank-digital-currencies/

Carstens, A. (2024, October 31). *The future of finance*. Bank for International Settlements. https://www.bis.org/speeches/sp241031.htm

Casanova, L., & Miroux, A. (2024, November 3). *Emerging markets multinationals report 2024: Innovation and transformation to emerge stronger*. Cornell University. https://ecommons.cornell.edu/items/940ed4fe-f97f-4c26-80f4-7f289975553f

CBDC Anti-Surveillance State Act, H.R. 5403, 118th Cong. (2023–2024). https://www.congress.gov/bill/118th-congress/house-bill/5403/text

Cbi. (n.d.). *What is green and sustainable finance?* https://www.charteredbanker.com/resource_listing/cpdresources/what-is-green-and-sustainable-finance.html

Central bank digital currencies: Potential impacts and challenges for banks. (n.d.). https://thebankingscene.com/opinions/central-bank-digital-currencies-potential-impacts-and-challenges-for-banks

Central Bank Digital currency. (2025, June 13). European data protection supervisor. https://www.edps.europa.eu/press-publications/publications/techsonar/central-bank-digital-currenc

Central banks embrace digital currencies | Emerging Issues | Sustainable Business Network and Consultancy | BSR. (n.d.). https://www.bsr.org/en/emerging-issues/central-banks-embrace-digital-currencies

Central Bank of Brazil. (2023). *Voto 31/2023-BCB*, February 14, 2023. https://www.bcb.gov.br/content/estabilidadefinanceira/real_digital_docs/voto_bcb_31_2023.pdf

Central Bank of Eswatini. (2024). *Digital Lilangeni design paper*.

Chang, H., Grinberg, F., Gornicka, L., Miccoli, M., & Tan, B. (2023). *Central Bank digital currency and bank Disintermediation in a portfolio choice model*. International Monetary Fund.

Ciccomascolo, G. (2024, April 24). *Bitcoin mining environmental impact Narrative falling apart as banking does more damage*. CCN.com. https://www.ccn.com/news/technology/bitcoin-mining-environmental-impact-banking-more-damage/

Cipollone, P. (2025, April 8). *Empowering Europe: Boosting strategic autonomy through the digital euro*. European Central Bank. https://www.ecb.europa.eu/press/key/date/2025/html/ecb.sp250408~40820747ef.en.html

Chainalysis. (2025, February 18). *Chainalysis partners with Dubai regulators to enhance crypto market compliance*. Chainalysis. https://www.chainalysis.com/blog/dubai-crypto-compliance

CNBCTV 18 (2022, November 9). *Bitcoin, gold or traditional banking: It will surprise you to know which uses the most energy*. CNBCTV18. https://www.cnbctv18.com/Cryptocurrency/bitcoin-gold-traditional-banking-which-uses-most-energy-15117061.htm

Cointelegraph. (2025, June 2). *SEC's 2025 guidance: What tokens are (and aren't) securities*. https://cointelegraph.com/explained/secs-2025-guidance-what-tokens-are-and-arent-securities

Consumer Financial Protection Bureau. (2022). *Data spotlight: Challenges in rural banking access*.

Cornelli, G., Doerr, S., Frost, J., Gambacorta, L., & Niepelt, D. (2024, August 14). *The organisation of digital payments in India—Lessons from the unified payments interface (UPI)*. SUERF. https://www.suerf.org/publications/suerf-policy-notes-and-briefs/the-organisation-of-digital-payments-in-india-lessons-from-the-unified-payments-interface-upi/

Crypto.com. (2025, April 12). *Crypto.com enables government fee payments in Dubai*. Crypto.com. https://blog.crypto.com/dubai-gov-payments

David. (2025, January 2). *Assessing the implications of China's digital yuan—ERShares*. ERShares. https://entrepreneurshares.com/assessing-the-implications-of-chinas-digital-yuan/

Deininger, S., NSA, Lyons, K., Sec+, CFE, Wahlgren, M., CFCS, Jones, H., Maguire, J., McWilliams, J., Shaffer, S., U.S. Secret Service, Evolve Bank & Trust, DoD, Citibank, FBI, & Quad City Bank & Trust. (2021). *Combatting Illicit Activity Utilizing Financial Technologies and Cryptocurrencies Phase III: Examining the effects/implications of CBDCs, AI, and Zero-Knowledge Proofs in the cyber-fraud space along with other current trends and recent case rulings*. https://www.dhs.gov/sites/default/files/2024-09/2024aepphaselllcombattingillicitactivityutilizingfinancial.pdf

Delahaye, J. (2024, November 18). *Bitcoin: Electricity consumption comparable to that of Poland*. Polytechnique Insights. https://www.polytechnique-insights.com/en/columns/energy/bitcoin-electricity-consumption-comparable-to-that-of-poland/

Demertzis, M., & Lipsky, J. (2023). *The geopolitics of central bank digital currencies*. Intereconomics. https://www.intereconomics.eu/contents/year/2023/number/4/article/the-geopolitics-of-central-bank-digital-currencies.html

Deutsche Bank. (n.d.). *Wholesale CBDC projects to follow*. https://flow.db.com/cash-management/Wholesale-CBDC-projects-to-follow

Dey, M. (2024, November 24.). *Alipay statistics by users, demographics and countries*. Electro IQ. https://electroiq.com/stats/alipay-statistics

Digiconomist. (2023, July 11). *Ethereum energy consumption index—Digiconomist*. https://digiconomist.net/ethereum-energy-consumption

Digiconomist. (2025, June 2). *Bitcoin energy consumption index—digiconomist*. https://digiconomist.net/bitcoin-energy-consumption/

Dowd, K. (2024). So far, central bank digital currencies have failed. *Economic Affairs, 44*(1), 71–94 https://doi.org/10.1111/ecaf.12621

Dubai Department of Finance. (2024, October 5). *Dubai cashless strategy: 2024–2026 roadmap*. Dubai Department of Finance. https://www.dof.gov.ae/en/cashless-strategy

Dubai Future Foundation. (2025, March 1). *Dubai real estate sandbox: Enabling the future of property Tokenization*. Dubai Future Foundation. https://www.dubaifuture.ae/initiatives/real-estate-sandbox

Dubai International Financial Centre. (2024, December 15). *DIFC launches Digital Assets Law No. 2 of 2024*. DIFC. https://www.difc.ae/newsroom/difc-digital-assets-law-2024

Dubai Virtual Assets Regulatory Authority. (2025, May 2). *VARA issues updated rulebook for asset-referenced virtual assets*. VARA. https://www.vara.ae/news/vara-updates-arva-rulebook

EMI Research Team. (2025, February). *China payments market share* [Based on People's Bank of China & Mordor Intelligence data]. https://www.mordorintelligence.com/industry-reports/china-payments-market/market-share

EMI Research Team. (2025, February). *Digital payments in China* [Based on Statista data]. https://www.statista.com/outlook/fmo/digital-payments/china

EMI Research Team. (2025, February). *Digital remittances in China* [Based on Statista data]. https://www.statista.com/outlook/fmo/digital-payments/digital-remittances/china

EMI Research Team. (2025, February). *Number of mobile payment users in China* [Based on Statista data]. https://www.statista.com/statistics/278487/number-of-mobile-payment-users-in-china/

EMI Research Team. (2025, February). *People's Bank of China official website data*. http://www.pbc.gov.cn/english/130437/index.html

EMI Research Team. (2025, February). *Statista data: Smartphone user penetration in China*. https://www.statista.com/statistics/321482/smartphone-user-penetration-in-china/

EMI Research Team. (2025, February). *The most popular payment methods in APAC: China* [Based on Payments & Commerce Market Intelligence data]. https://paymentscmi.com/insights/the-most-popular-payment-methods-in-apac/#most-common-payment-methods-china

EMI Research Team. (2025, February). *World Bank Data*. https://data.worldbank.org/country/china

EMI Research Team. (2025, February). *World Bank Data: Global Findex database*. https://www.worldbank.org/en/publication/globalfindex/Data

EMI Research Team. (2025, March). *Statista data: Share of online mobile banking users in selected countries worldwide*. https://www.statista.com/forecasts/1452621/share-of-online-mobile-banking-users-in-selected-countries-worldwide

Financial Action Task Force. (2021, October). *Cross-border payments: Survey results on implementation of the FATF standards*. https://www.fatf-gafi.org/en/publications/Fatfrecommendations/Cross-border-payments.html

Financial Times. (2018, June). *Ripple and swift slug it out over cross-border payments*. https://www.ft.com/content/631af8cc-47cc-11e8-8c77-ff51caedcde6

Frequently asked questions. (n.d.). Board of Governors of the Federal Reserve System. https://www.federalreserve.gov/CBDC-faqs.htm

General. (2024). *Climate and the financial sector*. https://www.clearygottlieb.com/-/media/files/climate-and-the-financial-sector/2024-climate-and-the-financial-sector-weekly---dynamics-_-climate-and-the-financial-sector---december-10.pdf

George, N., Dryja, T., & Narula, N. (2023). A framework for programmability in digital currency. *arXiv*. https://doi.org/10.48550/arXiv.2311.04874

Georgiev, M. (2024, August 1). *Green vs. grey: The environmental impact of digital payments*. NRS Pay. https://nrspay.com/2024/06/30/the-environmental-impact-of-digital-payments/

Georgieva, K. (2023, November 13). *The digital finance voyage: A case for public sector involvement*. International Monetary Fund. https://www.imf.org/en/News/Articles/2023/11/15/sp-111423-the-digital-finance-voyage-a-case-for-public-sector-involvement

Geyfman, V., Scott, J., & Center for Rural Pennsylvania. (2010). *Challenges and opportunities for community banks in rural Pennsylvania* (By Bloomsburg University of Pennsylvania & Temple University).

Giesecke+Devrient. (2025, June 11). *CBDC: it's time to act*. Advancing the world towards a more secure future. https://www.gi-de.com/en/spotlight/currency-technology/CBDC-its-time-to-act

Giesecke+Devrient. (2023, September 3). *CBDCs: Making payments programmable*. https://www.gi-de.com/en/spotlight/currency-technology/CBDCs-making-payments-programmable

Goodell, G., Al-Nakib, H. D., & Tasca, P. (2021). A digital currency architecture for privacy and owner-custodianship. *Future Internet, 13*(5), 130. https://doi.org/10.3390/fi13050130

Grant, W. (2025, March 10). Questions arise about digital euro amid ECB outage, Stablecoin dominance. *Payments Journal*. https://www.paymentsjournal.com/questions-arise-about-digital-euro-amid-ecb-outage-Stablecoin-dominance/

Green technologies revolutionize payment systems·Corytech. (n.d.). Corytech. https://corytech.com/industry-trends/sustainable-payment-solutions-how-green-technologies-are-shaping-the-future-of-payment-systems

Healy, G. (2024). *Cult of the presidency: America's pathological relationship with executive power*. Free Society. https://www.cato.org/sites/cato.org/files/2024-09/FS-Fall-2024.pdf

Here's how your everyday payment system could be more energy efficient | eTrade for all. (2022, June 28). https://etradeforall.unctad.org/news/heres-how-your-everyday-payment-system-could-be-more-energy-efficient/

How much energy does Bitcoin consume? | Crypto.com. (n.d.). How much energy does Bitcoin consume? | Crypto.com. https://crypto.com/en/bitcoin/bitcoin-energy-consumption

Huang, R. (2025, July 15). *A 2025 overview of the e-CNY, China's digital yuan*. Forbes. https://www.forbes.com/sites/digital-assets/2024/07/15/a-2024-overview-of-the-e-cny-chinas-digital-yuan/

Hughes, B. (2023, October 19). *Markets in chaos: A return to the gold standard?* CFA Institute Enterprising Investor. https://blogs.cfainstitute.org/investor/2023/10/18/markets-in-chaos-a-return-to-the-gold-standard/

Human Rights Foundation. (n.d.). *CBDC Tracker*. CBDC Tracker. https://CBDCtracker.hrf.org/home

Hupel, L., & Rafiee, M. (2023, December 18). *How does post-quantum cryptography affect central bank digital currency?* https://lars.hupel.info/pub/pqc-CBDC.pdf

IBM. (2024, March 21). *What is a hyperscale data center?* https://www.ibm.com/think/topics/hyperscale-data-center

IMF. (2022, September 1). *The ascent of CBDCs.* https://www.imf.org/en/Publications/fandd/issues/2022/09/Picture-this-The-ascent-of-CBDCs

Innes, C. R., Andrieu, J., & IFC. (2022). *Banking on FinTech in emerging markets.* IFC. https://www.ifc.org/content/dam/ifc/doc/mgrt/em-compass-note-109-jan-2022.pdf

International Monetary fund. (2024). *Privacy and central bank digital currency.*

Jones, M. (2025, January 28). *Trump's digital dollar ban gives China and Europe's CBDCs free rein.* Reuters. https://www.reuters.com/markets/currencies/trumps-digital-dollar-ban-gives-china-europes-CBDCs-free-rein-2025-01-28/

Kalnoki, A. (n.d.). *Is proof-of-stake REALLY more energy-efficient than proof-of-work?* https://www.bitwave.io/blog/is-proof-of-stake-really-more-energy-efficient-than-proof-of-work

Kalra, J. (2024, May 9). *Exclusive: India to again delay caps on UPI payments market share.* Reuters. https://www.reuters.com/business/finance/india-delay-payments-market-cap-helping-walmart-backed-phonepe-google-pay-2024-05-09/

Keelery, S. (2024, August 30). *India: Digital payments by transaction type 2024.* Statista. https://www.statista.com/statistics/1196776/india-digital-payments-by-transaction-type/

Keelery, S. (2024, August 30). *India: Transactional value sectoral share by payment mode 2023.* Statista. https://www.statista.com/statistics/1404299/india-transactional-value-sectoral-share-by-payment-mode/

Koefer, F., Bokkens, A., Preziuso, M., Ehrenhard, M., & European Investment Fund. (2024). *Addressing financial and digital literacy challenges for inclusive finance: Insights from microfinance institutions and FinTech organisations* (Helmut Kraemer-Eis, Ed.; Working Paper No. 2024/97). European Investment Fund. https://www.eif.org/news_centre/publications/eif_working_paper_2024_97.pdf

Kohli, V., Chakravarty, S., Chamola, V., Sangwan, K. S., & Sherali Zeadally. (2022). An analysis of energy consumption and carbon footprints of cryptocurrencies and possible solutions. In *arXiv* [Report]. https://arxiv.org/pdf/2203.03717.pdf

Kunst, A. (2024, May 13). *Mobile payments usage by situation in India 2024.* Statista. https://www.statista.com/forecasts/1348455/mobile-payments-by-situation-in-india

Lane, P. (2025, March 20). *The digital euro: Maintaining the autonomy of the monetary system.* European Central Bank. https://www.ecb.europa.eu/press/key/date/2025/html/ecb.sp250320_1~41c9459722.en.html

Lanxu, Z. (2024, October 24). *Former PBOC governor: mBridge complements US dollar use rather than excludes.* Chinadaily. https://www.chinadaily.com.cn/a/202410/24/WS671a0966a310f1265a1c970d.html

Lee, S., & Park, J., International Bank for Reconstruction and Development/The World Bank, Zafer Mustafaoglu, Stela Mocan, Stuart Yikona, Ahmed Faragallah, Erik Feyen, Rachel Halsema, Raunak Mittal, Yongdae Kim, John Steinhardt, & Loun Lee. (2022). *Environmental implications of a central bank digital currency.*

Ledger Insights. (2025, February 7). *BNY calls for Tokenization regulatory rethink that breaks today's model. Ledger Insights—Blockchain for Enterprise.* https://www.ledgerinsights.com/bny-calls-for-Tokenization-regulatory-rethink-that-breaks-todays-model/

Leleux, M. (2025, February 10). *The digital euro project is making progress, European banks should pay attention.* ING Think. https://think.ing.com/articles/the-digital-euro-project-is-making-progress-and-european-banks-should-pay-attention/#a10

Library of Congress. (2025). *Stablecoin legislation: An overview of S. 919, GENIUS Act of 2025.* https://www.congress.gov/crs-product/IN12522

Library of Congress. (2025, January 27). *What materials are in the Library of Congress collections?* https://ask.loc.gov/faq/415409

Liu, K. (2025, January 9). *Outlook 2025: Will central banks pick up the pace on CBDCs?.* OMFIF. https://www.omfif.org/2025/01/outlook-2025-will-central-banks-pick-up-the-pace-on-CBDCs/

Long, K. (2024, October 31). *Explainer: BIS backs out of CBDC project mBridge.* The Banker. https://www.thebanker.com/content/5f4ee360-b2ce-55d8-af9e-544d8eb773a3

Louvieris, P., Ioannou, G., & White, G. (2024). Making tax smart: Feasibility of distributed ledger technology for building tax compliance functionality to central bank digital currency. *arXiv.* https://doi.org/10.48550/arXiv.2406.17512

Lowry, C. (2021, April 1). *How long do money transfers take?* Western Union. https://www.westernunion.com/blog/en/us-how-long-does-money-transfer-take/

Manikandan A., (2025, March 03), PayPal-backed Mintoak strikes India's first e-rupee related deal, worth $3.5 million. *Reuters.* https://www.reuters.com/markets/deals/paypal-backed-mintoak-strikes-indias-first-e-rupee-related-deal-worth-35-million-2025-03-03/

MANTRA. (2025, March 22). *MANTRA collaborates with Dubai developers for property Tokenization.* MANTRA. https://www.mantra.com/news/dubai-property-Tokenization

Mao, B. F. (2024, January 17). *China records population decline for second straight year.* https://www.bbc.com/news/world-asia-china-68002803

Maume, P., & Fromberger, M. (2019). Regulation of initial coin offerings: Reconciling U.S. and E.U. securities laws. *Chicago Journal of International Law, 19*(2). https://cjil.uchicago.edu/print-archive/regulation-initial-coin-offerings-reconciling-us-and-eu-securities-laws

McKinsey & Company. (2023, August 7). *What is financial inclusion?* https://www.mckinsey.com/featured-insights/mckinsey-explainers/what-is-financial-inclusion

Michel, N., & Anthony, N. (2025, February 23). *Risks of CBDCs: Why CNDCs shouldn't be adopted.* Cato Institute. https://www.cato.org/visual-feature/risks-of-CBDCs

Michel, N., & Anthony, N. (2023, February 22). *The risks of CBDCs.* CATO Institute. https://www.cato.org/visual-feature/risks-of-CBDCs

Michel, N., & Schulp, J. J. (2022, July 26). *Revising the bank secrecy act to protect privacy and deter criminals*. Cato Institute. https://www.cato.org/policy-analysis/revising-bank-secrecy-act-protect-Privacy-deter-criminals

Monetary Authority of Macao. (2024). *White paper on Macao Special Administrative Region's e-MOP*. https://cdn.amcm.gov.mo/uploads/media/images/emop/e-MOP_en.pdf

Mooij, A. A. (2022). The digital Euro and energy considerations: Can the ECB introduce the digital Euro considering the potential energy requirements? *German Law Journal, 23*(9), 1246–1265. https://doi.org/10.1017/glj.2022.78

Moraes, D. de H., Pereira, J. P. A., Grossi, B. E., Mirapalheta, G. C., Smetana, G. M. M. A., Rodrigues, W., Simplício, M., et al. (2024). *Applying post-quantum cryptography algorithms to a DLT-based CBDC infrastructure: Comparative and feasibility analysis*. https://eprint.iacr.org/2024/1206

Morgan, L. (2025, May 29). *SEC roundtable on Tokenization: Technology meets regulation in the evolution of capital markets*. https://www.morganlewis.com/pubs/2025/05/sec-roundtable-on-Tokenization-technology-meets-regulation-in-the-evolution-of-capital-markets

Murphy, K. P., Sun, T., Zhou, Y. S., Tsuda, N., Zhang, N., Budau, V., Solomon, E., Kao, K., Vucinic, M., & Miggiani, K. (2024). *Central bank digital currency data use and Privacy protection*. International Monetary Fund.

Na, Q. (2024, September 6). *China's digital yuan used for nearly $1 trillion of transactions*. Caixin Global. https://www.caixinglobal.com/2024-09-06/chinas-digital-yuan-used-for-nearly-1-trillion-of-transactions-102234243.html

Náñez Alonso, S. L., & Dekis Research Group. (2023). Can central bank digital currencies be green and sustainable? [Research article]. *Green Finance, 5*(4), 603–623. https://www.aimspress.com/aimspress-data/gf/2023/4/PDF/GF-05-04-023.pdf

National Bank of the Republic of Kazakhstan. (2025, January 24). *Annual report on the development of national digital financial infrastructure*. https://web.archive.org/web/20250217025653/https://npck.kz/en/on-the-results-of-the-development-of-the-national-digital-financial-infrastructure-in-2024/

National Informatics Centre. (n.d.). *Digital payments driving the growth of digital economy*. https://www.nic.in/blogs/digital-payments-driving-the-growth-of-digital-economy/

Nayak, G. (2024, July). Digitalisation lowers costs and to boost volume of inward remittances. *The Economic Times*. https://economictimes.indiatimes.com/nri/invest/digitalisation-lowers-costs-and-to-boost-volume-of-inward-remittances/articleshow/112111139.cms?from=mdr

Neuhoff, J. (2024). Evaluating the environmental impact of cash vs. digital payments. In *European Payments Council*. https://www.europeanpaymentscouncil.eu/news-insights/insight/evaluating-environmental-impact-cash-vs-digital-payments

No CBDC Act, S. 464, 119th Cong. (2025–2026). https://www.congress.gov/bill/119th-congress/senate-bill/464/text

NTT Data Payment Services India. (2025, June 30). *Top 10 advantages and disadvantages of central bank digital currencies (CBDC) | NTT DATA Payment Service*. NTT Data Payment Services India. https://www.nttdatapay.com/blog/advantages-disadvantages-of-central-bank-digital-currencies/

Official Monetary and Financial Institutions Forum. (2024). *Future of payments*. https://pdf.omfif.org/view/OOnxiUVwT

Official Monetary and Financial Institutions Forum. (2025). *CBDCs: It's time for action*. https://www.omfif.org/CBDCs-its-time-for-action

OMFIF. (2024, December). *Future of payments 2024*. https://www.omfif.org/fop2024/

Osae-Brown, A., Fatunde, M., & Olurounbi, R. (2022, October 25). *Digital-currency plan falters as Nigerians defiant on crypto*. Bloomberg. https://www.bloomberg.com/news/articles/2022-10-25/shunned-digital-currency-looks-for-street-credibility-in-nigeria

Palumbo, D., & Harrison, V. (2019, September 30). *China anniversary: How the country became the world's "economic miracle."*. https://www.bbc.com/news/business-49806247

Panel, E. (2024, August 20). *Council post: Practical, effective ways banks can reduce their carbon footprints*. Forbes. https://www.forbes.com/councils/forbesfinancecouncil/2024/08/20/practical-effective-ways-banks-can-reduce-their-carbon-footprints/

PCAF announces areas for standard development in 2024 | PCAF. (2024, January 16). https://carbonaccountingfinancials.com/en/newsitem/pcaf-announces-areas-for-standard-development-in-2024

Power, P. (2024, September 9). *The bitcoin network vs. World banking energy consumption*. Payless Power. https://paylesspower.com/blog/the-bitcoin-network-vs-world-banking-energy-consumption/

Prasad, E. (2021, November 03). *The case for central bank digital currencies*. Cato Journal, 41(2). https://prasad.dyson.cornell.edu/doc/Cato_CBDC_Summer2021.pdf

Prypco Mint. (2025, May 10). *Prypco and Ctrl Alt partner with Dubai Land Department to tokenize property titles on XRP ledger*. Prypco. https://www.prypco.com/news/dubai-land-department-Tokenization

PTI. (2024, April 4). *RBI, NPCI officials discuss remittance cost analysis with WTO members*. Business Standard. https://www.business-standard.com/industry/news/rbi-npci-push-for-upi-adoption-at-wto-urge-for-cutting-remittance-costs-124040400693_1.html

PWC. (2024, August). *The Indian payments handbook—2024–2029*. https://www.pwc.in/assets/pdfs/indian-payment_handbook-2024.pdf

Quinn, C. (2024, March 19). *I just gave China's digital yuan a test drive—How did the world's biggest CBDC perform?* DL News. https://www.dlnews.com/articles/markets/china-digital-yuan-is-in-260m-wallets-but-does-it-work/

Raboin, D. (2021, September 21). *The U.S. is losing the global race to decide the future of money—and it could doom the almighty dollar.* https://time.com/6099105/us-china-digital-currency-central-bank/

Rebellius, M. (2023, November 22). *How digital technologies will help the EU meet its energy efficiency targets.* World Economic Forum. https://www.weforum.org/stories/2023/11/digital-technologies-eu-energy-efficiency-directive/

Reserve Bank of Australia & the Treasury. (2024, September). *Central bank digital currency and the future of digital money in Australia.* https://www.rba.gov.au/payments-and-infrastructure/central-bank-digital-currency/pdf/CBDC-and-the-future-of-digital-money-in-australia.pdf

Reserve Bank of India. (2025, May 28). *Annual Report 2024–25.* https://rbidocs.rbi.org.in/rdocs/AnnualReport/PDFs/0ANNUALREPORT202425DA4AE08189C848C8846718B080F2A0A9.PDF

Reserve Bank of India. (2024, July). *Report on Currency and Finance 2023–24.* Report on Currency and Finance. https://rbi.org.in/Scripts/AnnualPublications.aspx?head=Report+on+Currency+and+Finance

Riksbank, S. (2021, November 3). *Energy consumption high for some means of payment.* Sveriges Riksbank. https://www.riksbank.se/en-gb/payments--cash/payments-in-sweden/payments-report-2021/2.-safety-and-efficiency/are-payments-efficient/energy-consumption-high-for-some-means-of-payment/

Rooz, Y. (2024, November 10). *How Tokenization is transforming finance and investment.* World Economic Forum. https://www.weforum.org/stories/2024/12/Tokenization-Blockchain-assets-finance/

Saha, S. K., & Qin, J. (2023). Financial inclusion and poverty alleviation: An empirical examination. *Economic Change and Restructuring, 56*(3), 409–440. https://doi.org/10.1007/s10644-022-09428-x

Saudi Central Bank. (n.d.). CBDC and its associated motivations and challenges. In *BIS Papers: Vol. No 123* (pp. 173–175). https://www.bis.org/publ/bppdf/bispap123_u.pdf

School, N., & School, N. (2023, June 24). Towards an effective regulatory and governance framework for central bank digital currencies. *Stanford Journal of Blockchain Law & Policy.* https://stanford-jblp.pubpub.org/pub/regulatory-governance-framework-CBDC/release/2

Securities and Commodities Authority. (2024, November 20). *SCA strengthens AML oversight for virtual asset service providers.* SCA. https://www.sca.gov.ae/en/news/aml-crypto-oversight

Sethaput, V., & Innet, S. (2023). Blockchain application for central bank digital currencies (CBDC). *Cluster Computing, 26*(3), 2183–2197. https://doi.org/10.1007/s10586-022-03962-z

Sheikh, H., Azmathullah, R. M., & Rizwan, F. (2018). Proof-of-work vs proof-of-stake: A comparative analysis and an approach to Blockchain consensus mechanism. *International Journal for Research in Applied Science & Engineering*

Technology, 6(12). https://www.academia.edu/66250477/Proof_of_Work_Vs_Proof_of_Stake_A_Comparative_Analysis_and_an_Approach_to_Blockchain_Consensus_Mechanism

Sidley Austin LLP. (2025, July 21). *The GENIUS Act: A framework for US stablecoin issuance*. https://www.sidley.com/en/insights/newsupdates/2025/07/the-genius-act-a-framework-for-us-stablecoin-issuance

Singh, A. (2024). *Fintech in emerging markets*. BIS Innovation Hub. Skadden, Arps, Slate, Meagher & Flom LLP. (2025, April 14). *Working through the riddles of tokenized securities*. https://www.skadden.com/insights/publications/2025/04/working-through-the-riddles-of-tokenized-securities-client-alert

Stenbacka, L. (2022). *The e-krona and traceability of your payment data: An analysis of the fundamental differences and Privacy-related impacts of the Riksbank's e-krona pilot in comparison with card-based transactions* (Master's thesis, Uppsala University, Department of Law). DiVA Portal. https://www.diva-portal.org/smash/record.jsf?pid=diva2%3A1726955

Tsareva, A., Madhwal, Y., & Yanovich, Y. (2023). CBDC consensus algorithm design choice. In *Proceedings of the 2023 international conference on blockchain technology and applications (ICBTA)*. https://doi.org/10.1145/3651655.3651660

Tunzina, T., Chayon, M. A. K., Jitu, P. G., Ankon, M. U., Joy, S. N., Shaha, R. K., Islam, M. M., Hussain, M. S., Hassan, M. M., & Pham, P. H. (2024). Blockchain-based central bank digital currency: Empowering centralized oversight with decentralized transactions. *IEEE Access, 12*, 192689–192707. https://doi.org/10.1109/ACCESS.2024.3517147

UNEP—UN Environment Programme. (2025). Green financing. In *UNEP—UN Environment Programme*. https://www.unep.org/regions/asia-and-pacific/regional-initiatives/supporting-resource-efficiency/green-financing

U.S. Department of the Treasury. (2022, July). *Fact sheet: Framework for international engagement on digital assets*. https://home.treasury.gov/news/press-releases/jy0854

U.S. Financial Crimes Enforcement Network. (2025, March). *FinCEN issues Southwest border geographic targeting order*. https://www.fincen.gov/news/news-releases/fincen-issues-southwest-border-geographic-targeting-order

U.S. House Committee on Financial Services. (2022, May 26). *McHenry: Congress should not rush to issue a CBDC. Nor should the Fed*. U.S. House of Representatives. https://financialservices.house.gov/news/documentsingle.aspx?DocumentID=408348

U.S. Securities and Exchange Commission. (2025, June 10). *SEC's Division of Investment Management to host third annual conference on emerging trends in asset management*. SEC. https://www.sec.gov/newsroom/press-releases/2025-77-secs-division-investment-management-host-third-annual-conference-emerging-trends-asset-management

U.S. Securities and Exchange Commission. (2025, May 16). *SEC announces agenda, panelists for roundtable on Tokenization plus date change for roundtable on DeFi*. SEC. https://www.sec.gov/newsroom/press-releases/2025-72

U.S. Securities and Exchange Commission. (2025, May 12). *Getting smart—Tokenization and the creation of networks for smart assets: Opening remarks for Tokenization roundtable*. SEC. https://www.sec.gov/newsroom/speeches-statements/peirce-remarks-crypto-roundtable-Tokenization-051225

Varghese, J. (May 9, 2025). Can't afford a whole property in Dubai? Buying a piece of one just got easier! *Gulf News*. https://gulfnews.com/your-money/saving-investment/cant-afford-a-whole-property-in-dubai-buying-a-piece-of-one-just-got-easier-1.500120696

Waliczek, S. (2023, November 7). Privacy concerns around CBDCs—Are they justified? *World Economic Forum*. https://www.weforum.org/stories/2023/11/Privacy-concerns-around-CBDCs/

Waller, C. J. (2021, August 5). *CBDC: A solution in search of a problem?* Board of Governors of the Federal Reserve System. https://www.federalreserve.gov/newsevents/speech/waller20210805a.htm

Weinberg, A. I., Petratos, P., & Faccia, A. (2024). *Will central bank digital currencies (CBDC) and Blockchain cryptocurrencies coexist in the post-quantum era?*. https://doi.org/10.48550/arXiv.2411.06362

Weston, G. (2025, March 17). *Privacy and security implications of CBDCs*. 101 Blockchains. https://101Blockchains.com/Privacy-and-security-in-CBDC/

White House. (2025, July 18). *Fact Sheet: President Donald J. Trump Signs Genius Act Into Law*. https://www.whitehouse.gov/fact-sheets/2025/07/fact-sheet-president-donald-j-trump-signs-genius-act-into-law/

Winston & Strawn LLP. (2025, May 29). *SEC hosts roundtable with Crypto Task Force on Tokenization*. https://www.winston.com/en/blogs-and-podcasts/capital-markets-and-securities-law-watch/sec-hosts-roundtabl

World Bank. (n.d.-b). *India. World Bank Open Data*. https://data.worldbank.org/country/india

World Bank (n.d.). *GDP (current US$)—China*. https://data.worldbank.org/indicator/NY.GDP.MKTP.CD?locations=CN

World Bank. (n.d.). *Global findex database*. https://www.worldbank.org/en/publication/globalfindex

World Bank. (n.d.). *Overview*. https://www.worldbank.org/en/topic/financialinclusion/overview

World Bank. (n.d.). *World Bank SME finance*. https://www.worldbank.org/en/topic/smefinance

World Bank. (2024). *Interoperability between central bank digital currency systems and fast payment systems: A technical perspective*. Technology & Innovation Lab. http://hdl.handle.net/10986/41812 (License: CC BY-NC 3.0 IGO)

World Bank Group. (2024, April 4). *Global Findex database. World Bank*. https://www.worldbank.org/en/publication/globalfindex/Data

World Bank Group. (2024, June). *Remittance prices worldwide quarterly* (Issue 50). https://remittanceprices.worldbank.org/sites/default/files/rpw_main_report_and_annex_q224.pdf

References

World Bank Group. (2022, July 21). *COVID-19 boosted the adoption of digital financial services*. World Bank. https://www.worldbank.org/en/news/feature/2022/07/21/covid-19-boosted-the-adoption-of-digital-financial-services#:~:text=Globally%2C%20some%201.4%20billion%20adults,go%2C%20much%20more%20is%20needed

World Bank Group. (2017). Financial access. In *World Bank*. https://www.worldbank.org/en/publication/gfdr/gfdr-2016/background/financial-access

World Economic Forum, Research Center for Wealth Management, Tsinghua University, PBC School of Finance, Zhang, X., Iskenderian, M. E., & Allibhoy, F. (2024). *Global financial inclusion practices: Case studies from China, India and the USA* [Report]. https://www3.weforum.org/docs/WEF_Financial_Inclusion_Cases_2024.pdf

World Economic Forum. (2024, July). *Why financial inclusion is the key to a thriving digital economy*. https://www.weforum.org/stories/2024/07/why-financial-inclusion-is-the-key-to-a-thriving-digital-economy

Worldpay. (n.d.). *GPR 2025*. https://www.worldpay.com/en/global-payments-report

Xie, Y. (2024, October 23). *Multi-country digital currency platform is worth the effort: Central Bankers*. South China Morning Post. https://www.scmp.com/business/banking-finance/article/3283528/central-bankers-say-mbridge-multi-country-digital-currency-platform-worth-effort

YCharts. (2025). *Visa Inc (V)—Total transaction volume (quarterly)*. https://ycharts.com/indicators/visa_inc_v_total_transaction_volume_quarterly

Zhang, T., & Huang, Z. (2022). Blockchain and central bank digital currency. *ICT Express, 8*(2), 264–270. https://doi.org/10.1016/j.icte.2021.09.014

Zodia Markets. (2025, January 29). *Zodia markets secures ADGM license for institutional crypto trading*. Zodia Markets. https://www.zodiamarkets.com/news/adgm-license

Index

A

Accessibility 7, 15, 50, 76, 79, 81, 84, 89, 98, 100, 113, 120, 138, 139, 141, 166, 174, 191, 215, 222

Account 11, 29, 31, 33–35, 49, 50, 64, 66, 70, 72, 81, 90, 91, 96, 98, 100, 101, 106, 107, 109, 112, 114, 117, 118, 120, 128, 130, 132–134, 138, 140, 142, 144, 145, 151, 158, 187–189, 191, 194, 205, 210, 222, 232

Account-based 49, 50, 66, 117, 118

Agent 29, 32, 35, 133

Agreement 112, 117, 134, 143, 202, 230, 231

Algorithm 52, 56–58, 63, 64, 167, 171, 231

Anonymity 9, 39, 50, 108, 120, 163, 202

Anti-Money Laundering (AML) 49, 54, 55, 142, 172, 188, 210, 213, 214, 217, 225, 229

API 55, 105, 114, 161, 215

Application Programming Interface. *See* API

Artificial intelligence (AI) 34, 37, 39, 48, 56, 57, 65, 76, 105, 150, 182, 183, 191, 206, 227

Auditability 41, 42, 51, 52, 107

Authentication 22, 51, 74, 75, 105, 106, 112, 113, 139, 196, 229

Authorization 205

Automated 52, 54, 113, 166, 168, 170, 204, 227

Automation 37, 53, 54, 56, 66, 107, 159, 161

B

Banking 4, 5, 7, 9, 15, 23, 30–32, 35, 37, 47, 52, 56, 59–63, 65, 72, 73, 75, 86, 95–100, 105, 110–113, 126, 127, 132, 133, 136, 137, 139

Banknote 19, 59, 61, 141, 186, 191, 196

Benchmark 25, 62, 104

Index

Blockchain 4, 6, 15, 37–44, 53, 55, 75, 76, 79, 80, 89, 107, 118, 122, 134, 150, 156, 160, 161, 163, 166, 167, 171, 175, 179, 180, 182–184, 204, 206, 208, 211, 213–219, 223, 226, 230, 231

C

Central Bank Digital Currencies (CBDC) xi, 3–16, 23, 24, 27, 37–49, 51–66, 69–71, 75, 77–79, 81, 82, 84, 85, 87–96, 98, 106–109, 115–123, 125–127, 130–135, 137–139, 142, 144, 145, 149–156, 158–160, 162, 163, 165, 166, 170, 173, 174, 185–208, 211–213, 219, 221–228, 230, 231
CIBC (Customer Initiated Bank Credit) 234
Clearing house 113, 137, 204
CNBC (Common Name-Based Computation) 235
Consensus mechanism 37, 38, 40, 43, 44, 46, 47, 61, 62, 65, 230, 231
Convertibility 20, 196
Credit risk 179
Cross-border payments 4, 8, 13, 82, 116–118, 144, 149, 150, 155, 157, 160–162, 169, 179, 183, 186, 190, 203, 222, 224, 227
Cryptocurrency 23, 43, 59, 60, 62, 63, 85, 90, 168–170, 179, 181, 182, 203, 206, 208, 211, 215
CSD (Central Securities Depository) 234
Custody 172, 178, 181
Cybersecurity 3, 9, 11, 13, 38, 48, 52, 56, 89, 106, 108, 109, 139, 185, 187, 195, 196, 198, 212, 213, 217

D

Data privacy 34, 35, 38, 54, 106, 192, 193
Debt 21, 179, 183, 227
Default 33
Denomination 120, 187, 189, 227
Digital asset 4, 6, 7, 15, 24, 82, 96, 166, 168, 170, 175, 176, 178, 179, 181, 193, 203, 206, 208–211
Digital cash 5
Digital currency 5, 12, 13, 41, 44, 46, 49–51, 56, 58, 59, 63–65, 71, 78, 80, 82, 87, 107, 121–123, 125–127, 131, 134, 135, 138, 141, 151, 165, 170, 173, 174, 187, 189, 195, 197, 203, 204, 206, 207, 223–225, 227, 232
Digital identity 34, 108, 109, 188, 189, 225
Digital ledger 39, 42, 218
Digitization 7, 8, 108, 165, 195, 216–218
Disintermediation 9, 10, 108, 151, 185, 194, 212
Distributed Ledger Technology (DLT) 38, 40, 42–44, 88, 89, 106, 107, 118, 134, 157, 176, 177, 200, 218, 230, 231

E

Economy 16, 20, 24, 25, 34, 47, 54, 71–73, 77, 83–87, 89, 95, 98, 101, 102, 105–107, 109, 116, 125, 127, 133, 135–137, 139, 140, 142, 145, 152, 167, 171, 173, 189, 191, 192, 197, 199, 200, 214

Encryption 48, 51, 58, 159

F

Financial inclusion 4, 6, 7, 13, 14, 29–32, 36, 38, 49, 66, 69, 70, 72, 78, 79, 85, 87, 92–95, 98, 101, 102, 104–109, 116, 122, 125–128, 130, 132, 133, 135–140, 144, 145, 153, 185–187
Financial sovereignty 145, 207
Financial stability 10, 13, 21, 81, 142, 151–154, 158, 171, 195, 198, 200
Fintech 3, 13, 14, 34, 84, 85, 95, 99, 100, 104, 106, 111, 115, 122, 126, 130, 131, 133, 136, 140, 179, 180, 182, 185, 189, 193, 196, 204, 224, 226
Fungibility 237

G

Governance 34, 40, 43, 44, 46, 47, 52, 55, 66, 108, 111, 122, 123, 158, 161, 174, 193, 198, 216–218, 227

H

Hybrid model 46, 50

I

IMF 9, 10, 13, 31, 90, 135, 139, 230
Inclusion 5, 13, 30, 46, 49, 87, 93, 112, 119, 122, 125, 126, 130, 140, 144, 173, 187–189, 193, 196, 198, 201, 205, 221, 222, 224, 226
Infrastructure 5, 7–11, 13, 14, 16, 29–32, 36, 37, 41, 42, 47–49, 51–55, 58, 59, 61–65, 69

Instant payments 7, 103, 110
Interbank 5, 9, 88, 107, 112, 117, 121, 137, 204, 210, 229, 230
Intermediary 49, 157, 188, 203
Interoperability 15, 27, 34, 39, 54, 55, 66, 102, 104, 107, 115, 120, 122, 123, 138, 144, 150, 157, 161, 171, 174, 180, 200, 215, 219, 221–223, 231
Issuance 20, 50, 89, 107, 118, 120, 135, 138, 172, 178, 183, 196, 204, 206–208, 211, 229, 232

J

Jurisdiction 54, 55, 149, 171, 172, 174, 175, 177, 182, 191, 196, 207, 209

K

KYC (Know Your Customer) 34, 49, 84, 130, 225, 230

L

Ledger 14, 37–42, 47, 50, 55, 58, 65, 80, 149, 161, 162, 176, 195, 201, 206, 218
Legal tender 3, 5, 11, 16, 19, 24, 121, 128, 131, 141, 152, 153, 174
Liquidity 9, 10, 53, 87, 107, 121, 130, 152, 155, 159, 162, 170–172, 182, 183, 194, 212, 217

M

Machine learning 56, 57
Monetary Base 238
Monetary policy 3, 8, 10, 13, 20, 53, 55, 64, 65, 78, 83, 87, 92, 94, 106, 116, 118, 121, 134,

140, 158, 173, 190, 194, 222, 225, 227, 229, 230, 232

N
Network Effect 238
Non-bank 130

O
Off-Chain 238
On-chain 168, 172
Operational risk 10, 167

P
Payment processor 194, 195
Payment Rail 239
Payment system 4, 6–8, 12–14, 16, 23, 57, 61, 63, 73–75, 80, 86–88, 92, 93, 95, 96, 98, 100–102, 104, 106, 110, 116, 117, 125–127, 129, 132, 133, 136, 145, 149, 150, 159, 165, 166, 173, 186, 189, 195, 202, 224, 227, 231, 232
Payment Token 239
Peer-to-peer 23, 42, 79, 101, 105, 112, 114, 117, 129, 188, 194
Peer-to-peer payments 188
Permissioned 37–39, 41–44, 53, 63, 66, 157, 214, 216
Permissioned Ledger 37, 43
Privacy 3, 5, 8–11, 14, 34, 35, 38, 39, 41, 42, 47, 49–52, 54, 55, 58, 65, 66, 74, 77, 106–108, 120, 139, 143, 149, 159, 163, 173, 174, 185, 192, 193, 197, 198, 200–202, 205, 207, 208, 212, 214, 221, 223, 225, 227
Programmable currency 7, 11, 27, 55, 107, 180, 221, 225
Programmable money 27, 225
Programmable Payments 239

Protocol 34, 38, 40, 51, 55, 81, 82, 106, 142, 167, 196
Public key 51, 120

Q
Quantum computing 52, 57, 58, 196

R
Real-Time Gross Settlement (RTGS) 55, 61, 113, 232
Real-time payments 95, 100–103, 110, 111, 122, 132, 145
Reconciliation 129, 161
Regulation 5, 6, 84, 88, 92, 102, 153, 159, 171, 173, 174, 177, 199, 203, 208, 209, 211, 213, 230, 232
Remittances 54, 77, 78, 87, 108, 115, 117, 131, 144, 158, 168, 169, 173, 190, 203
Reserve currency 190
Reserves 20, 26, 83, 117, 137, 138, 140, 141, 162, 166, 167, 170, 172, 177, 201, 206, 208–211, 232
Retail 5, 12, 43, 46–48, 79, 88, 89, 103, 105, 107, 108, 112, 114, 115, 117–120, 125, 126, 128, 129, 134–137, 140, 143, 150, 152, 154, 158, 162, 181, 186, 189, 194, 195, 197, 200–202, 205, 211, 215–218, 231
Retail CBDC 5, 12, 43, 46, 48, 79, 88, 89, 117–119, 125, 126, 128, 135, 137, 140, 143, 154, 158, 162, 186, 195, 197, 201, 202, 205
Retail payment 129, 136, 150, 158, 194, 200

S

Scalability 10, 34, 38, 40–42, 44, 46, 47, 56, 80, 81, 88, 105, 107, 115, 120, 218, 221
Settlement 5, 26, 44, 55, 84, 88, 116, 120, 121, 155, 161, 173, 178, 183, 190, 192, 195, 209, 230, 232
Smart contracts 37, 38, 52–54, 65, 76, 107, 149, 157, 160–162, 167, 168, 225, 227
Stablecoin 4, 6, 88, 117, 143, 145, 157–159, 165–173, 180, 183, 184, 209, 210
Stakeholder 12–14, 84, 87, 90, 111, 114, 122, 128, 130, 143, 156, 160, 162, 176, 178, 201, 204, 226

T

Tokenization 74, 107, 160, 161, 165, 175–178, 184, 213–218, 226
Traceability 8, 39, 49, 88, 120, 188, 191, 192, 195, 228
Transparency 3, 7, 8, 14, 15, 35, 39–42, 44, 47, 50, 51, 66, 86, 88, 98, 108, 117, 137, 155, 161, 166, 167, 170, 171, 176, 180, 181, 188, 190, 191, 193, 214, 217, 222, 226, 227

U

Unbanked 6, 7, 29–31, 33, 35, 91, 98, 101, 102, 105–107, 132, 137, 138, 152, 188, 189, 201, 203, 222

V

Validator 40, 42, 46, 230
Value transfer 117, 166, 167

W

Wallet 9, 11, 13, 23, 42, 49, 50, 57, 74, 80–82, 85, 86, 89, 90, 98–100, 104, 112, 113, 120, 121, 125, 126, 128, 131–135, 137–139, 142, 153, 160, 168, 172, 188, 189, 191, 194, 195, 201, 202, 232
Wholesale 5, 9, 79, 88, 107, 108, 117–121, 134, 137, 143, 149–152, 154, 156, 158, 160–162, 186, 194, 201, 203
Wholesale CBDC 5, 9, 79, 88, 117–119, 121, 143, 149, 154, 156, 162, 163, 186, 194

GPSR Compliance

The European Union's (EU) General Product Safety Regulation (GPSR) is a set of rules that requires consumer products to be safe and our obligations to ensure this.

If you have any concerns about our products, you can contact us on

ProductSafety@springernature.com

In case Publisher is established outside the EU, the EU authorized representative is:

Springer Nature Customer Service Center GmbH
Europaplatz 3
69115 Heidelberg, Germany

www.ingramcontent.com/pod-product-compliance
Lightning Source LLC
LaVergne TN
LVHW021339080526
838202LV00004B/239

9 783032 028181